Gender and Lynching

Gender and Lynching

The Politics of Memory

Evelyn M. Simien

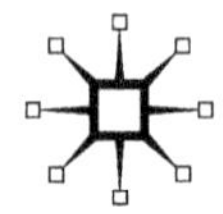

GENDER AND LYNCHING

Softcover reprint of the hardcover 1st edition 2011 978-0-230-11270-4

First published in 2011 by
PALGRAVE MACMILLAN®
in the United States—a division of St. Martin's Press LLC,
175 Fifth Avenue, New York, NY 10010.

Where this book is distributed in the UK, Europe and the rest of the World, this is by Palgrave Macmillan, a division of Macmillan Publishers Limited, registered in England, company number 785998, of Houndmills, Basingstoke, Hampshire RG21 6XS.

Palgrave Macmillan is the global academic imprint of the above companies and has companies and representatives throughout the world.

ISBN 978-1-349-29463-3 ISBN 978-1-137-00122-1 (eBook)
DOI 10.1057/9781137001221

Library of Congress Cataloging-in-Publication Data

Gender and lynching : the politics of memory / edited by
Evelyn M. Simien.
p. cm.
Includes bibliographical references and index.
1. Lynching—Sex differences—United States—History.
2. African American women—Violence against—United States—History.
3. Rape—United States—History. 4. Lynching in literature.
5. Lynching in art. 6. Sexism—United States—History.
7. Racism—United States—History. I. Simien, Evelyn M., 1974–
II. Title.
HV6457.G46 2011
364.1'34—dc23 2011016902

A catalogue record of the book is available from the British Library.

Design by Integra Software Services

First edition: November 2011

10 9 8 7 6 5 4 3 2 1

Transferred to Digital Printing in 2012

For my son, Roman Marcellus
I love you very much, unconditionally.

Contents

List of Figures

Acknowledgements

This book evolved out of the 2008 National Endowment for the Humanities (NEH) Summer Institute entitled "African American Struggles for Civil Rights in the Twentieth Century," sponsored by the W.E.B. Du Bois Institute at Harvard University. The institute was managed and directed by Henry Louis Gates, Jr., Waldo E. Martin, Jr., and Patricia Sullivan. I owe a special debt to this group, including fellow participants and visiting faculty who provided me with an intellectually engaging and thoroughly rewarding experience that revitalized my approach to teaching civil rights history. Leon Litwack's guest lecture on lynching—particularly, his discussion of Mary Turner—inspired this project. The four-week program promoted collaboration between participants and visiting faculty, as evidenced by the working groups that took place on-site and continued long after we left Cambridge, MA. I wish to thank Todd Allen, Bill Huntzicker, Wanda Jackson, Erika Molloseau Pryor, Sherrow Pinder, Janie Ward, and Rychetta Watkins for their warmth and kindness. Our in-depth conversations were both meaningful and thoughtful, as we routinely reflected upon our classroom experiences over breakfast, lunch, and dinner. I am especially grateful to Brenda Edgerton-Webster, Frances Jones-Sneed, and Barbara McCaskill who met with me on a weekly basis to discuss the book project. They proofread the original call for papers and made editorial suggestions. They also commented on the earliest drafts of manuscripts. Barbara, in particular, read a disproportionate share and provided superb feedback.

Given the interdisciplinary focus of *Gender and Lynching*, I solicited the help of several readers from a range of disciplines outside my area of expertise so that the collection of essays would meet the highest intellectual standards. I am especially thankful to those readers who were not among my friends or colleagues, but were virtual strangers who willingly volunteered to review manuscripts both carefully and thoughtfully, often more than once. I owe a huge debt to all of the following, from close friends to mere acquaintances who obliged my requests: Lawrence Davis, Alice Deck, Tiffany Gill, Dayo Gore, Angeletta Gourdine, Micki McElya, Robin Muhammad, Shawn Salvant, Judith Stephens, Christel Temple, Bernell Tripp, Christopher Waldrep, and Stephanie Wright. I must also thank the contributors. If it were not for their original research and intellectual curiosity, this project would not have been made possible. For the privilege and opportunity to work with them, I am eternally grateful.

I must also thank my friends and colleagues: Michele Tracy Berger, Sharon Harris, Shareen Hertell, Shayla Nunnally, and Melina Pappademos for their professional guidance and collegial support. Michelle read the book's proposal before it was sent to the editor at Palgrave. Shareen was kind enough to proofread the introduction at a moment's notice, as did Sharon and Shayla. Melina lent me her ears when I needed to vent. I benefited enormously from our candid conversations about how to balance competing demands of work and family. An associate professor with tenure in the Department of Political Science, I hold a joint appointment with the Institute for African American Studies and I am affiliated with Women's Studies. I am also Acting Director of the University of Connecticut's Humanities Institute. I believe one of the greatest challenges facing joint hires like me is the ability to so manage time effectively and skillfully that you fulfill your service obligations, but not to the detriment of your research agenda or family. Pregnant with my first child, the book's proposal along with sample chapters were delivered to the press for external review days before I went into labor.

Finally, I must thank the two most important people in my life. First, I have to thank my husband, Steven, for the extra hours of sleep in the morning, his willingness to become a full-time stay-at-home dad to care for our son, and his unwavering support of my academic career. Secondly, I have to acknowledge the way in which our son, Roman Marcellus, has changed my life. I have never felt as productive as I do now. Every single day he greets me with the biggest smile and heartiest laugh. He brings me such joy. I never knew that I could love another human being quite so much, unconditionally.

Permissions

Grateful acknowledgment is made to the following for granting permission to quote from and reprint the copyrighted material listed below:

Permission to use the photo of the Mary Turner Historical Marker is granted by Julie Buckner Armstrong.

Permission to use the poem "dirty south moon" is granted by Honoreé Fanonne Jeffers and Southern Illinois University Press.

"Mary Turner, Hidden Memory, and Narrative Possibility," is adapted from *Mary Turner and the Memory of Lynching* by Julie Buckner Armstrong and reprinted by permission of The University of Georgia Press.

Permission to use the photograph of Rubin Stacy, a lynching victim, Fort Lauderdale, Florida, from the Ku Klux Klan & Lynching Photograph Collection dated July 19, 1935 is granted by Photographs and Prints Division, the Schomburg Center for Research in Black Culture, The New York Public Library, Astor, Lenox, and Tilden Foundations.

Permission to use lines of poetry from the work entitled "Lines to Ida B. Wells" by Katherine Davis Chapman Tillman, published in July 5, 1894 is granted by *The Christian Recorder.*

Permission to use lines of poetry from the work entitled "A Southern Incident" by Katherine Davis Chapman Tillman, published in her 1902 book *Recitations* (Philadelphia: A.M.E. Book Concern) is granted by the Moorland Spingarn Research Center at Howard University, Washington, DC 20059.

Permission to use the Laura Nelson Photo, Without Sanctuary, Page 97 is granted courtesy of theNational Center for Civil and Human Rights.

Permission to use the photo of the sculpture of Mary Turner (A Silent Protest against Mob Violence) by Meta Wassick Fuller is granted by the Museum of African American History, Boston, MA.

Permission to use the Image of Art Installation "A Woman Was Lynched the Other Day . . . " is granted courtesy of Kimberly Mayhorn, "A Woman Was Lynched the Other Day . . . ," 1998–2001.

Permission to use the photograph of Billie Holiday singing at Café Society in 1939 is granted by the Institute of Jazz Studies, Rutgers University.

Permission to use song lyrics from "Strange Fruit", words and music by Lewis Allan Copyright 1939 (renewed) by Music Sales Corporation (ASCAP). All Rights for the US controlled by Music Sales Corporation (ASCAP) International. Copyright secured from Carlin America, Inc. All Rights Reserved. Reprinted with permission.

Permission to use image VV1488, African Americans March in Protest (c) Underwood & Underwood/CORBIS and image U60270INP, Mob Beating Black Man (c) Bettmann/CORBIS.

Permission to use the flag photo, *A Man Was Lynched Yesterday*, courtesy the Library of Congress, Prints & Photographs Division, Visual Materials from the NAACP Records.

All other material is in the public domain.

Introduction

Evelyn M. Simien

Mister, you ought to've heard the nigger wench howl![1]

The conventional approach to (or master narrative of) American civil rights history has focused almost exclusively on Black male victimhood during the era of lynching, encompassing nearly five decades from 1880–1930. Rather than broaden and deepen our understanding of racial discrimination, however, such an approach often simplifies and distorts the more complex and devastating history of lynching in the United States.[2] Indeed, both academic and popular discussions of lynching are dominated by a static, fixed understanding of deprivation that is principally racially based. Far less common is an association of the era with a richer, more nuanced understanding of deprivation that is critical of hierarchal relationships determined by interlocking systems of oppression—namely, racism and sexism.

Although the ritual of lynching claimed many lives, *Gender and Lynching* is not so much about Black female victimhood as it is about reclaiming the life stories of African American women via public remembrance, oral history, and community narratives. This book examines the musical, theatrical, literary, photographic, and artistic representations of women and lynching that involved either black-white audiences or coalitions between black and white women against lynching. This volume also recognizes the efforts of individual African American women as well as those of institutional actors such as the Association of Southern Women for the Prevention of Lynching (ASWPL) and the National Association for the Advancement of Colored People (NAACP) to properly document and spotlight lynching. In doing so, the essays that follow reveal the unique ways in which African American women's victimization at the hands of angry mobs and their participation in anti-lynching campaigns alter our popular understanding of lynching in the United States.

Rather than sidestep or avoid some of the most vexing or controversial issues inherent in civil rights history, this introduction will explore how scholars of lynching have typically ignored the ways in which African American women experienced racial-sexual violence in the South, where at least 150 women were lynched between 1880 and 1965. In fact, the overwhelming majority of these cases involving African American female victims—that is, 130 in total—occurred before 1930.[3] For the most part, historians who write about lynching address the practice as it occurred during the post-Reconstruction era and when it was geographically limited to the South: the primary targets were African American men, and the punishment inflicted resulted in death to the victims. It is therefore essential that we re-conceptualize such extralegal violence as both gendered and racialized for the purpose of writing a corrective history that accounts for ways in which African American women have been erased from the extant literature on lynching. To date, African American women have suffered racial-sexual violence without explosively emerging as the most gripping examples of hate crimes, even as stories of extraordinarily heinous offenses against African American men—from Emmett Till to James Byrd, Jr.—have left an indelible mark on civil rights history.

Public memory, created by newspaper accounts and oral testimony, has remembered lynch victims who were African American and female in specific ways, featuring both racial and sexual terms. Described as "fiends," "assassins," "prostitutes," and "negress brutes," African American women lived under the shadow of assumption that, by virtue of their race, they were so morally deprived and violent that they seemed as dangerous as their male counterparts. Their rape and torture were ideologically sanctioned to enforce white supremacy. Mary Turner was eight months pregnant when a mob of several hundred men and women murdered her in Valdosta, Georgia. The Associated Press reported that she had made "unwise remarks" and "flew into a rage" about the lynching of her husband, Hayes, insisting that she would press charges against the men responsible. Her death in May of 1918 prompted a widespread, multifaceted response that continues to evolve today. Laura Nelson confessed to shooting a sheriff to protect her son, L.W. The officer was searching her cabin for stolen goods as part of a meat pilfering investigation. Members of a mob seized Laura along with her son, and both were lynched in Okemah, Oklahoma, in May of 1911—however, not before Laura had been raped by several men. Their bodies were hung from a bridge for hundreds to view.[4] To the extent that Turner and Nelson are symbolically represented among other masculine narratives of lynching, it is as tragic characters or "collateral victims" whose supportive efforts were aimed at defending the men in their lives. Such deaths, however, were not incidental. They were essential to maintain white supremacy, as a form of punishment for defying the social order.

Though women represent a minority of lynching victims, their stories challenge previous interpretations and dominant conceptualizations of lynching as justified protection for white women from Black male rapists. If we are to fully understand lynching and the motives behind it, scholars must begin to include analyses of African American women who were robbed of dignity, respect, and bodily integrity by a weapon of terror used to maintain a caste system that assigned inferior roles to African American men and women alike. By including women centrally within the historical narrative of lynching, we not only avoid reinforcing the rape/lynch myth (i.e., the emasculated Black man as the only visible victim) but, in doing so, also reveal a more complete understanding of this devastating social practice.

The term "lynching" evokes an image derived from a collective memory which African American men and women both share, but to which only African American men claim entitlement—i.e., a charred male figure swinging from a tree or telegraph pole amidst an angry mob. Such an image has overshadowed the equally representative experience of African American women who were similarly tortured and mutilated, as well as raped and killed, by angry mobs. Moreover, this highly stylized, one-dimensional form of representation also fails to capture contemporary forms of lynching, such as the Jena Six episode and the Megan Williams case discussed below, which critically connect the past with the present and contextualize the ongoing legacy of lynching.

In August 2006, Kenneth Purvis—an African American high school student in Jena, Louisana—asked his principal whether Black students could sit beneath a tree that most believed was reserved for whites only at the local high school in Jena.[5] In this case, the separation of the two races was widely accepted by the majority of teachers, parents, school administrators, and the student body. The tree marked the separation and re-inscribed the lack of social equality between the two races. Thus, it is significant that white students hung nooses from the tree on the very next morning after their African American classmates—Kenneth Purvis and his cousin Bryant Purvis—sat under the tree and violated norms of social etiquette that directly invoked Jim Crow. Three nooses were found hanging from the tree's branches, draped in school colors.[6] A flagrant act, it was dismissed by the local superintendent and majority white school board, which overturned the principal's original decision to expel the culprits involved and, instead, imposed suspensions on the grounds that the tree display was an innocent, youthful prank. The fact remains, however, that the noose invokes a torrid history of lynching in the United States.

Between the late 1800s and early 1900s, the reported incidents of lynching rose sharply and occurred most frequently in the southern states—namely, Georgia and Mississippi.[7] The term "lynching" has been used to denote hanging and other types of executions carried out with inhumane cruelty by self-appointed mobs to assert the supremacy of white masculinity for a presumed offense. Such offenses included, but were not limited to, arson and poisoning, as well as burglary and self-defense.[8] Allegations of rape involving Black male offenders and white female victims resulted in cruel and unusual punishment—specifically, castration—and figure most prominently in narrow discussions of lynching that invoke the sole image of African American men as primary targets.

The myth of the Black male rapist functioned as a means of social control as it served to regulate the behaviors of African American men and white women in relationship to each other. African American men lived under the shadow of assumption that, by virtue of their race, they were so bestial and immoral that lynching was ideologically sanctioned to enforce white supremacy. In light of the rape myth, lynching has been interpreted as a sexually perverse public performance of hegemonic masculinity spawned by both repulsion and desire between men on account of racist stereotypes that evoke envy on the part of white men for the supposed sexual potency and virile strength of Black men.[9]

As African American men had been denied the rights of manhood and the privileges of patriarchy, the violent act of lynching made it possible for white men to exhibit exaggerated masculinity before a live audience that exalted them for serving as guardians of white womanhood.[10] Scholars have considered such a ritualistic practice of public emasculation and sadistic torture an extralegal means to affirm the supremacy of white masculinity and to reinforce the African American male's inferior status in the social, economic, and political structure of the United States. Lynching differed from ordinary murder or assault. The individual victim was denied due process and equal protection under law, as evidenced by mob coercion of judicial proceedings, special doctrinal rules, and the language of court opinions.[11]

Like execution by guillotine, lynching was celebrated as a spectacular event and drew large crowds of people who tortured, burned alive, and dismembered their victims. Participants and onlookers left the scene with grisly souvenirs, mostly body parts, including genitalia. People fought each other for bits of burnt flesh, teeth, nails, and hair.[12] Photographs were taken, and postcards were mailed to friends and family. Mothers held their babies in tow, standing next to the corpse of a dead body and smiling for a photo opportunity.[13] Such a gruesome spectacle gripped the imagination and enjoyed widespread public approval with extensive media coverage in local and national newspapers.

Lynching thereby constituted a form of domestic terrorism that inflicted individual harm upon the African American male and collective injury upon an entire race of people simultaneously, with the purpose of instilling fear. It served to give dramatic warning, emphasizing the fact that the iron clad system of white supremacy was not to be challenged by word, deed, or even thought.[14] Lynching could therefore be understood as the ritualistic reenactment of a historically scripted and rehearsed hierarchy that oppressed the Black male victim and empowered the white assailant in the most masculine terms, using honor and chivalry as well as white female frailty as a defense for mob violence. Yet such an explanation or interpretation of lynching effectively conceals the fact that not all victims were African American men, and rape was not the leading motive. African American men, women, and children were lynched for a range of alleged crimes and social infractions—from petty theft to labor disputes over debt, credit or wages, as well as arson and murder. Thus, the designation of African American women as symbolic representatives of lynching challenges often taken-for-granted assumptions about lynching and its victims.

Today, the noose has come to symbolize an era of terror when lynching was used as a tool of oppression to maintain white supremacy. The act of hanging nooses from a tree presumably reserved for white students in Jena, Louisana, served a similar purpose: it gave dramatic warning to African American students like Kenneth Purvis and his cousin, Bryant Purvis, who dared to resist marginalization in public spaces. The case of the Jena Six spotlights the dynamic interplay between race, crime, and punishment in the United States, invoking three salient themes: an earlier era of Jim Crow, when separate but equal accommodations were legally sanctioned by the Supreme Court's *Plessy v. Ferguson* decision; the legacy of lynching, when African American men, in particular, were punished excessively for a presumed offense without due process of the law;

and racial disparities in the US criminal justice system, whereby judges and juries imposed harsher sentences upon African American men who stood trial for crimes committed against white victims than they did upon whites.

Mychal Bell, one of the African American students involved in the Jena Six case, was initially arrested and charged with attempted second-degree murder (though this charge was later reduced to aggravated battery and conspiracy). Tried as an adult, Bell was age 16 at the time of the assault, when he and other members of the Jena Six reportedly beat their white classmate, Justin Barker, on school grounds. Accused of ambushing Barker and knocking him unconscious, Bell was convicted by an all-white jury and faced up to 22 years in prison.[15] Such a charge as aggravated battery requires the use of a dangerous weapon, and District Attorney Walters argued that the shoes Bell wore and used to kick his victim (Barker) were deadly weapons. Mychal Bell's African American public defender, Blane Williams, urged him to accept a plea bargain versus going to trial. Unlike civil rights attorneys of the past—namely, Thurgood Marshall and Robert Carter—Williams was not hailed as a hero by the African American community as he failed to challenge the composition of the all-white jury pool and rested the defense's case without calling upon any witnesses or offering counter evidence.[16] Fortunately, Louisiana's Third Circuit Court of Appeals overturned Bell's battery conviction as the minor had been tried as an adult.

Had District Attorney Walters had his way, however, Bell would have surely been made an example of, taught a lesson, and punished excessively for a presumed offense—i.e., a crime committed against his white classmate. In fact, Walters forewarned Bell and his accomplices of the unusually harsh punishment that awaited them upon conviction and following criminal sentencing. He is quoted as having stated that "I can be your best friend or your worst enemy . . . I can take away your lives with a stroke of my pen" in the context of a public forum on school grounds.[17] Such a powerful statement served to remind the African American community in general, and African American men, in particular, of their disparate treatment in the American criminal justice system. At once, the privileges and immunities of putative first-class citizenship were trumped by the penalties and restrictions of second-class citizenship in Jena, Louisiana.

Yet, the most disappointing feature of the Jena Six case was neither the mean-spirited attacks of the local District Attorney, J. Reed Walters, nor the racial bias evident in the criminal sentencing of Mychal Bell.

Both aspects of the case revealed the historically troubled relationship between race, crime, and punishment in the United States. Rather, what was particularly disappointing was the way in which six young African American men came to occupy privileged victim status in anti-racist discourse. Racial suffering was singularly represented by six presumably innocent African American males: Robert Bailey, Jr., Jesse Beard, Mychal Bell, Carwin Jones, Bryant Purvis, and Theo Shaw, all of whom stood accused of physically assaulting their white classmate, Justin Barker. By all accounts, the Jena Six were squarely situated within the civil rights struggle and regarded as the Scottsboro Boys of their generation.[18] With the help of such radio personalities as Michael Baisden and Joe Madison, the Jena Six captured the attention of mainstream media outlets—both print and television. In fact, the Jena Six became an important topic of discussion for most Americans when thousands of demonstrators descended upon Jena, Louisiana, and the likes of Al Sharpton, Jesse Jackson, and Martin Luther King III appeared on site to rally the masses.[19]

At the same time, Megan Williams, an African American woman who was kidnapped, raped, and tortured in West Virginia by six white assailants, was unable to muster the same level of public outcry from much of the Black community, including well-known opinion leaders and spokespersons mentioned above.[20] Despite its spectacular features, the case of Megan Williams lacked the press coverage and notoriety that would accompany such a sensational story—one where the female victim was stabbed repeatedly, scorched with hot water, forced to drink from a toilet, and eat rat droppings for an entire week until the police responded to an anonymous tip.[21] Despite moving appeals from the victim's mother, silence prevailed with the press devoting far less time and attention to reporting the facts of this case and the special circumstances surrounding the African American woman as a rape victim—i.e., the process of recognizing sexual violence as a particularly salient race and gender issue, as well as a criminal justice issue. Instead, the media, as well as the African American vanguard of leadership, focused its attention upon Black male victimhood and the more appealing narrative of racial injustice by privileging the plight of six young African American males who became popularly known as the Jena Six. This disproportionately gendered attention speaks volumes about the persistence of views held by the adult African American population that, when given the choice between being attentive to allegations of Black male victimization and being attentive to claims of Black female victimization, African Americans—men and women alike—prioritize the plight of their wounded Black male.[22]

Such neglect renders the sexual violation and torture of countless African American women invisible. In fact, it can be argued that the gendered construction of Black male victimhood is emblematic of patriarchal values that legitimize the subordination of African American women in particular, as evidenced by historical and contemporary trends in the recording (or retelling) of civil rights history.[23] Hence, *Gender and Lynching* contributes to our practical and theoretical understanding of Black female victimization and contextualizes the way in which the past influences the present, especially with regard to a hierarchy that privileges the plight of African American men at the expense of erasing African American women from the historical record. It obliges scholars who either willfully ignore or mischaracterize African American women as "collateral victims" to reconsider their fundamentally flawed approach.

Gender and Lynching challenges scholars and teachers to reframe a discussion of the long Civil Rights Movement through engagement with civil rights activism before the classic years of 1954–1965. Individual chapters traverse traditional disciplinary boundaries, from American cultural studies and English literature to journalism and history, as well as theater. Contributors consider how and why African American female victims of lynching have not been accurately documented, but rather conveniently forgotten. They rely on such methodological approaches as content and media analyses, comparative historical work, as well as literary criticism. To be sure, this book is poised to advance an interdisciplinary and cumulative research agenda that brings African American women to the fore as victims and martyrs, characters in works of art and literature, as well as activists and change agents.

In Chapter 1, "Mary Turner, Hidden Memory, and Narrative Possibility," Julie Buckner Armstrong examines recent attempts to remember Turner by artist Freida High Tesfagiorgis, poet Honorée Fanonne Jeffers, and a local organization, The Mary Turner Project. These efforts demonstrate how Turner continues to disrupt conventional narratives of racial violence, leading artists, writers, and activists to new ways of thinking about gender, healing, and representation. In Chapter 2, "Sisters in Motherhood (?): The Politics of Race and Gender in Lynching Drama," Koritha Mitchell examines Black women's lynching drama. It is a genre initiated by Angelina Weld Grimké's three-act play *Rachel* (1916), which is set in a Black home and traces its deterioration years after the man of the house is lynched. Grimké believed that "if anything can make all women sisters underneath their skins, it is motherhood," so she worked to touch her sisters' hearts with depictions of Black mothers' pain. The 1930 founding of the Association of Southern Women for the Prevention of Lynching (ASWPL) suggests that Grimké's hope was well placed; white women took responsibility for helping to end lynching. However, May Miller's *Nails and Thorns* (1933), which was honorably mentioned in an ASWPL drama competition, is set in a white household that is devastated when townspeople hang a Black man. Focusing on how lynching could bring destruction to white homes, Miller seems much less optimistic than Grimké had been about white women's interest in Black women's pain. Mitchell frames both plays—Grimké's *Rachel* (1916) and Miller's *Nails and Thorns* (1933)—as responses to lynching themes and motifs in the mainstream theatrical and literary productions that informed them.

In Chapter 3, "The Antislavery Roots of African American Women's Antilynching Literature," Barbara McCaskill looks back to the literature of abolition to understand how Black women writers of that era discussed violence. Taking a page from the antislavery movement, these writers examined the social, economic, and political underpinnings of lynching and took both apathetic blacks and whites to task while pushing back against portrayals of Black southern women as primarily victims. In Chapter 4, "A Woman was Lynched the Other Day: Memory, Gender, and the Limits of Traumatic Representation," Jennifer D. Williams examines literature published at the height of mob violence that bears witness to lynching. The author reads Angelina Weld Grimké's *Goldie* (1920), Carrie Williams Clifford's *Little Mother* (1922), and Jean Toomer's *Kabnis* (1923) as narrative acts of witnessing that seek to redress the silencing of Mary Turner and Laura Nelson. By locating these works within a broader context of Black women's anti-lynching cultural production and activism, Williams lays claim to a Black feminist discourse of lynching. The selected texts also reflect an overarching concern with trauma and the limitations, possibilities, and ethics of representing it.

In Chapter 5, "The Politics of Sexuality in Billie Holiday's 'Strange Fruit,'" Fumiko Sakashita analyzes the complicated politics of sexuality in Holiday's live performance of "Strange Fruit." By examining its reception by audiences and the media, the meanings and symbolism of its lyrics, and the historical context of lynching and rape, her essay examines how Holiday's "Strange Fruit" offered audiences a vicarious experience of lynching and unwittingly helped them consume a stereotypical image. This essay also demonstrates how Holiday's performance was meant to subvert such commodification of lynching and the sexual stereotyping of

Black men and women. In Chapter 6, "Gender, Race, and Public Space: Photography and Memory in the Massacre of East Saint Louis and the Crisis Magazine," Anne Rice examines a *Crisis* special issue that covers the 1917 East St. Louis race riot and includes "Massacre of East St. Louis," a photo essay by W.E.B. DuBois and white suffragist Martha Gruening. Foregrounding women as victims, survivors and militants, the issue parallels coverage by African American female investigators who saw the riot as an assault against the family demanding a specific gendered response. Through their visualization of Black female bodies, both as victims of violence and rightful inhabitants of public space, the *Crisis* images help to recover women's history and exemplify a history of resistance in Black visual culture yet to be fully explored.

Taken together, the essays in this edited collection raise important questions for all who study lynching in the United States. Most importantly, they pose a challenge to much of the extant literature on lynching. By forcing scholars to grapple with a legacy of exclusion and to consider the impact of that exclusion on civil rights history, the edited volume sheds critical light on a flawed approach that wrongfully characterizes African American men as the sole victims of lynching and prioritizes the rape/lynch narrative over others that provide an equally compelling motive to justify white supremacy. Thus, this book addresses lynching specifically, but more broadly for anyone interested in the cultural complexities of race and gender. While *Gender and Lynching* aims to rescue African American women from their obscurity in civil rights history—specifically, the history of lynching in the United States—it does so through careful analysis of musical, theatrical, literary, photographic, and artistic representations of their lives.

Notes

1. Walter White, *Rope and Faggot: A Biography of Judge Lynch* (Notre Dame, IN: University of Notre Dame Press, 2001): 28.
2. The edited volume, *Gender and Lynching,* rounds out leading books on the subject of lynching—for example, it is more focused on gender and women's history than Philip Dray's *At the Hands of Persons Unknown: The Lynching of Black America* (New York: Random House, 2002)—and offers an interdisciplinary perspective rather than the regional focus of books such as *Lynching to Belong* (College Station, TX: Texas A&M University Press, 2007);*Carnival of Blood: Dueling, Lynching, and Murder in South Carolina, 1880–1920* (Columbia, SC: University of South Carolina Press, 2006); *Lynching in the West, 1850–1935* (Durham, NC: Duke University Press, 2006); *Rough*

Justice: Lynching and American Society, 1874–1947 (Champaign, IL: University of Illinois, 2004); *A Lynching in the Heartland: Race and Memory in America* (New York: Palgrave, 2001); *Under Sentence to Death: Lynching in the South* (Chapel Hill, NC: University of North Carolina Press, 1997); *Lynching in the New South: Georgia and Virginia, 1880–1930* (Champaign, IL: University of Illinois Press, 1996); and *A Festival of Violence: An Analysis of Southern Lynchings, 1882–1930* (Columbia, SC: University of Illinois Press, 1995). By virtue of being more focused on gender and female victims, as well as being more interdisciplinary, it also complements such discipline specific books as Amy Wood's *Lynching and Spectacle: Witnessing Racial Violence in Black America, 1890–1940* (Chapel Hill, NC: University of North Carolina Press, 2009), and Sandra Gunning's *Race, Rape, and Lynching: The Red Record of American Literature, 1870–1912* (New York: Oxford University Press, 2006). While some books obviously take up single aspects of lynching, from theatrical plays to photographic images and literary expression—for example, Kathy Perkins and Judith Stephens's *Strange Fruit: Plays on Lynching by American Women* (Bloomington, IN: Indiana University Press, 1998); Dora Apel's *Imagery of Lynching: Black Men, White Women, and the Mob* (Piscataway, NJ: Rutgers University Press, 2004); James Allen's *Without Sanctuary: Lynching Photography in America* (Sante Fe, New Mexico: Twin Palms, 2000); and Trudier Harris's *Exorcising Blackness: Historical and Literary Lynching and Burning Rituals* (Bloomington, IN: Indiana University Press, 1984)—this book features a series of chapters bound by a common theme aimed at advancing an interdisciplinary and cumulative research agenda that brings African American women to the fore. It does not qualify as a standard reference text or sourcebook like *Lynching in America: A History in Documents* (New York: New York University Press, 2006); *Witnessing Lynching: American Writers Respond* (Piscataway, NJ: Rutgers University Press, 2003); or *Lynching and Vigilantism in the United States* (Santa Barbara, CA: Greenwood, 1997)—but, rather, a collection of original essays, developed by scholars in dialogue with one another across various disciplines.

3. Crystal Feimster, *Southern Horrors: Women and the Politics of Rape and Lynching* (Cambridge, MA: Harvard University Press, 2009): 159.
4. Leon Litwack, *Trouble in Mind: Black Southerners in the Age of Jim Crow* (New York: Vintage Press, 1998): 288–290; White, *Rope and Faggot*: 28; Feimster, *Southern Horrors*: 171–174.
5. Marisol Bello, "Jena Six Supporters Plan Rally After Verdict Vacated," *USA Today*, September 17, 2007; Marisol Bello, "Civil 'Jena 6' Town Feels Time Warp: Huge Rally Over Hate-Crime Case Promises Hint of '60s," *USA Today*, September 19, 2007; Gary Younge, "Jena is America," *The Nation*, October 8, 2007.
6. Raquel Christi, "Double Whammy," *American Journalism Review*, 30, no. 1 (2008): 16–25; Younge, "Jena is America,".

7. Patricia Schechter, *Ida B. Wells-Barnett and American Reform, 1880–1930* (Chapel Hill, NC: University of North Carolina Press, 2001); White, *Rope and Faggot.*
8. Fitzhugh W. Brundage, *Under Sentence of Death: Lynching in the South* (Chapel Hill, NC: The University of North Carolina Press,1997); Patricia Hill Collins, *On Lynchings: Ida B. Wells-Barnett* (Amherst, NY: Humanity Books, 2002); Litwack, *Trouble in Mind*; Schechter, *Ida B. Wells-Barnett*; Stewart E. Tolnay and E.M. Beck, *A Festival of Violence: An Analysis of Southern Lynchings, 1882–1930* (Champaign, IL: University of Illinois Press, 1995).
9. Angela P. Harris, "Gender, Violence, and Criminal Justice," *Stanford Law Review* 52, no. 4 (2000): 777–807.
10. Harris, "Gender."
11. Anita Hill and Emma Coleman Jordan, *Race, Gender, and Power in America: The Legacy of the Hill-Thomas Hearings* (New York: Oxford University Press, 1995).
12. Brundage, *Under Sentence of Death*; White, *Rope and Faggot.*
13. Collins, *On Lynchings*; Litwack, *Trouble in Mind*; White, *Rope and Faggot.*
14. Brundage, *Under Sentence of Death*; Collins, *On Lynchings.*
15. Darryl Fears, "Louisiana Appeals Court Throws Out Conviction in Racially Charged 'Jena 6' Case," *The Washington Post,* September 15, 2007.
16. Kenneth Mack, "Law and Mass Politics in the Making of the Civil Rights Lawyer, 1931–1941," *Journal of American History* 93, no. 1 (2006): 37–62.
17. Younge, "Jena is America."
18. In 1931, the Scottsboro Boys (nine African American male teenagers) were falsely accused of rape in Alabama. After several retrials, massive protests, international press attention, and two landmark decisions from the U.S. Supreme Court, only four of the nine gained their freedom after having served six years in prison. The Scottsboro case came to symbolize a great miscarriage of justice, and its defendants were widely considered innocent victims of Southern racism.
19. Bello, "Jena Six Supporters"; Bello, "Civil 'Jena Six' Town Feels Like Time Warp; Fears," *Louisiana Appeals Court*; DeWayne Wickman, "Jena Six Case Awakens Civil Rights Movement," *USA Today,* September 18, 2007; Christi, "Double Whammy"; Mark Sorkin, "Justice after Jena," *The Nation,* October 22, 2007; Younge, "Jena is America."
20. Chappell, Kevin, "Black Woman in W. VA Enslaved, Tortured by White Captors: Police," *Jet,* October 1, 2007, 11–12; Robert Gavin, "Rally Supports Nonwhite Women," *The Times Union,* November 1, 2007; Francie LaTour, "Hell On Earth: The Wooded Hills of West Virginia and a Housing Complex in West Palm Beach, Florida, Where Two Black Women Experienced Unimaginable Horror, So Where is the Outrage?" *Essence,* November 2007, 210–216.

21. Chappell, "Black Woman in W. VA"; LaTour, "Hell On Earth."
22. Jane Mansbridge and Katherine Tate, "Race Trumps Gender: Black Opinion on Thomas Nomination," *PS: Political Science and Politics* 25, no. 3 (1992): 488–492; White, *Rope and Faggot*; Evelyn M. Simien, *Black Feminist Voices in Politics* (Albany, NY: State University Press of New York, 2006).
23. Joan Scott, *Gender and the Politics of History* (New York: Columbia University Press, 1999).

CHAPTER 1

Mary Turner, Hidden Memory, and Narrative Possibility

Julie Buckner Armstrong

In October 2002, students arrived at Georgia's Lowndes County High to find several Barbie dolls painted black and hung in a tree outside the school's main entrance. For several weeks afterwards, public opinion in newspapers and community meetings split between two positions common to such noose incidents: hate crime or harmless prank? Conspicuously absent from the debate was acknowledgement of racial violence in Lowndes County's past.[1] Twenty miles from the high school, Mary Turner's body remains buried where she was lynched along with her fetus in May 1918. Turner was one of at least 11 African Americans killed during a spree of mob violence following a white farmer's murder. When she expressed outrage over her husband Hayes' lynching, the mob went after her. Several hundred spectators watched as the men hung her upside down, set her on fire, shot her, then removed the eight-month fetus and stomped it into the ground. After digging a hole for the bodies, someone marked the makeshift grave with a whiskey bottle, a smoldering cigar stump rammed into its neck.[2] For almost 90 years this incident remained a taboo subject. Local archives contained little to no information. Community historians claimed no knowledge, and people who did know spoke privately, if at all.[3] By May 2009, the situation had changed. Local residents, students, and faculty at Valdosta State University (VSU), also in Lowndes County, held a public ceremony to place a cross at the lynching site, where an official historical marker would go in 2010 (See Figure 1.1).

What happened to break the silence? Scholarship by VSU faculty made facts available, but the Barbie incident itself wound up calling attention

Figure 1.1 Historical marker describing the 1918 Brooks-Lowndes lynchings (Photograph courtesy of Julie Buckner Armstrong)

to a trauma that many could not name and giving birth to the memorial group called The Mary Turner Project.[4]

Beyond the local community, Turner plays a complex role within lynching history. A female victim whose death generated widespread response during the late 1910s and 1920s, she disappeared from the national spotlight by the early 1930s. During the past two decades, academics, artists, and writers have defined Mary Turner's story as a significant counter to male narratives of the past and a traumatic event within African American historical memory. However, a large amount of primary material devoted to Turner remains understudied. If, as Amy Louise Wood and Susan V. Donaldson contend in a recent special issue of *Mississippi Quarterly*, "the history of lynching is inseparable from the history of rhetoric and representation," then these valuable Turner resources merit more attention.[5] News reports and editorials about her death reveal the range of public opinion on lynching during World War I, when the United States entered the international arena as a defender of justice and rights.[6] Accounts from theNational Association for the Advancement of Colored People (NAACP) Walter White, the Anti-Lynching Crusaders, and others show how activists successfully cast lynching as a national shame during the 1920s and 1930s.[7] Creative responses by Meta Warrick Fuller, Angelina Weld Grimké, Anne Spencer, and Jean Toomer powerfully engage the struggle to assert a collective humanity in the face of oppressive violence.[8] More recent works by Freida High Tesfagiorgis and Honorée Fanonne Jeffers explore Turner's story in the context of what Tesfagiorgis calls "hidden memory" that is necessary, painful, and challenging to access.[9] The local and the national converge on this ground of hidden memory as The Mary Turner Project joins similar groups across the country to work through legacies of racial violence. Turner's story—sensational news item, national shame, local taboo, hidden memory, reconciliation project, counter-narrative—thus becomes a microcosm for charting a century's worth of lynching discourse.

A word that Wood and Donaldson might use is "prism," a particularly apt metaphor in Turner's case. Building on Jonathan Markovitz's assertion that lynching serves as a lens through which Americans view contemporary race relations, Wood and Donaldson explain that the term "prism" may be more accurate given the way lynching has been misremembered, misunderstood, and misrepresented. A prism multiplies and refracts; "it can obfuscate as much as it clarifies."[10] The history of Turner responses likewise reveals a history of representational difficulty. A female victim challenged the usual lynching justifications, initially a boon for activists such as White. But a woman's story also challenged the usual conventions for depicting lynching victims. If Turner was no Black rapist, neither was she a Black Christ. Fuller, Grimké, and others who portrayed her as a sentimental mother-to-be found little room for anger and pain, their subject's or their own. Invariably, form and syntax ruptured. Fuller never finished the sculpture that she subtitled "A Silent Protest Against Mob Violence." Grimké worked obsessively on multiple drafts of multiple stories that eventually saw publication as "Goldie." Modernists such as Spencer and Toomer comment reflexively upon tensions between silence and voice, using rupture as aesthetic strategy. Fragmented bodies testify to the destruction of souls, communities, and, potentially, texts themselves. Yet these works insist upon the power of art to speak out. Tesfagiorgis, Jeffers, and The Mary Turner Project, products of a postmodern age, carry the struggle forward. Such responses reveal a story whose limits and possibilities emerge from the same place. As hidden memory, it appears in parts, in traces, through a prism at best. Shaping that prism's refracted images into a coherent picture presents its own multifaceted challenges—intellectual, creative, and emotional. More positively, Turner continues to disrupt conventional narratives of racial violence, leading artists and activists to new ways of thinking about gender, healing, and representation. This essay focuses on contemporary responses to Mary Turner because they encourage the kind of work that literary scholar Jacqueline Goldsby suggests is needed in lynching studies today: breaking apart the "narrative molds" that have controlled the discourse for far too long, so that more productive insights might emerge.[11]

Freida High Tesfagiorgis, *Hidden Memories*

In 1985, Freida High Tesfagiorgis' *Hidden Memories* became the first work of art to address Mary Turner by name since the 1920s. What does it mean to call Turner's memory "hidden"? When family and friends buried Hampton Smith, the white farmer who died in May 1918, they marked his grave with his name, the dates of his birth and death, and the symbols of his Masonic tribe. They wanted a substantial obelisk (still the tallest in Brooks County's Pauline Cemetery) to be visible and to last. When some of the same people participated in Turner's lynching, they marked her grave, and thus her life, as disposable. The whiskey bottle would eventually break; the cigar, burn down to ash.[12]

Active attempts to silence Turner and other local Blacks did not succeed in burying her memory, however. Her story soon took on a new life in oral history, journalism, pamphlets, poetry, fiction, and the visual arts. During the late 1920s, through the early 1930s, Turner's story got buried in a different, subtler way. One by one, creative and activist responses disappeared into archives. In Walter White's foundational study, *Rope and Faggot* (1929), her's is among a handful of women's stories in an overwhelming list of atrocities against men. Pamphlets of the 1930s refer to her only as "a pregnant colored woman," lynched and mutilated in Georgia. By the late 1940s, urban legend had conflated her story with another woman's lynching at Moore's Ford Bridge, near Monroe.[13] Such is knowledge of the history of violence against Black women that Turner could make front page news in 1918, generate multiple creative responses, and then become the footnote trail that one follows behind Jean Toomer's fictional Mame Lamkins in the revised edition of *Cane*: "This is an account of an actual lynching."[14] Even many who are heavily invested in Black women's history grew up knowing nothing about Mary Turner. Artist Kara Walker, educated in Atlanta, drew upon images of a lynched pregnant woman and a crushed fetus in her 1997 notebook sketches without knowing Turner's name or her story. Honorée Fanonne Jeffers, a writer who spent much of her youth in Georgia, learned about Turner not from local sources but from Philip Dray's 2002 book, *At the Hands of Persons Unknown*.[15]

Mary Turner's memory became "hidden" in two ways: some actively suppressed or repressed it; others deemed it disposable or less important. Either way, for Tesfagiorgis, a Black feminist critic as well as artist, that memory still occupies a liminal space in history. It may be "visible" or "accessible" in an archive, but male-dominated narratives overshadow or bury it completely. It may be violent and ugly, but refusing to acknowledge it not only robs Black women of their history, it also prevents members of the local community from claiming a shared past.

By juxtaposing Turner's story, as text, against her composition's title, Tesfagiorgis suggests that *Hidden Memories,* although traumatic, must be recalled and named.[16] Historical erasure, however it happens, constitutes a double crime. First comes the violence; then, denying or forgetting its existence.

Doing the opposite—recovering—involves two steps as well. First comes remembering, then the healing, although the process is more recursive than the idea of linear "steps" would imply. *Hidden Memories,* an abstract piece, echoes these themes: strong vertical lines, like a forest, form the field. Against this background sits the focal point—a long tree-like column, with a darker noose-like form inside. The rounded end of the noose causes the tree to bulge out as if pregnant. The noose form might also be interpreted differently, as a medieval torture implement or malformed insect. No matter how one views it, the imagery evokes visceral pain. This tree is dying—blighted and scarred. Underneath its rounded "belly," circles within circles uncover the "hidden memory" text of "MARY TURNER," written in upper-case letters along with "GEORGIA" below to drive the point home. This painting announces, in bold strokes and bold letters, that it will bear witness to a history of violence against women such as Turner. Their stories will be acknowledged and named so that healing can begin.

With *Hidden Memories* and works such as *Homage to Ida B. Wells* (1990), Tesfagiorgis joined a wave of artists, writers, historians, and others initiating similar feminist recovery projects. Significantly, one of her critical essays helped pave the way for another such project, the defining exhibition *Bearing Witness: Contemporary Works by African American Women Artists.*[17] Curated by Jontyle Theresa Robinson in 1996 and first housed at Spelman College, the show gathered works by Lois Mailou Jones, Elizabeth Catlett, Betye Saar, Faith Ringgold, Barbara Chase Riboud, and many more, including Tesfagiorgis. Robinson's introduction credits Tesfagiorgis' idea of "Afrofemcentrism," coined in 1993 and later folded into the category "Black feminism", with forming the exhibition's ideological framework. *Bearing Witness,* Robinson explains, depicts the world and speaks the truth from a Black woman's perspective. Even when the artists convey very difficult images, the end result can be empowering for Black women control the representation and, thus, do the naming. Rather than historical erasure, *Bearing Witness* constituted an important act of historical and artistic recovery: reclaiming memories, myths, images, even genres, styles, and materials. Black women did not stumble upon stories such as Turner's during these years by accident. Violence against women was itself a "hidden memory," an unspoken truth. Women's stories and voices were buried, too, mere footnotes to "real" history, literature, and art. If Mary Turner's and Hampton Smith's graves are actual locations, they serve as appropriate metaphors. Works like *Hidden Memories* and exhibitions like *Bearing Witness* counter such territorial markings of life and death, history and memory, by saying Black women will no longer be disposable.

One result of bringing hidden memories to light is a changed picture of history. The static becomes dynamic as one considers new data. Granted men fell victim to mob violence at rates substantially higher than women: an NAACP report published the year after Turner's death lists 3,224 male deaths since 1889, and 61 female.[18] Even though Turner and other women were statistical anomalies, their stories still count. Feminist recovery projects such as *Hidden Memories* saw scholars and artists centering work around women rather than treating their stories as peripheral. As Elsa Barkley Brown explains, focusing on historically marginalized figures like Turner raises some provocative questions. Brown wonders why millions of women suffered along a continuum of violence, but the history of racial oppression remains male centered:

> Why it is that the other experiences of violence that have so permeated the history of Black women in the United States—the rape, the sexual and other forms of physical abuse as employees in white homes, the contemporary domestic and public sexual and other physical violence—are not as vividly and importantly retained in our memory. Why it is that lynching (and the notion of it as a masculine experience) is not just remembered but is, in fact, central to how we understand the history of African American men and, indeed, the African American experience in general. But violence against women—lynching, rape, and other forms of violence—is not.[19]

Much effort has gone into rectifying such historical omissions since Brown's essay was written. Efforts include trailblazers such as Tesfagiorgis, Kathy A. Perkins and Judith L. Stephens, Crystal Feimster, and now a volume on gender and lynching.[20] Still, work remains to be done. As Goldsby explains, breaking lynching's narrative molds is difficult, especially when they have been around since Ida B. Wells called them "a threadbare lie."[21]

Hence, the reason for recovering Mary Turner's story: the NAACP sent Walter White to South Georgia because her lynching showed the potential to shatter one narrative mold. A generation of artists and writers in the late 1910s and early 1920s, then another contemporary one, responded creatively as Turner raised provocative questions about the place of women in the bigger picture of lynching.

To return to Barkley Brown, why *is* this nation so fully invested in male narratives of race that few can "see" a story like Turner's when it is "hidden" in plain sight, in places like page 29 of *Rope and Faggot*? What are the chances that Kara Walker and Honorée Jeffers went through graduate school never hearing the names Leo Frank or Sam Hose?

The questions that Turner's story raises are not just about women as victims: her story and reactions to it show women playing multiple roles—as victims, as loved ones left behind, and as those who fought back using grassroots, institutional and artistic forms of resistance. Each role reveals new complications, however. Narrative disruptions have rewards and consequences. Conventional wisdom on lynching posits that turn-of-the-century Black women had greater leeway for speaking out.[22]

Surely what happened to Turner shows otherwise, as do the creative responses where textual and archival evidence document Black women struggling with what they could and could not say. Just as some have viewed women's memories as disposable, others have assumed their voices to be problem free. Yet race, class, gender, aesthetic traditions, and more mediate expressions of anger and pain. When a new generation of artists and writers recovered Turner's "hidden memory," they faced the same old problems. If the story does not fit the narrative, then how does one find the form to fit the story? How does an individual artist craft a work of communal mourning and healing? How does a Black woman speak her truth about a Black woman killed for speaking her truth?

The irony is that not long after creating such a moving tribute to Turner, Tesfagiorgis retired *Hidden Memories* from circulation. She was not the first to make such a move: Meta Warrick Fuller had walked that path before.

Honorée Fanonne Jeffers' "dirty south moon"

For some historians, Mary Turner has come to epitomize horrific injustice.[23] For some artists and writers, she has come to symbolize what happens when creative expression meets brutal oppression. One result can be silence, even among the most courageous. Conversely, creative responses to Turner reveal moments of profound insight and beauty. Sometimes the successes and the struggles are hard to tell apart. Fuller created one of the earliest works of visual art to depict a lynching, and certainly the first to focus on a woman. Tesfagiorgis helped to lead a vanguard of feminist artists recovering difficult subjects in innovative ways. After breaking new ground, both pulled their works from view.

Contemporary writer Honorée Fanonne Jeffers shares affinities with these artists. She does not read her Turner poem "dirty south moon" at public appearances because it remains too close. However, she did publish the piece in her collection *Red Clay Suite* so that it could go out into the world and accomplish its cultural work.[24] In a telephone interview, Jeffers was forthcoming about her writing process and her intentions. "I'm just trying to honor my ancestors," Jeffers said. "People want you to write pretty little poems that document but don't upset. But how can you write a poem about a woman who was killed and her baby ripped from her womb and not upset?" The result, a technically and emotionally jarring piece, reveals the difficulties involved in recovering painful, hidden memories such as Turner's.

The poem started out as a very different work. Jeffers first composed a pantoum, a quatrain-based form, where the second and fourth lines of each stanza become the first and third lines of the next. Jeffers thought the piece was "plodding" and sat on it for some time. The poem was too tight, Jeffers said; she was not allowing herself to feel grief. She wanted the poem to be "visceral," to "rip off the scab." Her solution: take her own advice to a student writer and let go. She shattered the structure, abandoning narrative for a series of loosely connected images. "dirty south moon," now in tercets, holds together rhythmically through the staccato beat of repeated phrases and multiple caesuras:

> the moon is here   the moon
> don't believe the sun arriving for its own sake
> thrall of nostalgia beating
>
> out *out* spot of moon   don't believe the sun
> or the tattoo of beauty   childhood tableaux
> thrall of nostalgia beating   white dress on clothesline

Opening up the pantoum's formal structure allowed Jeffers to go directly for the scab. These first two stanzas capture a key point, that one cannot trust received notions of the past. The moon illuminates something wrong with sunny, nostalgic tableaux that hold viewers in thrall. The words "out *out*," evoking Lady Macbeth, guilt and blood, point toward the "white dress on clothesline." Another memory hides in plain sight.

The poem holds accountable those who hide such memories, whether through commission or omission. Through its title, images, and the "brother" it addresses, "dirty south moon" talks back specifically to men and male-dominated cultural productions. "dirty south moon" as a title mixes Toomer's "Blood-Burning Moon," the lynching story that closes *Cane*'s first part, and "Dirty South," the hip-hop genre popularized by rappers from Atlanta, Memphis, New Orleans, and other New South cities. The poem begins by confronting a specific legacy of Southern violence, rooted in lynching culture, which criminalizes Black men and erases Black women. Women appear to be absent from the Old South pastoral that opens "dirty south moon." They are hinted at only through allusion ("out *out*") and outline ("white dress on clothesline"), as if a body has been removed from a crime scene. In Toomer's "Blood Burning Moon," women are not absent, but highly present and objectified: Louisa's role is a prize between competing men. Similarly, in Dirty South song lyrics, women take center stage, often on the dance floor. Simultaneously, while rappers in this mostly male industry confront, even flaunt, Southern stereotypes about Black men, they do so at the expense of Black women, who they relegate to roles as sexy 'shawties', predatory baby mamas, 'hos', and bitches.[25] For them, Jeffers speaks out.

The poem's moon illuminates what the "dirty south," whether Old or New, refuses to recognize: how much women give and, more importantly, give up for men. Here, the sacrifice is two lives, of mother and child. Like many early antilynching works, "dirty south moon" employs a Black Christ motif, directly engaging the subject matter's inherent religious potential— "her name is mary."[26] The poem complicates easy attempts at redemption, however. The lynching scene contains mostly verbs, with no blood of the lamb to wash the sinner clean: "a falling child starts/stops crying knife unlocking its mother." When all is over, "nothing holy said." The sin of denial compounds the sin of murder. The speaker asks the brother—adamantly in the last lines—to acknowledge this sacrifice:

look *look here*

The caesura directs the brother and, by implication, readers to two painful realities: the gruesome caesarean abortion that prompted this poem's making and the historical gaps where memories like Turner's lie, hidden in plain sight. "don't you refuse her," the poem commands the brother, "don't commit old sins." These truths need to be acknowledged, these stories need to be mourned. Or, to use the poem's terms, these "old blues" need a proper singing.

Jeffers challenges readers to look and, by looking, to join her in singing those blues. Her poem, along with her willingness to talk about writing it (even if reading it publicly remains too difficult), accomplishes something significant within the trajectory of Turner responses. Overt expressions of anger and pain vexed an artist like Fuller to the point of silence, and Grimké, to the point of obsession. Jeffers first composed what she called a "plodding . . . message poem" until she allowed the truth she needed to speak to fracture form and syntax. The result is a powerful work that owns its outrage and demands accountability from readers, too.

Tesfagiorgis and Jeffers use similar strategies as postmodern feminists. The visual artist interrupts the otherwise linear field with the circle that tells Turner's story. She points the way into the hidden memory's pain, and the way out, through the recursive mourning process. The poet interrupts text with visible fragmentation, image phrases separated by caesuras and stanzas, its trajectory difficult to follow as a gruesome denouement unfolds. Upon closer inspection, the white dress on a clothesline becomes the lynching victim's body.

Both artists mean to confront, to rip off the scab, to use Jeffers' term. The difference between the two is one of audience and approach. *Hidden Memories* focuses on forgotten women and their stories. "dirty south moon" also targets those who have done the forgetting. If mourning and healing remain to be done for the legacy of racial violence, everyone whose life it has touched, past and present, must take an active role in the process.

The Mary Turner Project

Remembering Mary Turner and her baby as part of a traumatic local incident is very different from remembering them as victims in their own right or as paradigmatic stories. A wide gulf separates the response of an artist outside the community and that of someone whose ancestors may have been involved on some level, or someone who, as a newer local resident, feels invested in speaking out or preserving civic pride. Different frames of reference may be necessary in talking about national and local memory. As complex as trauma is, community stakeholders may even need different frames of reference for discussing their own experiences before coming together as one group.

Parallels do exist, however. The significant amount of work on cultural trauma and collective memory demonstrates that wounds of the mind and spirit, unlike wounds of the body, are not direct and knowable.[27] Nor can they be reached in ways direct and familiar. The routes to hidden memory, as Tesfagiorgis and Jeffers have shown, are circuitous and fragmented. What does it mean when local residents must travel the same routes? It is relatively easy for scholars to demonstrate how artists recover women's voices using phrases such as "breaking the silence," "talking back," and "fracturing form and syntax." How does a community perform similar actions? In this case, the narratives that get disrupted involve a shared sense of identity. Stories about the past that elide the traumatic memory must be taken apart and reshaped to include all stakeholders. Such work does not come easy because different groups have conflicting interpretations. Feelings run high. Not everyone agrees that the recovery process is even necessary. Successfully working through that process as a community therefore means radically altering how groups relate to one another. Local residents cannot change their narratives without changing the way they talk. Form and syntax shift here, too, as old modes of discourse make way for the new.

When university and community members launched The Mary Turner Project, they became part of a growing movement. Similar groups have formed across the United States to work toward justice and healing. Their missions are location specific. An early organization, The Rosewood Heritage Foundation, formed after survivors of a 1923 massacre, won a reparations suit against the State of Florida in 1994. In 1999, the Moore's Ford Memorial Committee near Monroe, Georgia, put up one of the first historical markers to commemorate a lynching. In 2005, Mississippi's Philadelphia Coalition played an instrumental role in the conviction of Edgar Ray Killen for the 1964 deaths of civil rights workers Andrew Goodman, James Chaney, and Michael Schwerner. These groups do share ideals. An umbrella organization, The Alliance for Truth and Racial Reconciliation describes the common goal as "truth-seeking and reconciliation on issues of racial violence."[28] Sherrilyn A. Ifill outlines what that process entails in her book *On the Courthouse Lawn: Confronting the Legacy of Lynching in the Twenty-First Century*. Drawing from the successes and struggles of the South African Truth and

Reconciliation Commission during the mid-1990s, Ifill explains the importance of replacing ideas of justice rooted in retribution with those rooted in restoration.[29] Two points are key: First, restorative justice does not imply that a society will be restored to an illusory prior state of wholeness or peace. Loved ones cannot be returned; destroyed locations or communities, replaced. Restorative justice acknowledges rifts and fractures, and attempts to build something new rather than recreate what has been lost forever. Second, restorative justice does not dispense with prosecution or reparations, but sees them within a framework of possibilities. Telling the truth and accepting responsibility are key elements of the healing process. Ifill offers several different alternatives for doing those things: acknowledging lynching in public spaces, teaching about it in public schools, putting gravestones at unmarked burial sites, and eliciting apologies from institutions that were complicit in local incidents.

Prosecutions or reparations, however, are not the main goal of reconciliation. The goal is a new community, Ifill says, where "formerly excluded stories become part of the history, identity, and shared experience of all the residents" (133). The process of healing from violence is complex, as The Mary Turner Project's efforts show. One level of resistance includes local whites. As Ifill explains, "Whites fear or resent being branded as racist, or they simply refuse to see themselves as responsible in any way for incidents in which they were not involved" (134). Both The Mary Turner Project and *The Valdosta Daily Times* worked to demonstrate that the May 2009 commemoration service was intended to bring the community together, not divide it. "Discovering the Truth to Heal from the Past," the program announced. Editorials concurred: "this weekend's ceremony is about recognizing that past, not reliving it, not demonizing anyone." Still, local television stations would not cover the event, and one letter writer fulminated to the *Times,* "Shame on the professor at VSU [organizer Mark George of Valdosta State University] . . . . This community needs to be aware of what liberal professors are teaching our young adults."[30]

Whites are not the only ones who perpetuated 90 years of local silence, however. Ifill states, "The silence that followed a lynching denied blacks the opportunity to confront their fears, anger, and confusion. The lynching became more powerful because it was taboo" (146). Survivor reticence prevented talk in subsequent generations—at least publicly. A journalist who grew up in the area, and later moved away, spoke off record about adults discussing the lynchings when he was young, but never telling him anything directly. "It's not the kind of story you tell the children," he said. During the commemoration ceremony, many local Blacks came forward to talk openly for the first time; others found it hard to do so. One woman barely got out, through huge sobs, a story about her grandmother, also pregnant, being mistaken for Mary Turner and getting pulled from a wagon, then being let go as she was "just Aunt Polly." A local descendent of the Turners tried to speak, broke down, and stopped. Almost 90 years later, the violence of 1918 still has the power to silence.

That power will not diminish until the healing process has moved further along. A commemoration service provides only one step, albeit a significant one. The historical marker does symbolic work that radiates outward, standing in contrast to what James Loewen calls a "landscape of white supremacy." Speaking about the need for such markers more generally, Loewen states, "All across America, the landscape suffers from amnesia, not about everything, but about many crucial events and issues of our past."[31] Prior to the May 2009 service, the area near Turner's lynching site remained pretty much as the lynch mob left it: a forgotten space off a river bridge, collecting beer bottles, cigarette butts, and other detritus from passing automobiles. A sign that tells the story of what happened to Turner and the other victims of the May 1918 lynching rampage, in a now fully cleared and cleaned site, counters other local symbols that give the impression the only valid history is celebratory or white. Hampton Smith's visibly phallic headstone stands as one reminder of whose memory was meant to dominate this story. Beyond his grave, street and business signs still bear mob members' surnames. Linking the area's past to a long-contested racial terrain, Valdosta's water tower proclaims, "Southern Charm, Not *Gone With the Wind*." A statue of a Confederate soldier stands guard over the Lowndes County courthouse downtown. Confederate iconography (the "Stars and Bars") remains part of Georgia's flag, which flies before all state buildings, including the libraries and historical museums where it was difficult, if not impossible, to find information about local lynchings before 2001. I know because I looked. We never had any lynchings here, I was told, again and again.[32] It ultimately took some white boys from the local high school, a can of black spray paint, and some Barbie dolls to begin shattering that myth. As Turner's story demonstrates, however, fracturing old narratives does not lead automatically to new, improved substitutes.

The Mary Turner Project, a group made up of VSU students and faculty along with local civil rights activists, was formed in 2007, determined to tell this story openly—not in secret; not in uncanny, symbolic acts involving dolls. With the marker in place as of May 2010, their work is not yet done. For the healing process to be successful, for the goals of restorative justice to be met, the story of the May 1918 lynchings must be told beyond a backroad plaque: it must become a fully acknowledged part of local history.

Ifill points out that for a community to be a real community, each of its members must have an actual stake. All stories must be heard and acknowledged. Where cases of lynching and other forms of violence are involved, this includes the stories of victims, perpetrators, beneficiaries, and bystanders. Each holds a piece of the truth that must be aired. And each gains in some way from telling that piece of the truth: perpetrators, beneficiaries, and bystanders acknowledge responsibility and let go of guilt. Victims acknowledge pain and let go of anger. All exchange the silence that controls them for speech that acknowledges and mourns, as a community, what happened.

To move beyond that silence, everyone whose voice the historical marker represents must feel empowered to speak, especially within the institutional arenas that control and mediate local discourse. Ifill describes those institutions—the media, the business community, faith communities, educational systems, and legal systems—as a final, significant piece of the puzzle. Institutions should be part of reconciliation dialogues and accept responsibility for the roles they played historically in perpetuating racism, racial violence, and the silence surrounding these issues. Ifill explains, "The individual actor is emboldened because he believes that his community's institutions . . . will ultimately support his actions" (155). Lynching was, after all, community sanctioned punishment of a person perceived at the time to be a criminal. Even if contemporary society does not judge Mary Turner's act—expressing anger over her husband's lynching—as a crime, local and state authorities in 1918 did, and they stood behind the men who killed her. Such a widely-witnessed event touched the lives of all who lived in the immediate area, no matter how they were related to the victim. Healing and reconciliation efforts must touch their descendents' lives as well.

Narrative Possibilities

Turner's death resonated well beyond the local area. In an address before the 1919 National Conference on Lynching, James Weldon Johnson cited it as "a national crime," that should make his audience members "hang your head in shame."[33] What made Turner's story stand out for Johnson is also what made it become a hidden memory for others years later. A mob brutally lynched a pregnant woman for reasons unrelated to "the usual crime" of rape. Even though Ida B. Wells and other activists had been working tirelessly since the 1890s to break the connection between white mobs, Black men, and white women, fear of what Johnson called the "Burly Black Brute" still dominated public opinion in 1919. Turner's story did not fit that larger narrative and, for a time, seemed to challenge it effectively. By the early 1930s, she was no longer a sensational headline, but a nameless colored woman whose story joined the ranks of other shameful acts, usually male and usually named. Even though statistical analyses today bear out Wells and Johnson's arguments, Black male criminality and lynching still seem intrinsically linked.[34]

When lynching is perceived as a national event or recalled in historical memory, the bodies in question are male. If any death was felt as a national trauma, it was Emmett Till's. Historians credit Clarence Thomas for bringing lynching back into public consciousness after claiming to be the victim of a "high-tech" one during his Supreme Court confirmation hearings.[35] When men become the focal point of such public spectacles, women get relegated to the margins, even when they play central roles. Scholars writing about the Anita Hill-Clarence Thomas incident from multiple disciplines generally agree that he won the rhetorical battle because he had a powerful narrative to manipulate and she did not. In 1991, Thomas could stand before a Senate subcommittee to recall, in one short phrase, a long history of white-male-on-Black-male victimization. However, as Elsa Barkley Brown pointedly asks, does his reconstruction of Black history include women like Mary Turner?[36]

Her question is rhetorical, implying that it does not but should. As scholars, activists, artists, and everyday people begin to think seriously about the legacy of racial violence, Turner's story merits particular attention. Not because it represents the norm, but because, as a story from the margins, it offers critical insights into the center. Statistically, mobs lynched women far less than they did men. But the presence of female victims, especially in gruesome spectacles such as Turner's, has much to say about the ways that lynching supporters defended the act to others and to themselves. The recurring, yet underexamined presence of Turner's story in art, literature, and oral history also prompts questions about the continuing dominance of male-centered narratives. Why is she a "hidden memory," and why is her situation paradigmatic for those of other women? Beyond numbers lie hard questions about why Black women remain marginal to the history of racial violence. Yet Turner's story is not just about female victimization: its richest perspectives come from the complex ways people respond to racial violence—as current threat or traumatic past.

Turner paid for her outrage over lynching with her life. Those whom her story compelled found themselves confronting a crisis of representation. Turner's death defied sense and conventional lynching discourse. The most effective way to tell her story, ironically, was to do what Turner herself had done: disrupt the narrative. Contemporary artists, writers, and activists face similar circumstances as they seek to create inclusive, healing stories. Those old narratives still need disrupting. Freida High Tesfagiorgis, Honorée Fanonne Jeffers, and The Mary Turner Project employ a significant woman's story toward that goal. Bringing Turner's memory from its hidden place into the light does not provide all the answers, but it does offer a more nuanced way of seeing.

Notes

1. Jingle Davis, "FBI May Join Probe of Mock Lynching: Students Suspended for Act Using Black Doll," *Atlanta Journal Constitution,* Wednesday Home Edition, October 9, 2002, Metro News, sec. 1B; Viki Soady, "Women's Studies 'Where Civil Rights Never Made It,' " *Chronicle of Higher Education,* November 22, 2002, sec. B12; Jessica Pope, "Speakout Hosted by VSU Addresses Diversity," *The Valdosta Daily Times,* November 19, 2002; "Parents, Others Must Bring School Changes," *The Valdosta Daily Times,* November 24, 2002, http://www.valdostadailytimes.com (accessed June 6, 2010).

   In addition to its news and editorial coverage of the story, *The Valdosta Daily Times* runs a column called "Rants and Raves," where anyone may call in commentary on any subject. What locals call the "Barbie lynchings" was discussed there for about six weeks afterwards.
2. Walter White, "Memorandum for Governor Dorsey from Walter F. White," National Association for the Advancement of Colored People, Papers, Group 1, Box, C-353, Manuscripts Division, Library of Congress. See also Walter White, "The Work of a Mob," *The Crisis,* September 1918, 221–23; and Christopher C. Meyers, " 'Killing Them by the Wholesale': A Lynching Rampage in South Georgia," *Georgia Historical Quarterly,* 90.2 (Summer 2006): 214–235.
3. I lived and worked in the area, as Assistant Professor of English at Valdosta State University, from 1997 to 2001. During that time I did some of the research for the book from which this essay is taken, *Mary Turner and the Memory of Lynching* (Athens: University of Georgia Press, 2011). The noose incident involving the dolls took place the year after I moved away.
4. Julie Buckner Armstrong, "The Infamous, Neglected, But Not Forgotten Story of Mary Turner," African American Studies Lecture Series, Valdosta State University, Valdosta, GA, February 8, 2001; Meyers, "Killing Them by the Wholesale"; Dean Pohling, "Putting the Past to Rest," *The Valdosta Daily*

Times, May 13, 2009. The Mary Turner Project, *Remembering Mary Turner*, http://www.maryturner.org (accessed June 6, 2010).

Both Pohling and Mary Turner Project spokesperson Mark George directly connect the organization's founding to the noose incident.

5. Wood and Donaldson, "Introduction: Lynching's Legacy in American Culture," Special Issue on Lynching and American Culture, *Mississippi Quarterly* 61.1–2 (Winter-Spring 2008), 8.
6. For news accounts of the story, see the NAACP Papers, Group 1, Boxes C-353 and C-355, Manuscripts Division, Library of Congress (also available on microfilm); and The Tuskegee Institute News Clippings File, 1899–1966, Microfilm, Reel 221.
7. White, "The Work of a Mob," and *Rope and Faggot: A Biography of Judge Lynch* (1929, South Bend: University of Notre Dame Press, 2001), 29; The Anti-Lynching Crusaders, "A Million Women United to Suppress Lynching," 1922, Grace Nail Johnson Correspondence, James Weldon Johnson Papers, Series II, Box 26, Folder 6, Beinecke Rare Book and Manuscript Library, Yale University.

   Other references to Turner can be found in NAACP, *Thirty Years of Lynching in the United States, 1889–1918* (1919, New York: Arno Press, 1969); Commission on Interracial Cooperation, "Mob Murder in America: A Challenge to Every American Citizen," 1929; Commission on Interracial Cooperation Papers, 1919–1944, Microfilm Series V, Literature 1920–44, Reel 29; and Harry Haywood and Milton Howard, "Lynching: A Weapon of National Oppression" (New York: Labor Research Association, 1932).
8. Meta Warrick Fuller, *Mary Turner: A Silent Protest Against Mob Violence* (Boston, MA: Museum of African American History, 1919); Grimké, "Goldie," *Selected Works of Angelina Weld Grimké*, Ed. Carolivia Herron (New York: Oxford University Press, 1991), 282–81; Carrie Williams Clifford, "Little Mother," *The Widening Light, The Writings of Carrie Williams Clifford and Carrie Law Morgan Figgs*, Ed. P. Jane Splawn (New York: G.K. Hall, 1997), 57–58; Anne Spencer, "White Things," *The Crisis*, March 1923: 204; and Jean Toomer, "Kabnis," *Cane*, Ed. Darwin T. Turner (1923, New York: Norton, 1988).
9. On Tesfagiorgis, *Hidden Memories*, see Robert Henkes, *The Art of Black American Women: Works of Twenty-Four Artists of the Twentieth Century* (Jefferson, NC: McFarland, 1993), 113; Jeffers, "dirty south moon," *Red Clay Suite* (Carbondale, IL: Southern Illinois University Press, 2007), 33–4; and Jeffers, "If You Get There Before I Do," *Story Quarterly* 41 (2005): 199–219.

   Contemporary responses also include multiple items on the Internet and a graphic but well-contextualized display of Hayes and Mary Turner at Baltimore, Maryland's National Great Blacks in Wax Museum.

Several works reference the lynching of a pregnant woman or a related image without mentioning Turner by name. See Kara Walker's notebook sketches in *My Complement, My Enemy, My Oppressor, My Love*, Org. Philippe Vergne (Minneapolis, MN: Walker Art Center, 2007); Alice Walker, *The Third Life of Grange Copeland* (New York: Washington Square Press, 1970), 322; and Octavia Butler, *Kindred* (Boston, MA: Beacon Press), 191.

10. Wood and Donaldson, 8–10; Jonathan Markovitz, *Legacies of Lynching: Racial Violence and Memory* (Minneapolis, MN: University of Minnesota Press, 2004), 7.
11. Jacqueline Goldsby, *A Spectacular Secret: Lynching in American Life and Literature* (Chicago: University of Chicago Press, 2006), 8.
12. White's "Memorandum for Governor Dorsey" names the ringleaders of the mob that killed Turner, among them members of Smith the local coroner's family, and the foreman of the coroner's jury, which insured no charges would be brought in the matter. See also Meyers, "Killing them by the Wholesale."
13. See CIC, "Mob Murder in America"; Haywood and Howard, "Lynching: A Weapon of National Oppression"; and White, *Rope and Faggot*, 29.

    Local residents near Monroe, Georgia, insist that Dorothy Malcolm was seven months pregnant when she was killed at the Moore's Ford Bridge in 1946, and that her fetus was removed, although Laura Wexler found no evidence in official investigations. See *Fire in a Canebrake: The Last Mass Lynching in America* (New York: Scribner's, 2003), 88.
14. *Cane*, 92.
15. Kara Walker, email to author, October 8, 2008; Honorée Jeffers, telephone interview, May 22, 2007; and Philip Dray, *At the Hands of Persons Unknown: The Lynching of Black America* (New York: Modern Library, 2002), 245–46.
16. My discussion of this piece comes from the image available in Henkes, *The Art of Black American Women*, 113. The artist chose not to sell or display it after this publication. Tesfagiorgis, email to author, March 23, 2005.
17. *Bearing Witness: Contemporary Works by African-American Women Artists*, Org. Jontyle Theresa Robinson (Atlanta: Spelman College and Rizzoli International Publishing, 1996). See especially Robinson's "Passages: A Curatorial Viewpoint," 15–18. Relevant critical works by Tesfagiorgis include "Afrofemcentrism and Its Fruition in the Art of Elizabeth Catlett and Faith Ringgold"; *Sage: A Scholarly Journal on Black Women* 4.1 (Spring 1987): 25–29; and "In Search of a Discourse and Critique(s) that Center the Art of Black Women Artists," *Theorizing Black Feminisms: The Visionary Pragmatism of Black Women*, Ed. Stanlie M. James and Abena P.A. Busia (London: Routlege, 1991), 228–266.
18. NAACP, *Thirty Years of Lynching in the United States*. A table on page 33 breaks down the number of women lynched by race and state.

19. Elsa Barkley Brown, "Imaging Lynching: African American Women, Communities of Struggle, and Collective Memory," *African American Women Speak Out on Anita Hill-Clarence Thomas*, Ed. Geneva Smitherman (Detroit, MI: Wayne State University Press, 1995), 100–24.
20. Kathy A. Perkins and Judith L. Stephens, eds., *Strange Fruit: Plays on Lynching by American Women* (Bloomington, IN: Indiana University Press, 1998) changed the way literary scholars think about women's responses to lynching. As Koritha Mitchell explains, these plays shift our gaze away from Black bodies into Black homes, forcing confrontation with the effects of violence on families and communities. See Mitchell, "Anti-Lynching Plays: Angelina Weld Grimké, Alice Dunbar Nelson, and the Evolution of African American Drama," *Post-Bellum, Pre-Harlem: African American Literature and Culture, 1877–1919*, Ed. Barbara McCaskill and Caroline Gebhard (New York: New York University Press, 2006), 210–30. Likewise, Crystal Feimster's *Southern Horrors: Women and the Politics of Rape and Lynching* (Cambridge: Harvard University Press, 2009) re-narrates lynching history from the perspective of its two most outspoken female figures, Ida B. Wells and Rebecca Felton. Feimster's work demonstrates Jim Crow's polarizing effects, showing how Wells and Felton could have similar goals for women (a stronger political voice and better protection against violence) yet remain separated across a wide racial gulf. What happens to the Black woman, Feimster's work suggests, caught in the intersections of Jim Crow's racism and sexism?
21. Goldsby, *A Spectacular Secret*, 8; Ida B. Wells, *Southern Horrors: Lynch Law in All its Phases, Southern Horrors and Other Writings: The Anti-Lynching Campaign of Ida B. Wells, 1892–1900*, Ed. Jacqueline Jones Royster (Boston, MA: Bedford Books, 1997), 52.
22. See W. Fitzhugh Brundage in "The Roar on the Other Side of Silence," *Under Sentence of Death: Lynching in the South*, Ed. W. Fitzhugh Brundage (Chapel Hill, NC: University of North Carolina Press, 1997), 280; Adam Gussow, *Seems Like Murder Here: Southern Violence and the Blues Tradition* (Chicago: University of Chicago Press, 2002), 164; and my response to this point in " 'The people . . . took exception to her remarks': Meta Warrick Fuller, Angelina Weld Grimké, and the Lynching of Mary Turner," *Mississippi Quarterly* 61.1–2 (Winter-Spring 2008): 113–141.
23. Historians point to the 1918 incident as a touchstone for understanding mob violence. In *Lynching in the New South: Georgia and Virginia, 1880–1930* (Urbana, IL: University of Illinois Press, 1993), W. Fitzhugh Brundage says that the lynchings "provided an extraordinary example of wanton slaughter" (35) and contributed to Brooks County's reputation as "the most mob-prone county in both the region and the state—and possibly even the South" (119). Leon Litwack writes that Turner's death was so brutal it "exceeded the most vivid of imaginations," *Trouble in Mind: Black Southerners in the Age of Jim Crow* (New York: Knopf,

1998), 288. Philip Dray remarks that it "introduced a new low in the level of degradation associated with lynching" (*At the Hands of Persons Unknown*, 246).

24. The poem was originally published in the journal *Meridians: Feminism, Race, Transnationalism*. Jeffers discussed her work with me in a telephone interview on May 22, 2007. She did not know most of her forebears' responses, having learned Turner's story from Philip Dray's book. Dray, like most historians, does not discuss the arts and literature.
25. On Dirty South as confrontation with lynching culture, see Riché Richardson, *Black Masculinity in the U.S. South: From Uncle Tom to Gansta* (Athens: The University of Georgia Press, 2007).
26. For a discussion of the controversial Black Christ figure, see Dora Apel, *Imagery of Lynching: Black Men, White Women, and the Mob* (New Brunswick: Rutgers University Press, 2004), 102–04; and Qiana Whitted, " 'In my flesh shall I see God': Ritual Violence and Racial Redemption in 'The Black Christ,' " *African American Review* 38 (2004): 379–94.
27. Cathy Caruth, *Unclaimed Experience: Trauma, Narrative, and History* (Baltimore, MD: Johns Hopkins University Press, 1996), 5–6. The essays in *Cultural Trauma and Collective Identity*, ed. Jeffrey C. Alexander et al. (Berkeley, CA: University of California Press, 2004) have been very helpful for understanding what has taken place locally in Brooks and Lowndes County, especially Alexander's "Towards a Theory of Cultural Trauma" and Neil J. Smelser's "Psychological Trauma and Cultural Trauma."
28. Information about and links to each group can be found on the Alliance Web site, which is housed at the University of Mississippi's William Winter Institute for Racial Reconciliation, http://www.winterinstitute.org/atrr/ (accessed June 6, 2010).
29. Sherralyn A. Ifill, *On the Courthouse Lawn: Confronting the Legacy of Lynching in the Twenty-First Century* (Boston, MA: Beacon Press, 2007). Subsequent page number references will be given in the text.
30. "Discovering the Truth to Heal from the Past: Remembering Mary Turner and the Lynching Victims of 1918," May 16, 2009, Hahira Community Center, Hahira, Georgia; "Our Opinion: Mary Turner: A Past Unearthed," *The Valdosta Daily Times,* May 13, 2009; and "Rant and Rave," May 20, 2009 *The Valdosta Daily Times*, http://www.valdostadailytimes.com.
31. James W. Loewen, *Lies Across America: What Our Historic Sites Get Wrong* (New York: New Press, 1999), 16–18.
32. Brundage, in *Lynching in the New South* (270–80), notes that Brooks County had 22, and Lowndes had 6 deaths, including the 1918 incident.
33. James Weldon Johnson, Address, May 5, 1919, NAACP Papers, Administrative Files, National Conference on Lynching, Group 1, Box, C-334, Manuscripts Division, Library of Congress.

34. Steward E. Tolnay and E.M. Beck, *A Festival of Violence: An Analysis of Southern Lynchings, 1882–1930* (Urbana, IL: University of Illinois Press, 1995), 47–48.
35. On Emmett Till and historical memory, see Harriett Pollack and Christopher Metress, eds., *Emmett Till in Literary Memory and Imagination* (Baton Rouge: Louisiana State University Press, 2008), especially the introduction on pages 1–15; and Christopher Metress, ed., *The Lynching of Emmett Till: A Documentary Narrative* (Charlottesville: University of Virginia Press, 2002). On Clarence Thomas and historical memory, see Joel Williamson, "Wounds Not Scars: Lynching, the National Conscience, and the American Historian," *The Journal of American History* 83 (1997): 1221–53, along with the round table Williamson's article occasioned, "What We See and Can't See in the Past," *The Journal of American History* 83 (1997): 1217–72.
36. Brown, 103. The Hill-Thomas hearings resulted in at least two essay collections, the Geneva Smitherman volume that contains Brown's article, and Toni Morrison, ed., *Race-ing Justice, En-gendering Power: Essays on Anita Hill, Clarence Thomas, and the Construction of Social Reality* (New York: Pantheon, 1992). Along with Brown's, another particularly useful essay is Wahneema Lubiano's "Black Ladies, Welfare Queens, and State Minstrels: Ideological Welfare by Narrative Means" in Morrison, 323–63.

    Wood and Donaldson draw from Markovitz to establish their idea that lynching may be used as a *prism* for viewing race. Markovitz draws from Lubiano to establish his idea that lynching may be used as a *lens* for viewing race. Her term is "synecdoche." Black women, Lubiano explains, have very few narratives to draw from when constructing themselves publicly. One is the "welfare-dependent single mother . . . the synecdoche, the shortest possible shorthand, for the pathology of poor, urban, black culture" (335). Likewise, for Markovitz, lynching becomes "the shortest possible shorthand" for racism. He, too, acknowledges the dearth of Black women's stories.

CHAPTER 2

Sisters in Motherhood(?): The Politics of Race and Gender in Lynching Drama

Koritha Mitchell

The founding of the Association of Southern Women for the Prevention of Lynching (ASWPL) was hailed as one of the most significant contributions to antilynching activism. Newspapers across the country commended the group's courage and grace,[1] and Black women (such as activist Nannie Burroughs) were pleased to see white women accept responsibility for changing public sentiment on mob violence. When considering the organization's November 1930 Resolution, it is no wonder that Burroughs later referred to the ASWPL as "the most effective organization now working...."[2] ASWPL members declared, "Distressed by the recent upsurge of [sic] lynchings, and noting that people still condone such crimes on the grounds that they are necessary to the protection of womanhood, we, a group of white women representing eight southern states, desire publicly to repudiate and condemn such defense of lynching, and to put ourselves definitely on record as opposed to this crime in every form and under all circumstances." They continue, "We are profoundly convinced that lynching is not a defense of womanhood or of anything else, but rather a menace to private and public safety...."[3] Indeed, founder Jessie Daniel Ames reported, "convinced by the consideration of the facts," these women resolved "no longer to remain silent" as the crime of lynching was "done in their name."[4]

In challenging conventional understandings of mob violence, these women built on the foundation laid by Black women activists. As historian Jacqueline Dowd Hall puts it, "For decades black women had filled the front ranks of the fight against lynching. . . . Together with black men, they had long sought the white southern support that . . . the ASWPL belatedly offered. Indeed, years of black struggle against lynching shaped the social and political climate that made the founding of the Anti-Lynching Association possible."[5] For instance, Ida B. Wells had made it clear in the 1890s that lynching had little to do with the rape of white women and that mobs created the myth of the Black male rapist to paralyze Black men just as they were becoming a political force. Wells argued that this strategy was effective because the charge of rape immediately "placed [African Americans] beyond the pale of human sympathy," making pleas for justice on their behalf seem like "an excuse for their continued wrongs."[6] Wells had also argued that a code of chivalry protecting white women while allowing for the rape and exploitation of Black women and girls was no chivalry at all. Equally important, she exposed the frequency with which southern men disrespected the white women teachers who had come south to educate freedmen and their children. That is, she identified the discourse of protection as a way of restricting white women's movement and dictating the scope of their activity.

While revising assumptions about what motivated the mob, Black women worked to awaken white women regarding their responsibility to oppose lynching and regarding the benefits of doing so. The ASWPL published pamphlets and otherwise educated the public to recognize that so-called chivalry simply restricted white women's freedom, but these ideas had been first articulated publicly by Black women in the nineteenth century. African American women had long been trying to pull white women into the fight against mob violence.

The ASWPL marked white women's willingness to shoulder the level of responsibility for ending lynching that their Black counterparts had been calling upon them to accept, so the group's efforts were in concert with those of Black women activists. The founding of the ASWPL in 1930 therefore provides an opportunity for thinking about Black and white women's cooperation in antilynching activism. Taking this opportunity does not mean that scholars will discover an "interracial" movement in the way modern readers might normally conceive of it, however. That is, it was not an example of Black and white women working side by side in any simple way. Firstly, the ASWPL emerged in 1930—decades after the initial height of mob violence in the 1890s and decades after

Wells and others had been working with a sense of urgency. Secondly, the ASWPL was expressly an organization for white women.[7] As a result, unique approaches are required for examining the relationship between this important group and the Black women who had long hoped that white women would become their true allies.

Here, I consider the organization's emergence through the lens provided by Black-authored lynching plays. In other work, I have discussed lynching drama as an archive that offers insights not to be gleaned from the sources that scholars typically consult.[8] If the ASWPL represents white women's willingness to join Black women in opposing lynching, it is significant that it took them decades to do so. Still, it seems that Black women never completely abandoned the hope of a true coalition with their white counterparts, and the unique genre of lynching drama offers a way of understanding the ebb and flow of that undying faith. I focus on two lynching plays by Black women: one that arose from the belief that white women would feel inspired to join the fight against lynching, and one written after white women had so fully accepted responsibility that they had formed an anti-lynching organization.

Written before and after the founding of the ASWPL, Angelina Weld Grimké's three-act drama *Rachel* and May Miller's one-act script *Nails and Thorns* illuminate Black women's understanding of lynching and their role as artist-activists as well as their assumptions about effective alliances. *Rachel* makes clear that Grimké viewed lynching as much a crime against Black families and households as against Black bodies. Because the homes devastated were so often those of upstanding individuals, not criminals, she seems to have felt a duty to break the silence caused by believing mainstream depictions of the race. As an artist-activist, she refused to be shamed into silence about the race's victimization; she did not accept the notion that opposing lynching was tantamount to excusing criminality. By not only writing the play, but also later publishing a rationale for it, she left archival evidence of the importance she placed on convincing white women to help end lynching. These documents also show that Grimké believed that whites would answer that call if they could see the pain of African Americans who reminded them of themselves.

Composed while the ASWPL was hard at work, *Nails and Thorns* reveals the degree to which Miller understood, as much as Grimké had, that mob violence devastates families and communities long after the physical violence has ended. However, while Grimké refused to let shame silence her, Miller seems to have avoided the silence that might be inspired by gratitude. Given that white women were very publicly taking responsibility to help end lynching, and were often encountering hate and harassment as they did so, many may have believed that white women who opposed mob violence should be applauded and never criticized. Yet *Nails and Thorns* exposes the limitations of placing too much faith in well-intentioned whites. While *Rachel* depicted the reverberating pain that mobs visited upon Black households, Miller's script is concerned with showing that mob violence can have tragic consequences for whites, not just Blacks. Thus, it seems to have been written with no assumption that white women would identify with African Americans or African Americans' pain.

Black-authored Lynching Drama's Founding Ethos: Grimké's Faith in White Women

Black-authored lynching drama was initiated when Angelina Weld Grimké[9] set out to convince white women that lynching was a grave injustice because (contrary to accepted rhetoric) even upstanding Black citizens were vulnerable to it. She therefore emphasized her characters' propriety, education, and appreciation for European culture. She also highlighted the far-reaching consequences of racial violence, understanding that the mob's destructive power reverberated long after the victim's death. *Rachel* focuses on 18-year-old Rachel Loving, her mother, Mrs. Loving, and her younger brother Tom. The action occurs in their northern home 10 years after the death of the missing father. The mob targeted the father because he had written an editorial denouncing racial violence. His article had exposed the fact that a group of "respectable people in the town" had lynched a Black man despite knowing that "a white man was guilty." The father was told to retract his words, but the next issue of his newspaper contained an even more searing indictment, so "some dozen masked men" came to the house.[10] His widow, Mrs. Loving, recalls that she and her husband had been in bed but not asleep when whites "broke down the front door and made their way to our bedroom" (41). When the mob had begun dragging her husband down the hall, her 17-year-old son, George, tried to intervene; "it ended in [the mob] dragging them both out" (41).

Upon hearing her mother's testimony, Rachel questions the wisdom of investing in marriage and motherhood, and doubts God's willingness to protect Blacks who do. As a result, though she cares for her suitor, Mr. Strong, and he has prepared a home for them, she rejects his proposal. She cannot bear the thought of bringing children into a racist society (77). In fact, after realizing that all Black males are potential lynch victims,

Rachel reasons: "Why—it would be more merciful—to strangle the little things at birth" (42). Later, she agonizes, "And so this nation—this white Christian nation—has deliberately set its curse upon the most beautiful—the most holy thing in life—motherhood!" (42). As the action progresses, Rachel is haunted by the sound of children begging not to be born,[11] and she promises them that she will not bring them into the world. Feeling forced to abandon her dreams of motherhood, Rachel becomes convinced that she hears God laughing at her pain. As her sanity deteriorates, her anger escalates and she tries to outlaugh God, clearly regarding Him as her worst enemy (76). In tracing this spiritual and psychological decline, Grimké insists that lynching destruction surpasses the physical realm and threatens the soul and psyche of the race. When the head of the Loving household is murdered, his wife and surviving children are forced to start over; then, his wrongful death haunts their new home in the North, continuing to weaken the already diminished family; finally, it prevents Rachel from creating a home with her suitor. Thus, the Black male absence inflicted by the mob does not simply destroy an existing household: it prevents the successful creation of new ones.[12]

This lynching play, which focuses much more on long-term effects than on physical brutality, inaugurated the genre because it helped spark discussion among African Americans about Black identity, racial violence, and about what Black drama should accomplish. The script had been penned by 1914 since Grimké's acquaintances at the National Association for the Advancement of Colored People (NAACP) were reading the drafts as early as January 1915.[13] Later that year, W.E.B. Du Bois created a drama committee within the NAACP, and in March 1916, that committee sponsored a semi-professional production of *Rachel* in Washington, D.C. This production made it the first Black-authored, non-musical drama to be executed by Black actors for a broad audience.[14]

The initial presentation of *Rachel* ran for just two days,[15] but Grimké's work inspired conversations that led to an increasing investment in Black-authored drama by some of the most important "New Negro" leaders of the day. Grimké circulated her manuscript before Du Bois formed the drama committee, so her work was not a response to his call for Black-authored plays, but more likely an inspiration for it.[16] Then, once the committee decided to sponsor its debut, Grimké's text helped others to identify their own artistic mission. Alain Locke (often called "the architect of the New Negro Movement") and his Howard University colleague Montgomery Gregory objected to the NAACP's "propagandist platform." They therefore vowed to create a space in which "purely artistic" concerns reigned. The more Locke and Gregory publicized their approach, the more Du Bois refined his articulation of the need for political art.[17]

Without question, then, *Rachel* deeply impacted the founders of both the NAACP drama committee and Howard University's theatre department—organizations that would encourage and train Black playwrights throughout the 1920s.[18] Thus, by 1916 and without reaching Broadway, Grimké's work rejuvenated Black drama. To the extent that New Negro Renaissance leaders invested in drama, Grimké set their agenda. Du Bois, Locke, and Gregory often took their disagreement to the pages of periodicals, and many joined them, including authors who entered the debate by simply executing their own vision of what Black drama should accomplish. Some, like Willis Richardson, became playwrights after the premiere of *Rachel* because they were convinced that they could do a better job than Grimké had.[19] Others simply seemed to believe that Grimké's perspective on lynching and Black family life was too important to leave unaddressed. By 1930, at least nine more lynching plays were written by African American authors.[20] Whether impressed or disappointed with Grimké's work, Black writers suddenly turned to drama and worked to develop conventions, cultivate themes, and overall perfect the craft.

Why did Grimké's work spark so many revisions that lynching plays proliferated enough to constitute a genre? Above all, Grimké's creative choices were shaped by her belief that showcasing middle-class Blacks was the best way to demonstrate the race's right to citizenship. Part of her goal was to convince whites to identify African Americans not with the image that had been so consistently proffered, but with the Black middle class, whose values, behaviors, hopes and dreams were no different from their own.[21] Grimké also centered her work on mothers, believing that "if anything can make all women sisters underneath their skins it is motherhood."[22] She wrote assuming that witnessing Black women's maternal pain would help white women to "see, feel, understand just what effect their prejudice and the prejudice of their fathers, brothers, husbands, sons" had on the "souls of the colored mothers everywhere."[23]

In operating under the assumption that human recognition across racial lines could end lynching, Grimké was certainly not alone. She did in drama what Black women had done in other forms. For example, in 1904, Mary Church Terrell insisted in the pages of the *North American Review* that white women had a responsibility to use their domestic influence for the greater good. She calls on white women to stand with her against violence, but the nation's history creates skepticism that she refuses to hide. She explains, "It is too much to expect, perhaps, that the children of women who for generations looked upon the hardships and the degradation of their sisters of a darker hue with few if any protests, should have mercy and compassion upon the children of that oppressed race now. But what a tremendous influence for law and order, and what a mighty foe to mob violence Southern white women might be, if they would arise in the purity and power of their womanhood to implore their fathers, husbands and sons no longer to stain their hands with the black man's blood!"[24]

The same cautious optimism perhaps gave rise to Grimké's drama. As theatre historian Judith Stephens puts it, "*Rachel* stands as an indictment of white women who subscribed to the dominant ideology of idealized motherhood but who ignored the particular pain of black mothers whose children were born into an environment of racial bigotry and violence."[25] Accordingly, the Grimké whom modern scholars often read as conciliatory to white readers may have been working more in the spirit of Charlotte Hawkins Brown.[26] In 1920, Brown addressed the Methodist Women's Missionary Council in Tennessee insisting, "The negro woman of the South lays everything that happens to the members of her race at the door of the Southern white woman. Just why I don't know but we all feel that you can control your men. We feel that so far as lynching is concerned that, if the white women would take hold of the situation, that lynching would be stopped. . . ."[27] Rather than catering to white women, Brown sought to convict them, and Grimké seems to have written with the same goal in mind.

Indeed, Grimké asserted in 1920: "Since it has been understood that 'Rachel' preaches race suicide, I would emphasize that that was not my intention. To the contrary, the appeal was not primarily to the colored people, but to the whites."[28] She continued, "The majority of women, everywhere, although they are beginning to awaken, form one of the most conservative elements of society. They are, therefore, opposed to change. For this reason and for sex reasons the white women of this country are about the worst enemies with which the colored race has to contend."[29]

Even as she wrote assuming that these "enemies" could be converted, Grimké had no illusions that making Black pain legible would be an easy task. She worked with a keen awareness of the images that threatened to overshadow in everyone's imagination the realities of Black life as she knew it. She explained: "Whenever you say 'colored person' to a white man he immediately [. . .] conjures up in his mind the picture of what he calls 'the darky.' In other words, he believes, or says he does, that all colored people are a grinning, white-toothed, shiftless, carefree set, given to chicken-stealing, watermelon-eating, always, under all circumstances, properly obsequious to a white skin and always amusing."[30]

Clearly, Grimké was responding to minstrelsy and the tremendous popularity of stage versions of Uncle Tom,[31] and she was attuned to the power of multi-layered representation. In her formulation, when one *hears* Blacks mentioned, a specific *picture* comes to mind. Thus, she was concerned not just about the written word, but also about gestures, movements, objects, tones of voice, etcetera. Surely, Grimké was pulled away from poetry and fiction to drama by the possibility of having at her disposal an endless array of meaning-making signs and symbols which dramatic texts ideally put into action. In other words, as she worked to present truths about African Americans that were erased in mainstream discourse, she was especially sensitive to how powerful stage images had become. She therefore adds to the efforts made by Black women in speeches, essays, poems, and fiction by maximizing drama.

In fact, while Grimké's 1920 rationale argues that she wrote primarily for the whites, *Rachel* illuminates her assumptions about her role as an artist-activist and the service that she could provide to Black communities. In an often overlooked passage, *Rachel* articulates fundamental assumptions regarding Blacks' obligation to speak with pride about fallen community members, suggesting Grimké's own belief that drama could be used to affirm Black identity as much as it had been used to denigrate it. Early in Act 1, Rachel says that she feels sorry for mothers whose children grow up to be bad. Her mother, Mrs. Loving asks, " . . . how do you happen to know all this? Mothers whose babies grow up to be bad don't, as a rule, parade their faults before the world." Rachel responds, "That's just it—that's how you know. They don't talk at all" (33).

Though Rachel and her brother Tom are nearly adults at the beginning of the play, neither of them knows how their father and elder brother died; they have simply noticed their mother's refusal to discuss the past. Mrs. Loving asks, "Did you think—that—perhaps—the reason—I—I—wouldn't talk about them—was—because, because—I was ashamed—of them?" (39). Rachel and Tom fumble for answers, and Mrs. Loving surmises that they have not broached the topic because, assuming that she was ashamed, they were too. Mrs. Loving exclaims, "You evade—both—of you. You have been ashamed. And I never dreamed until today you could take it this way. How blind—how almost criminally blind, I have been" (40). She now knows, she explains, that it is her duty to tell her story, and she describes the night that her husband and son were lynched. She gives her painful testimony.

Like Mrs. Loving, Grimké, the author, realized that she must tell her people's story. Black writers living at the turn of the century could not be content in using fiction, essays, or poetry; the historical moment demanded a dramatic response. While white writers were invested in using the stage to label Black men rapists,[32] the simple existence of Black-authored dramas would show that African Americans believed in the integrity of Black manhood. At a time when the stage was being used to cast Black men as buffoons—and, increasingly, as rapists—silence from Black playwrights would be tantamount to their expressing shame and accepting the dominant discourse about the race.

While resisting mainstream lies for herself, and African Americans more generally, Grimké's work also contributed to the effort among Black women to enlist white women as antilynching allies. Though the ASWPL was founded 14 years after *Rachel*'s debut and 10 years after Grimké's rationale, it suggested that Black women had succeeded in touching white women's hearts. Perhaps the experience described by ASWPL officer Carrie Parks Johnson had been the case for many: "... the cry of the mother heart of the Negro race leaped the chasm and found response in the mother heart of the white race."[33] Clearly, Grimké had not been alone in assuming that motherhood would inspire interracial cooperation in the fight to end lynching. As Grimké saw it, "if the white women of this country" were moved to help alleviate the pain of "the colored mothers everywhere" then "a great power to affect public opinion would be set free and the battle would be half won."[34] The ASWPL seems to have come into existence partly in response to efforts like Grimké's, and the organization had been active for years when May Miller wrote her lynching script. Nevertheless, Miller's 1933 play gives voice to skepticism about the wisdom of putting faith in white women allies.

"Half Won": May Miller's Critique

If the battle would be "half won" when white women joined the fight against mob violence, the founding of the ASWPL was reason to rejoice, indeed. ASWPL members not only repudiated the mob as lawless destroyers of US civilization, but they also insisted that lynching had nothing to do with Black sexual impropriety. Furthermore, they acknowledged that only an unjust double standard could demand that Black men die for intimacy with white women while white men who sexually exploit or coerce Black women do not even lose social standing. As importantly, the white women of this organization worked to change the minds of the entire nation, not just their fathers, husbands, and sons.

Even as the ASWPL did this important work, May Miller's *Nails and Thorns* emerged to expose the problems of relying on white empathy. Like other lynching dramas written by Black women, the play's focus remains inside the home. A lynching occurs during the dramatic present, but the script depicts only what happens within the domestic space—in this case, a white household. The text makes the reader privy to the conditions within the home before and after the lynching, demonstrating that though the violence occurs outdoors, its consequences reverberate everywhere.

The action begins in the living room of Stewart and Gladys Landers, the town sheriff and his wife. Gladys is anxious and Stewart is trying to ignore her fidgeting by pretending to read the newspaper. Gladys soon interrupts him, declaring, "I do wish you had notified the Governor this afternoon."[35] Stewart insists that the governor is busy and cannot be bothered with every "little outburst." Gladys counters, "you ought to understand your own home town well enough to know that a Negro's assault on a white girl is a pretty serious affair" (177). However, Stewart insists, "We don't even know yet that it was a Negro" (177). Because details remain unclear, officers have put Lem, the Black suspect, in jail only for his protection (178). As Stewart tries to lighten Gladys's mood, he shows her a comic that she does not find amusing. Shortly thereafter, Annabel, the Black woman who cares for their infant son, is heard frantically calling from outside. She has run across town because whites have been harassing Blacks in the streets. Most Black residents have locked themselves in their houses.

Annabel reports that Blacks are scared because of "what's happ'ned to po' daffy Lem" (179). Stewart says that her concern is "crazy," so she shares that, as a friendly gesture, whites have warned their Black acquaintances to stay off the streets because "they wouldn't lak to hafta burn up all the good cullud folks, too" (179). Stewart is still dismissive, reminding her that nothing happened to her on the way. At this point, Annabel reveals that she had been trying to conceal herself, but a man saw her and yelled at her; she began running and did not stop until she got there (179).

Gladys joins Stewart in trying to get Annabel's mind off what she has reported, but after sending Annabel to attend to the baby, she insists that Stewart at least check on conditions at the jail and in town more generally. Stewart says that "Negroes are excitable," so their reactions do not match the actual threat. He therefore regrets that they were unable to keep Blacks ignorant of Lem's situation. Finally, he leaves despite not believing what

Annabel says. He agrees to look into matters only because it will satisfy his wife.

In pleading with her husband, Gladys has been very clear about why she so desperately wants to prevent violence: there had been a lynching where she grew up, so she knew the damage that such barbarity would do to the entire town (180). Miller uses Gladys to explain her title: "For generations to come the children will be gathering the nails and thorns from the scene of that crucifixion" (180). After Stewart leaves, Annabel tells Gladys what she knows about the lynch plot, and it becomes clear that Stewart will find nothing at the jail; the violent ritual is already underway. Gladys therefore resolves to stop the lynching herself. She insists, "I'll tell that mob how I feel . . . I'll show them my baby—he is this town's tomorrow" (183). Gladys pushes past Annabel to get out of the door, for she maintains, "my son will show them the way" (183).

When Stewart returns home, his wife and baby are gone. Before Stewart can leave to look for them, Gladys returns with the assistance of the town doctor. She is completely hysterical because the mob has crushed her baby underfoot. Finally, Gladys bursts, "He's dead, dead, I tell you, and I'm glad. (*laughing hysterically*) He'll never have to see a lynching" (186). The action ends with a stunned Stewart admitting what he had previously refused to acknowledge about his Black servant: "Annabel's a very good woman—a very, very wise woman" (188).

With its emphasis on a white family's pain, May Miller's script quite eerily anticipates an NAACP advertisement that appears two years later, in 1935. At a time when photographs of lynch victims circulated as evidence of white power, the NAACP used them to create a counter-discourse designed to inspire shame about how whites chose to use their social and political power.[36] Reprinting a picture of Rubin Stacy, a Black man lynched in Florida, the advertisement points viewers' attention to the white children who surround the hanging victim (see Figure 2.1).

The reader is instructed by the NAACP's caption:

> Do not look at the Negro. His earthly problems are ended. Instead, look at the seven WHITE children who gaze at this gruesome spectacle. Is it horror or gloating on the face of the neatly dressed seven-year-old girl on the right? Is the tiny four-year-old on the left old enough, one wonders, to comprehend the barbarism her elders have perpetrated? Rubin Stacy, the Negro, who was lynched at Fort Lauderdale, Florida, on July 19, 1935, for "threatening and frightening a white woman," suffered PHYSICAL torture for a few short hours. But what psychological havoc is being wrought in the minds of the white children? . . . .[37]

Figure 2.1 NAACP antilynching advertisement that aims to mobilize readers by emphasizing that mob violence harms whites

To similar effect, Gladys tells her husband, ". . . I lived in a town once where they lynched a man and I can never forget how the town and the people suffered. It wasn't what they did to the unfortunate man alone. He was out of his misery."[38] Appealing to Stewart's sense of responsibility for white residents' quality of life, Gladys continues, "[the real tragedy] was what they did to every soul in that town. They crucified everything that was worthwhile—justice and pride and self-respect" (180). Not unlike the NAACP a couple years later, both Miller and her character Gladys clearly feel that an antilynching appeal based on the damage done to whites, not Blacks, will be most effective.

Many Black-authored literary works of the 1920s and 1930s, including lynching plays, offer victimized Black men as Christ figures,[39] but here, either abstract ideals or members of the white community are deemed to be crucified. In other words, both Gladys and Miller suggest that the "strange fruit" that will most disturb Americans is not that which later inspired Billie Holiday's famous lament.[40] Especially given that Gladys's own baby dies, Miller's text reveals her assumption that, even to liberal whites, Black pain is of secondary importance. Accordingly, when Annabel arrives to report to work, she rushes in because it is dangerous for Blacks to be on the streets. In response to her frantic explanation, Stewart is dismissive. While Stewart's response may not be surprising, his liberal wife Gladys is not very sympathetic either. Gladys insists, "All right, Annabel, now you're here safe and sound, and you need not worry any more. You go fix the baby's bottle and take it to him. And try to forget all about Lem and the affair."[41] The concern that the visibly unnerved Annabel expresses for Lem, his family, and the Black community simply does not register as relevant—even to Gladys. Although she immediately begins again to press Stewart to do something about the escalating tension, Gladys's inability to empathize with Annabel is undeniable.

Gladys is not only unable to relate to Annabel, she also proves incapable of truly hearing her. As Gladys convinces herself that she must stop the lynchers, she reasons that they will end the frenzy if she can get them to "forget the poor crazy fellow and look at themselves and the children."[42] Annabel immediately explains that they have the children with them. Gladys rages, "The children too! They can't do that to our children. They're all we have. They're our promise—our future." To this, Annabel replies, "Yes'm, mah chillun's all I got, too. If'twasn't foh 'em, I wouldn't be a-workin' all the time 'til I's ready to drop" (183). Annabel's loyalty to her children, not to Gladys, is apparent here, as are the labor demands that Gladys places on Annabel without regard for Annabel's family. None of this makes an impression on Gladys, but Annabel continues, "Then come a time lak tonight an' I get to thinkin' that mah sons has gotta grow up in this town, too, an' 'sposin' aftah all mah work they ends lak that" (183). As Annabel finishes with "a futile gesture," Gladys continues to insist that her *own* son is "this town's tomorrow" (183). In this scene, Gladys's behavior proves to be on a continuum with that of the lynchers, about whom Annabel says to Gladys, to no avail, "they ain't got no ears now, Ma'm" (183).

It is because Gladys has "no ears" for her dialect-speaking servant that lynching brings so much destruction to her home, so Miller's work reveals that the nation encourages its white citizens to be blind and deaf, seeing and hearing only what supports racial hierarchy. Quite explicitly, Miller's script engages the politics of representation, defined by cultural theorist Stuart Hall as the struggle over "whether a particular regime of representation can be challenged, contested and transformed."[43] While Grimké wanted the white middle class to acknowledge the Black middle class, Miller was interested in how both groups' ideas about propriety and criminality often leave racial injustice unaddressed because they do not challenge the assumption that whites are citizens and Blacks are not.

By placing a spotlight on a white family, Miller's work exposes the diffuse way in which power operates, and the text emphasizes the role that mainstream media plays in this distribution of power.[44] Early on, Miller explores the impact of the media as Stewart tries to calm Gladys by making her laugh. He tells her to sit down and read the newspaper because "the comic will be good for your nerves."[45] He declares, "I wouldn't miss an evening of 'Desperado Joe' for anything. (*enthusiastically bending over her shoulder*) Look here at the pickle he's in. They've just caught Joe who kidnapped Percy's girl. And look at this. It's a wow. (*laughing*) Here, the gang's got him, and is he scared!" (178). This "comic" plot resonates with the Lem situation currently overtaking the town, and the similarity is not lost on Gladys. At one point, she says to Stewart, "... I worry about the kind of world Junior will have to live in .... I hate the thought that he'll be reading about gangs and mobs and enjoy them" (180). Ultimately, if whites are citizens and Blacks are not—and white duty sometimes includes keeping Blacks subordinated—then Stewart's status as sheriff matters much less than the fact that average white residents feel empowered to police the neighborhood. Because power can emanate from several locations, Annabel runs through the chaotic streets to get to her employer's house, and Gladys later believes that she can change the mob's behavior by making them face her baby. Both Annabel's fear and Gladys's confidence align with mainstream discourses and practices regarding who should expect protection and who can expect punishment.

In fact, the broad connection that Gladys draws between Lem's predicament and the comic is important precisely because the only thing that Desperado Joe and the mentally impaired Lem have in common is that they will both likely die. As sheriff, Stewart is not convinced of Lem's guilt; he admits that Lem is in jail to prevent the mob from getting him. Nevertheless, Stewart is amused by the pickle that Desperado Joe is in, he does not seem to doubt that Joe kidnapped Percy's girl, and he claims that he would never miss an evening of this entertaining strip. Even in an officer of the law who acknowledges the likely innocence of his prisoner, there is a strong appetite for tales of "outlaws" and the "heroes" who subdue them.

Thus, Miller's play suggests that the desperado/hero narratives that saturate mainstream media maintain existing hierarchies. Importantly, such tales are linked to founding narratives of American distinctiveness. As Toni Morrison explains in *Playing in the Dark,* early Americans cast themselves as uniquely capable of facing a wide, dark expanse and taming it, and "the Africanist presence" proved to be an element requiring particularly fierce discipline.[46] Just as May Miller anticipated the NAACP's suggestion that the white children at Rubin Stacy's lynching were victims, she anticipated Morrison's argument. Through her white woman character Gladys, Miller advances her theory that the comic is not "just a funny," as Stewart claims. American realities are created in and through representation.

While acknowledging that representation shapes reality, Miller also insists upon the power of Black community networks and discourses. Annabel is sure that Lem will be kidnapped because she knows that a relative of the girl who was allegedly attacked has keys to the jail. Neither Stewart nor Gladys immediately believe her, so she later explains to Gladys, "I knows mo' bout this town n' you does, Mis' Landers, 'cause mah mammy nursed mos' o' these folks. She say one haf them's related an' those what ain't has got relatives what is."[47] Thus, Annabel suggests that whites represent themselves in one way, but Blacks know the truth behind the façade. Also, Annabel is better informed than Stewart, the sheriff, because "Ruby tole me an' she had it from Josh's Sarah an' Sarah got it from Josh from the store where he works on Main Street" (181).

This active undercurrent of Black information enables African Americans to understand events in ways that are not controlled by whites. (Recall that Stewart wanted the news about Lem withheld from Blacks.) Given the uncritical basis of "Desperado Joe" humor, African Americans would be in dire straits if they had access only to white-authored information. Miller's play is populated by white characters, but it nevertheless highlights the importance of Black voices—not the least of which is Miller's own.

Miller clearly valued the freedom to write about characters who were not Black. Even while exercising that freedom, though, she remains committed to preserving the alternative discourses that enable Blacks to understand themselves in ways not limited by dominant representations. Miller's play therefore bears witness to the importance of Black perspectives—whether whites have ears to hear them or not. *Nails and Thorns* contributes significantly to the history of lynching and antilynching activism because studying racial violence requires grappling with questions of whose testimonies matter and whose do not. Especially when considered alongside the founding text of Black-authored lynching drama, Angelina Weld Grimké's *Rachel,* Miller's script demands that scholars examine the factors determining which cultural artifacts have demanded attention and which have been allowed to fade into obscurity. With its portrayal of interactions between Gladys and her Black servant, Annabel, *Nails and Thorns* foregrounds questions about what can be heard, and its survival in the archive gestures toward the need to ask similar questions about the history of the ASWPL. As women of this important organization sought to educate the public (not just their husbands and sons), they developed extensive programming. One of the ways they sought to educate young people in particular was to initiate a playwriting competition. May Miller's 1933 one-act drama won third prize when they launched this initiative in 1936, but the most comprehensive work on the ASWPL gives no indication of its existence.[48]

Nails and Thorns is not part of the archive typically consulted by scholars of antilynching activism among American women. The play's absence from histories of the ASWPL in particular seems symptomatic of the very issues that the script highlights about the discourses and practices that most shape our society, even its most well-meaning members. As we have seen, Grimké believed that the barrier between white and Black women would crumble if white women saw Blacks who were not buffoons, rapists, and whores, but whose behavior, values, and tastes mirrored their own. Without question, the emergence of the ASWPL, and the tremendous risks that these white women took by standing against the mob's lies, gave reason to believe not only that lynching would end, but also that a more just society was in the making. If white women were willing to risk their reputations and their safety to oppose lynching, surely human compassion had been mobilized. And it is reasonable to conclude that the bond of motherhood had helped facilitate that change in society's "most conservative element," as Grimké had hoped. Yet, the archival imprint of Grimké's *Rachel* remains easily traceable, largely because of the play's link to the NAACP, not to white women activists. Miller's play was actually acknowledged by the ASWPL, but its importance seems to have quickly disappeared from histories of that organization.

As cultural artifacts of the early twentieth century, Grimké's *Rachel* and Miller's *Nails and Thorns* offer insight into Black women's ideas about their own activism and their alliances with white women. In *Rachel*, Grimké creates a Black mother who says that she had been "criminally blind" by not realizing that her silence would be interpreted as shame. Refusing to allow similar interpretations in real life, Grimké's work ensured that posterity would know that she believed lynch victims to be worthy of dramatic defense. They were not isolated brute rapists with no connection to institutions like marriage; they were often family men whose deaths were mourned by wives, sons, daughters, and entire communities.[49]

As Grimké's literary successor, Miller offers Annabel, who may think highly of her employers because they enable her to provide for her family—and she may appreciate Gladys's passion for wanting to prevent Lem's murder—but she does not let gratitude keep her from speaking the truth about why she works so many hours. Also, despite her relationship to the sheriff, Annabel expresses her fears about her sons' future in that town. Likewise, as an author, Miller gives indications of her doubts about relying on white empathy. Like Gladys, white women allies may mean well and, more importantly, they often accomplish much, but their work can never replace Blacks' efforts on their own behalf. In fact, white activism rarely has, even if mainstream conversations bear little trace of African American contributions.

Angelina Weld Grimké and May Miller would not allow themselves to be silenced by shame or by gratitude. They left evidence that, even in the midst of the most repressive violence, African Americans did not find silence to be acceptable. They affirmed for themselves that they were upstanding citizens and admirable men and women, whether they were servants or not. As they rejected silence, these writers offered their communities texts that bolstered their self-conceptions, enabling them to continue to believe their own truths despite the lies with which the nation bombarded them. Only this self-assurance could equip them to engage in social critique. And it was social criticism—and the cultural productions inspired by it—that allowed Blacks to convince whites to support the reform efforts to which they had been committed for decades. But more than that, what allowed African Americans to keep struggling in these movements, whether whites joined them or not, was that they had been preserving the community's truths all along. Early Black women lynching dramatists did not live to see the battle won, but their work survives to show succeeding generations how we came to have more of a fighting chance.

Notes

1. Newspaper reports on the ASWPL's founding include "Southern Women Attack Lynching," which was carried in the Dalton, Georgia *Citizen* on December 11, 1930 and the Cordele, Georgia *Dispatch* on December 10, 1930. Also see the Macon, Georgia *Telegraph* on November 4, 1930 and January 26, 1931. Other favorable reactions in the white Southern press include: Dallas *Times-Herald,* January 7, 1932 and the Hattiesburg, Mississippi *American,* November 11, 1930 and January 22, 1931. See Jacquelyn Dowd Hall, *Revolt Against Chivalry: Jessie Daniel Ames and the Women's Campaign Against Lynching* (Rev. ed., New York: Columbia University Press, 1993), 341 n.9 and 10.
2. "Nannie Burroughs Tells 'Why America Has Gone Lynch Mad,' " *Pittsburgh Courier,* December 23, 1933.
3. ASWPL Papers. Microfilm Reel 4, Appendix C of Minutes.
4. Ames quoted in Hall, *Revolt,* 164.
5. Hall, *Revolt,* 165.
6. Ida B. Wells, *A Red Record* in *Southern Horrors and Other Writings: The Anti-Lynching Campaign of Ida B. Wells, 1892–1900*, ed. Jacqueline Jones Royster (1895; New York: Bedford, 1997, 73–157), 78.
7. As Jacquelyn Dowd Hall explains, the most important feature of the organization's demographic was the women's race. "The decision to create an organization for white women only, which set the ASWPL apart from the interracial movement and shaped its rhetoric and style, flowed from a number of attitudes and perceptions" (180). As founder, Jessie Daniel Ames "stressed again and again that this was 'not an interracial movement, but a movement of Southern white women interested in law observance and law enforcement' " (181). Also, Ames "believed implicitly that social reform would come about not through the efforts of blacks but through the mediation of white interracialists between the black community and the white power structure" (182).
8. My book *Living with Lynching: African American Lynching Plays, Performance, and Citizenship, 1890–1930* (Urbana, IL: University of Illinois Press, 2011) is the first full-length study of the genre. I examine the scripts as access points to both the archive and the repertoire of U.S. culture at the turn into the twentieth century.
9. This is the great-niece of white activist Angelina Grimké Weld, after whom my Grimké is named.
10. Angelina Weld Grimké, *Rachel* in *Strange Fruit: Plays on Lynching by American Women,* ed. Kathy Perkins and Judith Stephens (Bloomington, IN: Indiana University Press, 1998, 27–78), 40.
11. Rachel's despair allies her with her biblical namesake: " . . . Rachel weeping *for* her children . . . would not be comforted because they are not" (Matthew 2:18).

12. In other work, I have called this "de-generation," meaning generation removal and prevention. See my "(Anti-)Lynching Plays: Angelina Weld Grimké, Alice Dunbar-Nelson, and the Evolution of African American Drama" in *Post-Bellum, Pre-Harlem: African American Literature and Culture, 1877–1919,* ed. Barbara McCaskill and Caroline Gebhard (New York: New York University Press, 2006), 210–30.
13. Gloria T. Hull, *Color, Sex, and Poetry: Three Women Writers of the Harlem Renaissance* (Bloomington, IN: Indiana University Press, 1987), 117–23.
14. Grimké's debut is significant not because she was the first to write serious drama, but because hers was the first Black-authored drama to be executed by Black actors for a broad audience on a semi-professional stage. Before *Rachel,* Black-authored dramas were either not produced or were brought to life by amateurs in churches and schools. Of course, such productions are important. In fact, lynching drama would not have existed without these small shows. Nevertheless, the impact of Grimké's work stemmed from the fact that it was not a musical, but it drew a relatively large interracial audience to formal theatrical productions about African Americans.
15. Production history of *Rachel* is as follows: It premiered in March 1916 at the Myrtilla Miner School in Washington, D.C. and then received productions in 1917 at New York City's Neighborhood Playhouse and at Brattle Hall in Cambridge, Massachusetts. See Hull, 119 and James Hatch and Errol Hill, *A History of African American Theatre* (New York: Cambridge University Press, 2003), 220.
16. Most assume that Du Bois motivated Grimké. For example, as he introduces *Black Thunder: An Anthology of Contemporary African American Drama,* theatre historian William Branch calls *Rachel* "the first produced play to result from Dr. Du Bois's call . . . " (xv). Samuel Hay's *African American Theatre* (Cambridge: Cambridge University Press, 1994) uses letters between NAACP drama committee members to show that Grimké's play was chosen when the organization wanted to sponsor a theatre production to improve race relations. Indeed, he suggests that Grimké's work may have been chosen because her father was an officer for the Washington, D.C. branch. Though Hay does not insist that the drama was *written* in response to the committee's desire to stage a play for "race propaganda," later scholars have read his work in exactly that way. As a consequence, for example, Lisa Anderson's *Mammies No More* (Lanham: Rowman & Littlefield, 1997) and Carol Allen's *Peculiar Passages* (New York: Peter Lang, 2005) argue that the play was penned in response to the committee's call, but years earlier, in 1987, Gloria Hull's classic study *Color, Sex, and Poetry* made it clear that Grimké's script was written before Du Bois founded the drama committee, given that a draft was circulating as early as January of 1915 (Hull, 117–23).
17. Locke and Gregory insisted that Black drama must be developed through folk plays, and their Howard University efforts advanced this belief which

Locke had articulated earlier in "Steps to a Negro Theatre" in *Crisis* magazine (December 1922): 66–68. In 1926, W.E.B. Du Bois had published, in *Crisis* magazine, "Krigwa Players Little Negro Theatre: The Story of a Little Theatre Movement" (July 1926): 134–36; "Criteria of Negro Art" (October 1926): 290–97; and "Paying for Plays" (November 1926): 7–8.

18. It is worth noting that Miller not only had Grimké as an English teacher in high school; she also attended Howard University, interacting often with Montgomery Gregory and Locke. Her journals, housed in the Emory University Manuscripts and Rare Books Library, contain many references to both men.
19. Richardson often said in interviews (with James Hatch, for example) that he returned from seeing *Rachel* determined to write drama of his own because he felt certain that he could do better. See Christine R. Gray's biography *Willis Richardson, Forgotten Pioneer of African-American Drama* (West Port, CT: Greenwood Press, 1999), 12–15 and 29.
20. Plays in which lynching is thematized first came from white authors. In 1906, Thomas Dixon, Jr. hired two acting troupes to bring a play version of his novel, *The Clansman,* to life. White-authored plays not expressly written to condone lynching include Edward Sheldon's *The Nigger* (1909) and Ridgely Torrence's *Granny Maumee* (1917).

    Black-authored plays begin with Grimké's *Rachel,* but quickly begin emerging in the one-act format; this formal shift has everything to do with Grimké's successors not prioritizing integrated audiences via formal productions. One-acts lent themselves to publication in periodicals, which made them available for amateur stagings or dramatic readings, and lynching dramas proliferated in this form: Alice Dunbar-Nelson's *Mine Eyes Have Seen* (1918); Mary Burrill's *Aftermath* (1919); Myrtle Smith Livingston's *For Unborn Children* (1926); and Georgia Douglas Johnson's *A Sunday Morning in the South* (1925), *Blue Blood* (1926), *Safe* (1929), and *Blue-Eyed Black Boy* (c. 1930). Black male authors contributed fewer plays before 1930: G.D. Lipscomb's *Frances* (1925) and Joseph Mitchell's *Son-Boy* (1928). Garland Anderson wrote a full-length play *Appearances* (1925), which he tailored for formal production before integrated audiences. Unlike most other plays by Black authors, Anderson's work is *not* as concerned with the consequences of lynching on Black homes. *Appearances* is set in a hotel and insists that Black men can overcome rape charges because transcending racism is simply a matter of controlling one's destiny through adherence to the ideals of Christian Science.

    Note that I prefer the term "lynching drama" to "antilynching drama," though I have used that term in earlier work. I want to move away from the easy assumption that these plays are reactions to violence—that they are primarily protest art—and toward an understanding that they affirm

African Americans. These scripts preserved truths about Black families and communities—truths that inspired reactions from whites. As Black men were proving to be admirable heads of household, for example, the mob sought to strip them of their success, destroying their homes and then denying that Black men ever cared to create and maintain domestic stability.

21. Even as I say that Grimké hoped to target "white audiences," I realize that she was interested in middle-class white audiences. She was very much immersed in middle-class respectability herself, and these are the people that she would most believe could effect social change. For insight into Grimké's life, social position, and beliefs, see Stephanie Shaw, *What a Woman Ought To Be and To Do: Black Professional Women Workers during the Jim Crow Era* (Chicago: The University of Chicago Press, 1996).
22. Angelina Weld Grimké, " 'Rachel' The Play of the Month: Reason and Synopsis by the Author" in *Lost Plays of the Harlem Renaissance,* ed. James Hatch and Leo Hamalian (1920; repr., Detroit: Wayne State University Press, 1996, 424–26), 424. [Hereafter, "Reason."].
23. Ibid., 425.
24. Mary Church Terrell, "Lynching from a Negro's Point of View," *North American Review* 178 (June 1904): 853–68, 862.
25. Judith Stephens, "The Anti-Lynch Play: Toward an Interracial Feminist Dialogue in Theatre," *Journal of American Drama and Theatre* 1 (1990): 59–69, 62. [Hereafter, "Interracial Feminist."].
26. In some ways, this may not forcefully disrupt assumptions about Grimké's tendency to agree with mainstream discourses because Hawkins Brown was known for taking pride in her white ancestry.
27. Charlotte Hawkins Brown in Gerda Lerner, *Black Women in White America: A Documentary History* (1972; repr., New York: Vintage Books, 1992), 470.
28. Grimké, "Reason," 424.
29. Ibid., 425.
30. Ibid.
31. Stage productions inspired by Harriet Beecher Stowe's novel *Uncle Tom's Cabin* (1852) were notoriously spectacular, borrowing from her famous characters but not her noble intentions. What became known as "Tom Shows" drew crowds as late as the 1920s, with several companies touring. As Alain Locke put it in 1940, "A plague of low-genre interest multiplied the superficial types of uncles, aunties, and pickaninnies almost endlessly, echoing even today in the minstrel and vaudeville stereotypes of a Negro half-clown, half-troubadour. The extreme popularity of these types held all the arts in so strong a grip that, after 70 or more years of vogue, it was still difficult in the last two decades to break through this cotton-patch and cabin-quarters formula." See *The Negro in Art: A Pictorial Record of the Negro Artist and of the Negro Theme in Art* (New York: Hacker Art Books, 1968).

32. At the last turn of the century, the mainstream American stage often cooperated with the mob, sometimes by explicitly legitimating racial violence. The most explicit example would be Thomas Dixon Jr.'s plays, which began touring the country in 1906, defining lynching as a patriotic duty. However, other media dehumanized Blacks, and those forms were more prominent than the country's still emerging (non-musical) mainstream drama. Therefore, when drama joins these forces, much of its strength comes from acting in unison with forerunners such as newspaper stories and comic strips in literary magazines. See Rayford Logan's *Betrayal of the Negro* (1965; repr., New York: Da Capo Press, 1997) as well as Henry Louis Gates, Jr.'s commentary on Black images in his seminal essay "The Trope of a New Negro and the Reconstruction of the Image of the Black," *Representations* 24 (Fall 1998): 129–51.
33. Quoted in Hall, *Revolt,* 105.
34. Grimké, "Reason," 425.
35. May Miller, *Nails and Thorns* in *Strange Fruit: Plays on Lynching by American Women*, ed. Kathy Perkins and Judith Stephens (1933; Bloomington, IN: Indiana University Press, 1998, 177–88), 177.
36. See Jonathan Markovitz, *Legacies of Lynching: Racial Violence and Memory* (Minneapolis, MN: University of Minnesota Press, 2004) and Amy Wood, *Lynching and Spectacle: Witnessing Racial Violence in America, 1890–1940* (Chapel Hill, NC: University of North Carolina Press, 2009).
37. NAACP advertisement quoted in Markovitz, 25–26.
38. Miller, *Nails,* 180.
39. The literature that casts lynch victims as Christ figures is plentiful. Examples include W.E.B. Du Bois, "Jesus Christ in Georgia" (1911 short story); Countee Cullen, "Christ Crucified" (1922 poem) and "The Black Christ" (1929 poem); and Langston Hughes, "Christ in Alabama" (1931 poem).
40. The famous ballad "Strange Fruit" began as a poem written by Lewis Allan (Abel Meeropol) that his wife sang publicly, but it was made famous when Billie Holiday lent her voice to it in 1939. For more, see David Margolick, *Strange Fruit: The Biography of a Song* (New York: Ecco Press, 2001). Holiday's influence has inspired numerous renditions, including Nina Simone's in 1965, Cassandra Wilson's in 1995, and Dwayne Wiggins' revision about police brutality, "What's Really Going On? (Strange Fruit)," released in 1999. See Margolick's appendix for a more complete list.
41. Miller, *Nails,* 179–80.
42. Ibid., 183.
43. Stuart Hall, *Representation: Cultural Representations and Signifying Practices* (London: Sage, 1997), 8.
44. Here, of course, I am suggesting that Miller also anticipates the theories of Jacques Derrida on how power is less likely to operate from some centralized authority base than in contingent, diffuse ways.

45. Miller, *Nails*, 178.
46. See Toni Morrison, *Playing in the Dark: Whiteness and the Literary Imagination* (New York: Vintage Books, 1992).
47. Miller, *Nails*, 182.
48. From reading *Revolt Against Chivalry*, the seminal history of the ASWPL and its founder, Jessie Daniel Ames, which has been updated and reprinted, one has no idea that May Miller's play won recognition in this contest. It is easy to understand how the play fell out of the historical record of the ASWPL because that organization's papers make little mention of it. However, there is much detail about the plans to launch the play contest and many letters between organizers and the playwriting judges that they recruited, especially University of North Carolina professor Frederick Koch. Plans dated January 30, 1936 indicate that the goal is to encourage one-acts on the subject of lynching, the "desire thereof to make active presentation of the problem to people of simple culture, without polemics or other blights upon artistic worth, which would ban the play from trained amateur groups." Also, plays should be "30 to 40 minutes" and "$100 [will be paid] for all rights."

    To encourage contest entries that fulfilled its goals, the ASWPL office sent educational material, including books on the history of lynching, to judges and other contacts who could generate plays. This material helped ensure that students and other amateur writers would have plenty of quality sources. (I could not help but notice), though, that the organization generously sent such materials to white contacts and told African Americans, such as Anne Cook at Spelman College, "We do not have an extra copy of [Author Raper's *The Tragedy of Lynching*] in the office but feel sure you may obtain a copy from the library of Atlanta University" (Letter dated February 6, 1936 by Jessie Daniel Ames's secretary, ASWPL Papers).

    Ultimately, it was in the May Miller papers at Emory University that I found the letter in which Miller was told "Your play was awarded third place; 'Country Sunday' by Walter Spearman of the University of North Carolina, took first place; and 'Lawd, Does Yo' Undahstan'?' by Ann Seymour of Strawn, Texas won second place" (May Miller Papers, Emory University, Box 7, Item 15).

    As first- and second-place winners, Spearman's and Seymour's plays were published by the ASWPL while Miller's fell off the radar. What is striking, though, is that there is much discussion about the need for artistic merit and realism if young people are to be moved to stage these plays, yet Seymour's script is so predicated on racist assumptions that it is hard to imagine that it would be viewed as realistic, even in 1936. Black characters have ridiculous names, such as "Fruit Cake," which is designated among characters as a real name, not a nickname (194). Also, according to stage directions, when one character is singing, "the other darkeys join in" (194). See Seymour's play in the anthology *Strange Fruit: Plays on Lynching by American Women,* edited by Perkins and Stephens.

49. Black-authored lynching plays generally focus on Black male victims, even though the playwrights clearly understood that Black women were lynched. In fact, Alice Dunbar-Nelson was part of the Anti-Lynching Crusaders, a group of Black women who helped pay for the *Shame of America* advertisement that insisted that lynching could not possibly be about rape, given that many women (including white women) had been lynched. See Markovitz and Mitchell, "(Anti-) Lynching Plays."

CHAPTER 3

The Antislavery Roots of African American Women's Antilynching Literature, 1895–1920

Barbara McCaskill

Are the candidates for lynching always found
among the men?
No, the fiends of human torture lynch a woman
now and then.

—Lizelia Augusta Jenkins Moorer[1]

Reflecting on the lynching scourge in 1900, Pauline Elizabeth Hopkins (1859–1930), one-time editor of the influential *Colored American Magazine* (1900–1904), added a sense of urgency to the campaign against it in the preface to her *Contending Forces: A Romance Illustrative of Negro Life North and South* (1900). "Let us compare," she wrote, "the happenings of one hundred—two hundred—years ago, with those of today. The difference between then and now, if any there be, is so slight as to be scarcely worth mentioning. The atrocity of the acts committed one hundred years ago are duplicated today, when slavery is supposed to no longer exist."[2] As passionately as Hopkins argued for calling out lynching's sad history, the absence of a key chapter in the serialized novel *Minnie's Sacrifice* (1869) by Frances Ellen Watkins Harper (1825–1911), where the female protagonist may have been lynched,[3] indicates a tension in African American literature between remembering and forgetting such brutal forms of vigilante justice. The installment describing the death of Minnie, an African American woman teaching school and bringing love and light and learning to the post-Civil War South, has been lost. Towards the end of the novel, she and her husband Louis have been receiving death threats from white racists. Directly after the missing scene of her death, among the descriptions of mourners viewing her body is that of a former slave woman. The elderly woman recalls how her daughter was beaten and hanged by Confederates for talking about her desire to marry a soldier of the Union Army. Perhaps it has been Minnie's murder at the hands of persons unknown that has triggered the old mother's memory.

Lynching rightfully has invited comparison to the "bad dream" of American slavery, whose memory "seemed unwise," as novelist Toni Morrison so vividly embodies in her masterpiece *Beloved* (1987). Lynching, like slavery, has "not" been "a story to pass on."[4] Yet in the decades between 1895 and 1920, Hopkins, Harper, and other Post-Reconstruction women like Lizelia Augusta Jenkins Moorer (quoted in the epigraph) did pass on this story and thus accomplished important literary and cultural work.

To expose, mourn, and raise an outcry against the lynching horrors of a new century, Post-Reconstruction literature by African American women reaches back to narrative methods from the earlier struggle against American slavery. In this essay, I track how African American women writing during four decades revisit strategies from abolition—indirection, substitution, transnationalism—to talk about lynching and Black women like themselves with frankness and dignity. From Harper's poetry and Hopkins's fiction, to the genteel verses of Katherine Davis Chapman Tillman (1870–?) and Moorer, to, finally, the unsettling stories of Angelina Weld Grimké (1880–1958), I trace a development from subtle to more clear representations of women and lynching. These writers return to the lessons of slavery days to take on the difficult challenges of describing the victimized without objectifying them, of speaking for the disempowered without diminishing their agency. For scores of silenced kin and neighbors, they spoke the unspeakable by demonstrating how African American women had been susceptible to lynching's brutalities.

American literature has often revisited lynching's pain and horror. Trudier Harris's *Exorcising Blackness* (1984), Sandra Gunning's *Race, Rape and Lynching* (1996), and Jacqueline Goldsby's *A Spectacular Secret* (2006) are influential, book-length, critical studies of lynching which demonstrate its presence in American literature.[5] An anthology of creative works, Anne P. Rice's *Witnessing Lynching* is the first collection to focus exclusively upon lynch law and its consequences.[6] As Goldsby states, "During the period 1882–1930 (the years, scholars agree, when the most reliable lynching statistics were kept), 3,220 African American men, women, and children were murdered by lynch mobs."[7] Over these years, according to the historian Leon F. Litwack, the "mob 'execution" ' of Black women, men, and families, "was not only a public spectacle but also public theater, often a festive affair, a participatory ritual of torture and death that many whites preferred to witness rather than read about."[8] Though in smaller numbers than poor Black men,[9] women did succumb before and well after the twentieth century's turn, to the rope, the whip, the bullet, and the bonfire—the perverse and prurient totems of lynching rituals.[10] Charged to speak for victims and the witnesses of this terror, African American women writers returned to and revised antislavery techniques in order to develop a variety of ways to articulate lynching and its impact on the printed page.

Two ballads by Frances E. W. Harper, initially published in 1895 yet with echoes of abolitionist rhetoric, rely upon the voices of African American women in order to condemn American society as a kind of lynch mob. The poetical elements of Harper's 14-stanza "Appeal to My Country Women" are those that she and other American writers perfected during the antislavery movement: solicitation of a white female audience; manipulation of sympathy; patriotic, sentimental, and Christian discourse; and prophetic warning. Their descriptions of women and lynching in Post-Reconstruction literature rhyme with those of women and bondage from a previous era. In her 14-stanza "Appeal," Harper enjoins her "well-sheltered" and "favored [white] sisters" to offer "a plea, a prayer or a tear" for the distressed South. There "[s]obs of anguish" and "murmurs of pain" have been raised. There "women heart-stricken are weeping/Over their tortured and slain." Relying upon Christian doctrine, Harper advises her privileged white female audience to extend "gentle compassion;/Your mercy and pity" beyond the Industrial Age's usual roster of fashionable charitable causes—war refugees, orphans, the temperance movement, animal cruelty. Relief must come to "men . . . still wasting/Life's crimson around our own doors," to "mothers who dwell 'neath the shadows/Of agony, hatred and fear."[11]

By naming neither individuals nor organizations, by branding lynchers as persons unknown who would "tread down the poor and lowly" and "crush them in anger and hate" (194), Harper's "Appeal" implicates in these violent crimes a swathe of white American men wider than merely various classes of southern white men. By not specifying the gender of the lynchers, Harper can also indict white women with the mob of haters she names—as long as they persist in their muteness about, and obliviousness to the lynching carnage. She extends the gutless thugs of lynching parties to include those men and women whose silence tacitly sanctions such violence as sure as if they swung a rope or severed a trembling hand.

Harper pivots from the role of poor victim, reliant upon appeals to privileged white women, to that of a portentous authority, whose prophetic announcement closes the poem:

> Go read on the tombstones of nations
> Of chieftains who masterful trod,
> The sentence which time has engraven,
> That they had forgotten their God.
>
> 'Tis the judgment of God that men reap
> The tares which in madness they sow,
> Sorrow follows the footsteps of crime,
> And sin is the consort of Woe.(194–95)

Harper is both vulnerable and ferocious. She could be next: another wretched Black mother cupped against a husband, a son, or father's charred, dismembered remains. Yet, by passing judgment against the nation in the tradition of the American jeremiad,[12]she also pushes back against the terrorism of the mob. Removed from the actual scenes of violence she recounts, yet possessing a racial identity that grants her urgency and authority, Harper can complicate lynching's impact on African American women who witness or succumb to such trauma. Her poem is a re-instantiation of how Black women writing in slavery "saw themselves as far more than victims of rape and seduction."[13]

Harper was a seasoned activist whose realization of the tough post-war campaign ahead for her people may have guided her to return to the narrative techniques that had proved so powerful in her antislavery writing. "In nineteenth-century African America," as Frances Smith Foster and Valerie Ruffin write, "a poet was the New World griot . . . . The two most popular and prolific nineteenth-century African American writers, Frances E. W. Harper and Paul Laurence Dunbar [1872–1906], were famous primarily for their poetry."[14] It was in her antebellum writing, concludes the scholar Carolyn Sorisio, that Harper "developed textual strategies to reveal slavery's corporeal nature without soliciting readers' voyeuristic spectatorship upon the bodies of slaves."[15] Such strategies and more are evident in Harper's earliest published abolitionist poems, such as "The Slave Mother" and "The Slave Auction," which appeared together in her *Poems on Miscellaneous Subjects* (1854). In both poems, Harper addresses a presumed audience of white mothers who might identify with the agony of a parent cruelly torn from her children. Sorisio has perceptively noted how these works force a connection between African American and white women, and persuade white Americans to "listen to the slaves, rather than merely watch them" by de-emphasizing the spectacle of Black bodies and challenging assumptions about Blacks' passivity.[16] "The Slave Auction," for instance, claims to white readers that—

> Ye who have laid your love to rest,
> And wept above their lifeless clay,
> Know not the anger of that breast,
> Whose lov'd are rudely torn away. (10)

Once Harper identifies supposedly beneficent slaveholders as nothing more than "cruel hands" that rudely "tear apart/[t]he . . . wreath of household love" ("The Slave Mother," 4), she prevents her white female readership from claiming ignorance of such abuses. Similarly, her race and gender connect her with the defenseless "sable forms" she writes about, "whose sole crime was their hue" ("The Slave Auction," 10), even as her freedom enables her to defend them. This attitude that silence condones oppression, and this speaker who is at once a victim and a liberator, are antislavery gestures anticipating Post-Reconstruction literature.

More important than the violence which Harper's poetry about lynching documents are the lessons they develop around the tragic products of public indifference and, inversely, the transformative power of public indignation. In the 21 stanzas of her "The Martyr of Alabama," the speaker reflects upon the death, in 1894, of a young African American boy named Tim Thompson. This innocent was beaten by white men "of cold and brutal cowardice" (147) because he would not violate his Christian beliefs and dance for their amusement. Although the poem eulogizes a murdered boy, readers can easily transpose a woman in his place. Tim's story is a variation of one of Harper's favorite subjects: Vashti, the Persian queen of the biblical *Book of Esther* (1:11–19) who refuses to obey the edict of King Xerxes to dance before his drunken dinner guests and is dethroned. In both plots, the integrity of the powerless—a boy, a wife—trumps the evil institutions of the powerful— of racism, sexism. Of the 21 stanzas of Harper's "The Martyr of Alabama," only 2 describe Thompson's actual murder. By comparison, Harper reserves eight stanzas, over one-third of the poem, to exhort pious readers to rise up and eradicate such "Christless" abuses (150): "Veil not thine eyes," she commands, "nor close thy lips/Nor speak with bated breath" (150).

In her indictment of apathetic Christians, the speaker expresses "an awareness of Christianity's complicity in the annihilation and/or subjugation of nonwhite cultures."[17]

Like Harper, Pauline Elizabeth Hopkins frequently revisited the history of slavery in her fiction at the turn of the century. In her essay "Raising the Stigma: Black Women and the Marked Body in *Contending Forces*" (2004), Jennifer Putzi describes how the "abolitionist legacy was crucial to Hopkins's own commitment to race uplift," and argues that female protagonists in Hopkins's *Contending Forces* announce a new era for African Americans by breaking from earlier representations of bondage composed by white writers such as Lydia Maria Child and Harriet Beecher Stowe.[18] I would add, in returning to slavery for narrative models, even if to demolish them, as Putzi argues, Hopkins participates in a collective development of lynching discussions rooted in abolitionist literature. Richard Yarborough and Hazel V. Carby, for example, have observed how the mulatta heroine Sappho Clark of *Contending Forces* exemplifies a saintly "chastity and self-control."[19] Her virtuousness references a strategy used during abolition in order to rebuke racist ideologies that blamed Black women's alleged promiscuity and immorality for their sexual victimization by white men. A squeaky clean Sappho conceals her violent past of rape and lynching until the evil seducer John Langley threatens to go public with her story and to break up her engagement to his rival, Will Smith. She withdraws into convent life (another social death) rather than tell the truth to Will. Yet, after a series of coincidental revelations, they reunite to marry and live, what one character calls, "a fairy tale of love and chivalry such as we read of only in books" (398).

"Hopkins used *Contending Forces*," writes Carby, "to demonstrate that the political issue behind the violence of lynching was not the threat of black sexuality, but the potential power of the black vote."[20] Where Sappho is muted in the novel about her own involvement in "the dark picture—lynching and concubinage" (15), she is outspoken to her friend Dora Smith on "race troubles" (124). A mouthpiece for Hopkins's own politics, Sappho's sexual virtue makes her political voice palatable to turn-of-the-century readers.

Post-Reconstruction African American women writers worked in tandem with African American men to organize sequential scenes of lynching and rape in order to reinforce what activists such as the journalist Ida B. Wells (1862–1931), the educator Anna Julia Cooper (1858–1964), and others had observed about the two-pronged nature of violence directed against Black men and women. While both men and women were lynched, the anxieties of white racists were also enacted on women through rape. For example, *Contending Forces* features a story-within-a-story with heroine Sappho Clark (née Mabelle Beaubean), a teenaged innocent, first being raped, then forced into sexual slavery by her father's white half brother. When her father protectively asserts his manhood and threatens legal action, he is lynched.

This scene resonates in "A Southern Scene" by Priscilla Jane Thompson (1871–1942), where a Black man struggles against the lynch mob in order to protect his lover from imminent assault.[21] Similarly, in "Of the Coming of John," the thirteenth chapter of *The Souls of Black Folk* (1903) by W.E.B. Du Bois (1868–1963), the rape of the protagonist's sister by a southern judge's indolent white son precedes the "tramp of horses and murmur of angry men" that foreshadow his own lynching. He is killed for acquiring the "education and Northern notions" of "a dangerous Nigger;"[22] for asserting what was "often called 'impudence.' "[23]

In the American South of the 1860s and 1870s, writes the historian Tera W. Hunter,

> Black men took great offense at the fact that while they were falsely accused of raping white women, white men granted themselves total immunity in the exploitation of black women . . . .Most whites refused to acknowledge the culpability of white men in abusing black women. "Rape" and "black women" were words that were never uttered in the same breath by white southerners. Any sexual relations that developed between black women and white men were considered consensual, even coerced by the seductions of black women's lascivious nature.[24]

Sexual assaults of Black women reinforced white supremacy as did lynching rituals organized against Black men. Both conveyed how white supremacists relied upon stereotypes and biases in order to oppress African Americans.

Post-Reconstruction women depict their gender as susceptible to another form of racial violence: physical and verbal abuse enacted on trains, in theaters, and at other public spaces. Essentialist notions that Black woman are unfeminine and unladylike are exposed as lies that sanction one group's domination over the other. Even before the Reconstruction ends, African American women excoriate in print what Cooper called "instances of personal violence to colored women travelling in less civilized sections of our country, where women have been forcibly ejected from cars, thrown out of seats, their garments rudely torn, their persons wantonly and cruelly injured."[25] For example, a "colored woman" that the title character meets in Harper's early novel, entitled *Minnie's Sacrifice,* recalls how she is routinely "insulted in different thoroughfares of travel."[26]

After the Reconstruction, such scenes of women's humiliations in Jim Crow cars are ubiquitous. The southerner Lizelia Augusta Jenkins Moorer (1861–?), for instance, dedicated an entire poem to what she called "[l]egalized humiliation," where a respectable Black woman or man pays "a first class passage and a second class receives."[27] Similarly, taking the train from Boston to New Orleans in Hopkins's *Contending Forces,* Sappho faces "the brutality of the conductor who ordered her out of the comfortable day-coach into the dirt and discomfort of the 'Jim crow' car, with the remark that 'white niggers couldn't impose on him; he reckoned he knew 'em.' "[28]

In her volume *Recitations* (1902), Katherine Davis Chapman Tillman joins her contemporaries in criticizing the compliance of white Americans with racist codes of etiquette, and their attendant indifference to human suffering and "charity true" (159). "A Southern Incident" describes an "old colored woman" who enters a streetcar to the contempt and ridicule of its white passengers, until one "young Southern woman" offers her a "cosy [*sic*] seat" (159). During slavery, "the Southern lady,/Who dared that act to do" (159) could have been matter-of-fact about disrespecting a Black woman, even an elder.[29] Abolitionist writers scrutinized such attitudes of the slaveholding aristocracy towards African American women. They concluded that the alleged promiscuity of slave women deflected the blame from white men who raped them. The alleged indifference of slave mothers and wives absolved white southerners of guilt and shame when they divided and sold anguished Black families in the marketplace. The southern woman's gracious gesture in Tillman's poem corrects such propaganda and levels a former imbalance of power. Whites must hold themselves and their peers to the "higher law" that abolitionists evoked in order to solve the race problem and end racial violence.

In my volume *Post-Bellum, Pre-Harlem* (2006), the scholar Paula Bernat Bennett examines the genteel aesthetic among late nineteenth-century African American women; an aesthetic which characterized most American poetry of the century. Bennett describes it as "[a]lmost another language, . . . announced not only by romantic vagueness and idealism but also by anachronistic turns of phrase . . . , exclamations and apostrophes, and frequently inverted syntax."[30] This genteel aesthetic privileged a Victorian, euphemistic approach to the human body. I would caution that this definition of the genteel belies the fact, as Bennett herself discusses, that Post-Reconstruction African American women poets did experiment with more bold and direct themes and techniques for reconciling these subtleties with lynching's realities of sexual mutilations, detached limbs, and torched corpses. Looking to abolition was one way in which such writers developed space to evaluate lynching's impact on African American women without re-objectifying and revictimizing themselves.

The movement that informed American antislavery literature benefited from a transnational community of agitators who galvanized political and religious support; mounted financial boycotts and fund-raising campaigns; aided escaping fugitives and their families; and intervened in cultural spectacles that reinforced stereotypes slaveholders tagged upon Africans in bondage. During the nineteenth century, a network of editors and publishers on both sides of the Atlantic reprinted fiction, poetry, letters, speeches, and proceedings of conventions and meetings that elaborated the perils of America's continued endorsement of plantation slavery. Douglass in Rochester, Child in New York City, Chapman and Garrison in Boston, and Tweedie in London are among those who published antislavery periodicals and books.[31]

The antislavery fairs or bazaars, which generally relied upon women abolitionists both to organize the events and to stock them with needlework, baked confections, jarred goods, and other domestic items for sale, became very popular annual events for many American antislavery societies. Such events combined fellowship, fun, and social activism. Yet, to pull off them successfully, women's committees devoted months of lamp-lit, ink-blotted evenings corresponding with sister societies in Great Britain. Female antislavery societies across the pond packed crates of merchandise to ship to their Yankee associates, and they solicited submissions from celebrated writers and artists to add a cosmopolitan glow to the gift books sold during the American fund-raisers. From Canada to England to France to Italy, sympathetic friends of abolition likewise opened their homes to fugitives and supported them financially and psychologically as they adjusted to freedom. The transatlantic abolitionist community regarded Great Britain, in particular, as an extension of the New England stage where fugitive men and women orated against American slavery. In turn, the British and European antislavery press monitored these former captives and interceded when they seemed to overreach economic and political bounds.[32]

As the antilynching movement gained momentum after the Reconstruction, a transnational perspective similarly informed African American women who wrote about lynching's impact on members of their gender. In the July 5, 1894 issue of the *African Methodist Episcopal (A.M.E.) Christian Recorder*, then the oldest circulating African American newspaper, Tillman published her paean "Lines to Ida B. Wells," which she revised for inclusion in *Recitations*. She also composed poems that recall the themes and aesthetics of antislavery writers, including "America's First Cargo of Slaves" (194–95), "Phyllis Wheateley [*sic*]" (165–66), and "Clotelle—A Tale of Florida" (155–58), which revives the tragic mulatta tale and nods to former slave William Wells Brown's 1853 novel.[33]

Tillman may have published "Lines to Ida B. Wells" to commend the activist's lecture tour that year in Great Britain, which raised international alarm over the epidemic of southern lynchings.[34] In the poem, she encourages the "brave woman leader" to "[s]pread our wrongs from shore unto shore" in a national campaign to "hurl the murderous lynch-law/Down to its dishonoured grave" (137, 136). Her initial stanza situates Wells within a global timeline of women warriors over the ages:

> Charlotte Corday for the English,
> Joan of Arc for the French,
> And Ida B. Wells for the Negro,
> His life from the lynchers to wrench. (136)[35]

Tillman's recitation sanctions Wells' activism by recognizing it as the latest in a sequence of noble grassroots insurrections begun across the Atlantic centuries ago. The publication of her poem so close to the annual Independence Day celebrations identifies Wells' legendary civil disobedience and confrontation of authority as, like abolition before it, a patriotic and inspired action to commit America to principles of justice and safety for all. By connecting America's historical enemies, the English and the French, to a social justice movement spearheaded by the "loving deeds" (137) of an African American, Tillman recalls how antislavery writers compared what William and Ellen Craft called the "mock-free Republic"[36] of America unfavorably with the English monarchies that had once oppressed it.[37] Tillman's second stanza directly reaches back to this antislavery conceit. She exclaims,

> Thank God, there are hearts in *old England* [emphasis mine]
> That feel for the Negro's distress,
> And gladly give of their substance
> To obtain for his wrongs a redress. (136)

Republishing her poem as "Ida B. Wells" in 1902, when its namesake had been exposing the truth behind "the butchery of blacks"[38] by white southerners for over a decade, Tillman chose to begin it with this stanza. Wells, herself, was willing to shame America by citing the British people's revulsion to lynching. As she noted, "The belief has been constantly expressed in England that in the United States, which has produced Wm. Lloyd Garrison, Henry Ward Beecher, James Russell Lowell, John G. Whittier and Abraham Lincoln, there must be those of their descendants who would take hold of the work of inaugurating an era of law and order."[39] Tillman likewise criticizes America's hypocrisy while applauding a principled, transnational community of antilynching activists.

In her *Prejudice Unveiled* (1907), Lizelia Augusta Jenkins Moorer, who taught in Claflin, South Carolina, from the mid- to late 1890s, does join her fellow writers Grimké, Hopkins, Harper, and the clubwoman Tillman, in linking her indignation about lynching and racial injustice to abolition. Like the fugitives who promised to unveil "the unvarnished truth" about bondage before incredulous audiences, she confides her purpose of telling the "unvarnished truth" about Black southerners to a white readership. In Moorer's portrayals of the social realities of Jim Crow, Bennett recognizes "something of the fierce energy and uncompromising anger of abolitionist poetry."[40]

Moorer has a great deal to say about lynching. She talks about a double standard where white men are exonerated for crimes Black men are lynched for ("The Southern Press"). She describes the ritualized tortures of the lynching party, and the cowardice of individual lynchers ("Lynching"). She illustrates how innocent African Americans are falsely accused, and prophesizes when the nation will be punished for this unmerited and savage spilling of blood ("Retribution"). She identifies how the southern courts uphold lynch law and convict the innocent with white-only juries ("Injustice of the Courts"). Yet the lynch victim in her verses is routinely male, even as she acknowledges the occasional woman who falls to the mob's frenzy.

Like her predecessors writing and orating during slavery, Moorer calls out the sexual assaults of African American women as parallels of the "awful, awful story" of lynching "that the Negro man relates" ("Lynching" 31). Her "Immorality" traces the blame game which labels rape victims as promiscuous to the *droit du seigneur* (right of the lord) planters once exercised:

> 'Tis a custom born of slavery when master's
> law and might,
> Was enforced upon the bondsman without
> question of the right,

And the parson preached on Sunday how the
servant should obey
All the mandates of the master, let them be
whate'er they may.

O, how sad the tales of bondage when persuasive measures failed,
How they tortured Negro women till their hellish plans prevailed!
Women faithful to their virtue were as martyrs sent to rest,
Others yielded to the tempter, weary, helpless
and distressed. (59)

Just as American law seems "powerless to hinder" lynchings and seems to uphold an atmosphere where "[s]imply to suspect a Negro is sufficient" for such bloodletting, so too does it offer "no protection" from sexual assault "that a Negro/girl can claim" ("Lynching" 35; "Immorality" 60). In a nation where "[t]o lynch a Negro is no crime," African American women face a similar "training school" where whites find it unfathomable to believe that they are virtuous and chaste, and therefore turn blind eyes to their sexual vulnerability ("Retribution" 37; "Immorality" 60). Moorer does not absolve white women of responsibility for this mess. She also applies the theme of miscegenation or racial amalgamation from antislavery literature to the "conditions in the Southland" of her own generation ("Immorality" 57).

In her study of the tragic mulatta figure in American literature, Eve Allegra Raimon notes how writing about masters' coercive relationships with female slaves enabled abolitionists "to follow acceptable fictional forms while challenging white supremacist representations of racial politics under slavery."[41] In this vein, but, I find, with more direct irreverence and sarcasm than her antislavery predecessors, Moorer poses rhetorical questions to invite scrutiny of how slavery's racial politics still hold sway during her generation:

Can you tell of these mulattoes, did they fall
here from the sky?
How is this that they're among us? Can you tell
the reason why?
Who's to blame for their existence? ("Immorality" 59)

The immorality of Moorer's title does not rest in Black bodies, where white Americans customarily have assigned it, but in a country and citizenry that cannot "do right" (61).

The economic and social changes engendered by World War I were accompanied by an uptick in racial violence on the American home front. As African Americans migrated northward from farms and towns to obtain more lucrative jobs and escape the indignations of Jim Crow, they ignited anxieties among working-class whites who were threatened by such prospective competition and unsettled by the prospect of living, working, worshipping, commuting, and learning in integrated environments. Tensions between white communities and African American migrants culminated in the Red Summer of 1919, when "race riots broke out in more than twenty cities, including Chicago, Omaha, Tulsa, Washington, D.C., Charleston, and Knoxville" and "seventy-six recorded lynchings of blacks" were documented.[42] Angelina Weld Grimké wrote antilynching literature against this backdrop. The scholar Carolivia Herron finds that "the subject of lynching is minor" in her poetry, yet "the entire corpus" of her "fiction, nonfiction, and drama focus almost exclusively on lynching and racial justice."[43] As Koritha A. Mitchell writes in her essay for this volume, Grimké staged antilynching plays which attracted sizeable attendance by whites and Blacks. Coming from a family of abolitionists,[44] Grimké examines the subject of women and lynching in ways that demonstrate antislavery influences. She favors graphic descriptions of violence—descriptions, as Herron states, "unknown in African American fictional literature prior to the work of Richard Wright"[45]—as if to convey a heightened urgency since enslavement: a modern's impatience with the plodding pace of justice.

As Julie Buckner Armstrong states in her essay for this volume, like many Americans writing and publishing during the 1920s—Carrie Williams Clifford, Anne Spencer, Jean Toomer—Grimké alludes to the May 1918 lynching of Mary Turner. Turner's martyrdom—her hanging (upside-down), burning (while still alive), and vivisection (while still alive, with an eight-month old baby in her body) occurred in Valdosta, Georgia—was reported by Walter White (1893–1955), longtime executive director of the National Association for the Advancement of Colored People (NAACP), as one tragedy among "a holocaust of lynchings" in the state.[46] The historian Philip Dray writes that "the mob killing of Mary Turner shocked even hardened antilynching activists. The atrocity was described in numerous articles and editorials, was discussed in Congress, and became an instant rallying point for further agitation.... It introduced a new low in the level of degradation associated with lynching."[47]

In a letter to the editors of the *Atlantic Monthly,* Grimké wrote that her "Blackness" was inspired by Turner's barbarous murder.[48] Sensing that a former lover and her husband are in trouble, the story's unnamed African American protagonist travels to the Deep South from Washington, D.C. As he walks in darkness towards his destination, the "tall black trees" framing his path—"nothing more, line on line, row on row, deep on deep"—foreshadow a grim discovery.[49] The next day, pushing aside branches and leaves, he finds the couple: "Each with a rope around the neck—strung up—onto the same limb—that made the creaking—. Their faces swollen, distorted, unrecognizable—awful!—and naked—both of them" (243). A special torture has been meted upon the wife's "beautiful golden body—swaying there" (243). Her abdomen has been "ripped open" (243), and "under her poor little swaying feet—her child—unborn—beautiful—tiny hands and feet perfect—one little hand reached up—as though—appealing—the little head—blotted out—crushed—its little brains" (244). The protagonist tracks down and murders their killer; then returns to the North. Later, as "brokenly in little gasps" (243) he recollects his saga to a close male friend, his colleague cries, "Oh Stop! And before I knew it I was on my feet. I could not keep still. Up and down I went luckily there was nothing for me to lash against . . . ." (243, 244). The imagery characterizing their responses suggests how Grimké might have expected readers to respond with a corresponding horror, revulsion, and rage.[50]

The protagonist describes his odyssey from North to South "being a sardine" in the Jim Crow car, "unable to sleep, to wash, or to shave" (235), as if he were a captive during the Middle Passage:

> Into it we were herded, men, women and children. At one time, a hundred of us, at least, were crowded into that little space, squeezed into the seats and into the aisles, body wedged in against body . . . I do not believe I could have moved much even if I had tried. If you remember, the weather at that time was far from cool. Can you imagine, then, something of the heat those hot bodies generated, in addition, jammed in close up against each other? And also something of those body odors they exhaled? (234)

At the end of this harrowing journey, the white station master, who has murdered the traveler's friends, evokes southern owners who are depicted as demons in slave narratives. His skin is "a horrible tallowy color," his eyes are "ratlike," his teeth are "yellow fangs," and his hands are "ten talons" (238, 246, 248). When the protagonist exacts his revenge and flees to his northern home, he declares himself "an outcast with a price upon my head, and . . . a wanderer over the face of the earth" (231). His language alludes to the verses of Isaiah 16:3–4 quoted widely in slave narratives and other abolitionist literature: "Hide the outcast. Betray not him that wandereth. Let mine outcasts dwell with thee. Be thou a covert to them from the face of the spoiler." Like the antebellum fugitives who found no security even after reaching the North, the protagonist of "Blackness" must hide from a detective who pursues him from "the far and sunny south" (230). His "bust of Wendell Phillips [1811–1884]" (222), the great Boston abolitionist and lawyer who defended many escaped slaves remanded to the South by the Fugitive Slave Act, underscores his vulnerability to the long arm of lynch law.

By transparently referencing the gruesome torture of Mary Turner, it may be that Grimké also returns to the visual iconography of enslavement in order to construct meanings about lynching and the continued oppression of African Americans. The dead child's "one little hand reached up—as though—appealing" (244) ironically may allude to the abolitionist icons of a kneeling African American woman or man, fettered hands held high in supplication, entreating "Am I Not a Woman and a Sister?" or "Am I Not a Man and a Brother?" to an ostensible white God or benefactor. This time around, Grimké implies that the Black community must rescue itself. The process will be retributive rather than just: "If there were any law in the South that protected a colored man or gave him any redress," her protagonist reflects, "I should have had no excuse for what I have done. But there is no law" (249).[51]

Published in *The Birth Control Review,* Grimké's story "The Closing Door" (1919) revives old scenes of infanticide from antislavery literature, meant to drive home the psychological toll of slavery. "A slave woman's sexuality and her reproductive organs," writes the historian Brenda E. Stevenson, "were key to her identity as a woman and she claimed a right to have power over that identity."[52] The story of Margaret Garner stood as an example of one slave woman who took this power to a horrific conclusion. With her husband Robert and four young children, Garner, a slave, crossed into free Ohio from Kentucky on the snowy night of January 27, 1856. Their hiding place was discovered by federal officials with warrants to fetch them back, but Garner managed to slash the throat of her two-year-old daughter Mary and wound her other children before she could be stopped. After hearings in Ohio to challenge the Fugitive Slave Law of 1850, which provided their owners the legal justification to reclaim her, Garner and her family were remanded back to slavery. In another instance of misfortune, a boat carrying Garner and her three remaining children down river to be sold capsized in a collision with another vessel, her infant daughter Cilla drowning in the calamity. Contemporaneous newspaper accounts describe Garner's joy upon learning of this second death.[53]

The uncommon murder of their children indicated the lengths a few slave mothers went to protect their offspring, particularly female infants who seemed destined for a future of sexual victimization, as well as to undermine their owners' control of their bodies. In "The Closing Door," Grimké transposes such stories of slavery and infanticide with the aftermath of a lynching. Agnes Milton's husband has been lynched for refusing to step down from the sidewalk and allow a white man to pass. After giving birth to their son, she smothers him rather than "bring children here—men children—for the sort—the lust—of possible orderly mobs—who go about things—in an orderly manner—on Sunday mornings" (274–75). Her husband Bob's burnt "ears, fingers, toes" have been dismembered and sold as "souvenirs": "His teeth brought five dollars each" (272). African American women do not themselves have to die, as Agnes learns, to suffer as victims of lynching. If her predicament is connected to slavery, her devotion to what Herron calls "the promulgation of racial self-genocide" (21) may not seem so unreasonable or extreme.

The abolitionist literature that produced African American women writers such as Harriet Brent Jacobs (1813–1897) and Julia C. Collins (d. 1865) modeled strategies that African American women writers later used to bring lynching into the homes, schools, churches, and literary societies of a wide American readership. Antislavery literature bequeathed to women writing against lynching its sense of urgency, the embrasure of biracial coalitions, and international scope. As Post-Reconstruction African American women wielded their pens, they lifted the atrocious acts of savagery that Pauline Hopkins challenged her readers to name from a history of unrecovered pages and awkward silences, and their grief, grievances, and arguments for justice gathered steam.

Notes

1. Lizelia Augusta Jenkins Moorer, "Lynching," from her *Prejudice Unveiled and Other Poems*, in *Collected Black Women's Poetry, Vol. 3,* ed. Joan R. Sherman (rpt. 1907, New York: Oxford University Press, 1988), 35. I make all further page references to Moorer's poems in this volume parenthetically within the text.

I would like to thank two generous colleagues for graciously reading a draft of this essay and offering very helpful revision guidance. Barbara Ryan pointed me to the lost chapter of *Minnie's Sacrifice*, and both she and Caroline Gebhard provided specific suggestions for sharpening and foregrounding my thesis on connecting narrative strategies in literature about lynching to the antislavery movement.

2. Pauline Elizabeth Hopkins, Preface to *Contending Forces: A Romance Illustrative of Negro Life North and South* (rpt. 1900; New York: Oxford University Press, 1988), 348. I make all further page references to *Contending Forces* parenthetically within the text.
3. See Chapters 19 and 20 of *Minnie's Sacrifice* in *Minnie's Sacrifice, Sowing and Reaping, Trial and Triumph: Three Rediscovered Novels by Frances E. W. Harper*, ed. Frances Smith Foster (Boston, MA: Beacon Press, 1994), 81–90.
4. Toni Morrison, *Beloved: A Novel* (New York: Alfred Knopf, 1987), 274.
5. See Trudier Harris, *Exorcising Blackness: Historical and Literary Lynching and Burning Rituals* (Bloomington, IN: Indiana University Press, 1984); Sandra Gunning, *Race, Rape, and Lynching: The Red Record of American Literature, 1890–1912* (New York: Oxford University Press, 1996); and Jacqueline Goldsby, *A Spectacular Secret: Lynching in American Life and Literature* (Chicago, IL and London: The University of Chicago Press, 2006).
6. Anne P. Rice, ed., *Witnessing Lynching: American Writers Respond* (New Brunswick, NJ: Rutgers University Press, 2003).
7. Goldsby, *Spectacular Secret*, 15.
8. Leon F. Litwack, *Trouble in Mind: Black Southerners in the Age of Jim Crow* (New York: Vintage, 1988), 287.
9. See Nell Irvin Painter, *Southern History across the Color Line* (Chapel Hill, NC and London: University of North Carolina Press, 2002), 130.
10. "Neither women nor entire families escaped the savagery of white mobs." Litwack, *Trouble in Mind*, 290.
11. Frances E.W. Harper, "An Appeal to My Country Women," in *Complete Poems of Frances E. W. Harper*, ed. Maryemma Graham (New York: Oxford University Press, 1988), 193–95. I make all further page references to Harper's poems in this volume parenthetically within the text.
12. It was during slavery that African American writers initially invoked the rhetoric of the American jeremiad to criticize the nation for its inequalities and to prophesy its imminent downfall unless it immediately reversed course. See, for example, the discussions of Frederick Douglass's oratory and writings in David Howard-Pitney, *The Afro-American Jeremiad: Appeals for Justice in America* (Philadelphia, PA: Temple University Press, 1990), 17–34.
13. Frances Smith Foster, " 'In Respect to Females . . . ': Differences in the Portrayals of Women by Male and Female Slave Narrators," in *Witnessing Slavery: The Development of Ante-Bellum Slave Narratives*, 2nd ed. (Madison, WI: The University of Wisconsin Press, 1979), xxxiii.
14. Frances Smith Foster and Valerie Ruffin, "Teaching African American Poetry of the Reconstruction Era: Frances E.W. Harper's 'Moses: A Story of the Nile,' " in *Teaching Nineteenth-Century American Poetry*, ed. Paula Bernat

Bennett, Karen L. Kilcup, and Philipp Schweighauser (New York: Modern Language Association, 2007), 142.
15. Carolyn Sorisio, "The Spectacle of the Body: Torture in the Antislavery Writing of Lydia Maria Child and Frances E. W. Harper," *Modern Language Studies* 30.1 (Spring 2000): 47.
16. Ibid., 63, 60–62.
17. Barbara McCaskill, " 'To Labor . . . and Fight on the Side of God': Spirit, Class, and Nineteenth-Century African American Women's Literature," in *Nineteenth-Century American Women Writers: A Critical Reader,* ed. Karen L. Kilcup (Oxford, UK: Blackwell Publishers, 1998), 166.
18. Jennifer Putzi, "Raising the Stigma: Black Women and the Marked Body in Pauline Hopkins's *Contending Forces,*" *College Literature* 31.2 (Spring 2004): 5, 1–21.
19. Richard Yarborough, Introduction to Pauline E. Hopkins, *Contending Forces,* xxxiii-xxxiv. See also Hazel V. Carby's discussion of Sappho Clark in *Reconstructing Womanhood: The Emergence of the Afro-American Woman Novelist* (New York: Oxford University Press, 1987), 140–43.
20. Carby, *Reconstructing Womanhood,* 141.
21. Priscilla Jane Thompson, "Ethiope Lays," in *Collected Black Women's Poetry, Vol. 2,* ed. Joan R. Sherman (rpt. 1900; New York: Oxford University Press, 1988), 29–35. See also Angelina Weld Grimké's "Blackness" and "Goldie," which I discuss later in this essay, in which an African American man murders a white lyncher.
22. W.E.B. Du Bois, *The Souls of Black Folk,* ed. Henry Louis Gates Jr. and Terri Hume Oliver (New York and London: W.W. Norton and Company, 1999), 153, 151.
23. Nell Irvin Painter, *Southern History across the Color Line,* 123. Along with Litwack, Painter evaluates the system of custom and etiquette, a carryover from slavery, which demanded Blacks' deference to whites in the postbellum, white supremacist South. After the Civil War, she writes, "[C]ontempt in [Black] employees . . . was occasionally a capital offense . . . . 'Impudence' threatened the employer-employee aspect of race relations and seemed to hint that the employee (actual or symbolic) was independent of the employer (actual or symbolic)."
24. Tera W. Hunter, Chapter Two, "Reconstruction and the Meaning of Freedom," in *To 'Joy My Freedom: Southern Black Women's Lives and Labor after the Civil War* (Cambridge, MA and London: Harvard University Press, 1997), 34.
25. Anna Julia Cooper, "Woman vs. the Indian," in *A Voice from the South. By a Black Woman of the South* (1892; New York: Oxford University Press, 1988), 91.
26. Harper, *Minnie's Sacrifice,* 46.
27. Moorer, "Jim Crow Cars," in *Collected Black Women's Poetry, Vol. 3,* 14.

28. Hopkins, *Contending Forces,* 348.
29. Claudia Tate, ed., *The Works of Katherine Davis Chapman Tillman* (New York: Oxford University Press, 1991), 158–59.
    I make all further page references to Tillman's works parenthetically within the text.
30. Paula Bernat Bennett, "Rewriting Dunbar: Realism, Black Women Poets, and the Genteel," in *Post-Bellum, Pre-Harlem: African American Literature and Culture, 1877–1919,* ed. Barbara McCaskill and Caroline Gebhard (New York: New York University Press, 2006), 147–48.
31. Among the many newspapers that Frederick Douglass (c. 1818–1895) founded and published was *The North Star*, which he edited at Rochester, New York. Lydia Maria Child (1820–1880) served as editor-in-chief of the *National Anti-Slavery Standard* for several years. In Boston, Maria Weston Chapman (1806–1885) spent nearly two decades editing the annual *Liberty Bell* for the Boston Female Antislavery Society, and William Lloyd Garrison (1805–1879) founded and edited *The Liberator* (1831–65), the longest-running and largest-circulating antislavery newspaper. The Quaker William Tweedie published antislavery and temperance books, including *Running a Thousand Miles for Freedom* (1860) by the fugitive slaves William and Ellen Craft (1824–1900; 1826–91).
32. See, for instance, Daphne A. Brooks's discussion of reactions by the transatlantic abolitionist press to Henry Box Brown's traveling panorama, *The Mirror of Slavery*, in *Bodies in Dissent: Spectacular Performances of Race and Freedom* (Durham, NC and London: Duke University Press, 2006), 94–102.
33. Tillman, *Works*, 136–37.
34. Philip Dray, *At the Hands of Persons Unknown: The Lynching of Black America* (New York: Random House, 2002), 103–8.
35. Marie Ann Charlotte de Corday d'Armont (1768–1793) was an aristocrat who assassinated the Jacobin leader Jean-Paul Marat (1743–1793) in order to end the bloodbath of the Reign of Terror. Here, Tillman identifies de Corday with the English people perhaps because of her monarchist views. Joan of Arc (1412–1431) brought the French army to victory against the English who had conquered them and restored Charles VII to the French throne.
36. William Craft and Ellen Craft, *Running a Thousand Miles for Freedom: The Escape of William and Ellen Craft from Slavery* (1860; Athens, GA and London: The University of Georgia Press, 1999), 57.
37. In his essay " 'I Was Born': Slave Narratives, Their Status as Autobiography and as Literature," James Olney states that it was conventional for former slaves to introduce their memoirs with a "poetic epigraph, by preference from William Cowper," which expressed such sentiments. *The Slave's Narrative*, ed. Charles T. Davis and Henry Louis Gates, Jr. (New York: Oxford University Press, 1985), 152.

38. Ida B. Wells-Barnett, *A Red Record*, in *On Lynchings* (1895; New York: Humanity Books, 2002), 59.
39. Ibid., 150.
40. Bennett, "Rewriting Dunbar," 152.
41. Eve Allegra Raimon, *The "Tragic Mulatta" Revisited: Race and Nationalism in Nineteenth-Century Antislavery Fiction* (New Brunswick, NJ and London: Rutgers University Press, 2004), 17.
42. Dray, *Persons Unknown*, 254.
43. Carolivia Herron, Introduction to *Selected Works of Angelina Weld Grimké*, ed. Herrron (New York: Oxford University Press, 1991), 5.
44. Ibid., 5–6.
45. Ibid., 21.
46. Patricia Sullivan, *Lift Every Voice: The NAACP and the Making of the Civil Rights Movement* (New York and London: The New Press, 2009), 74.
47. Dray, *Persons Unknown*, 246.
48. Grimké, *Selected Works,* 417–18.
49. Ibid., 139. I make all further page references to Grimké's works in this volume parenthetically within the text.
50. In "White Islands of Safety and Engulfing Blackness: Remapping Segregation in Angelina Weld Grimké's 'Blackness' and 'Goldie,' " Anne P. Rice discusses how Grimké uses landscape and other natural imagery in these works of short fiction to protest Jim Crow; preserve the memory of lynching rituals; and articulate the retribution angry African Americans threatened to shower upon white America. In *African American Review* 42.1 (Summer 2008): 75–90.
51. In 1920, Grimké revised and published this story as "Goldie". This time, she names the protagonist "Victor Forrest" along with his white nemesis, "Lafe Coleman". It is Victor's sister, the "Goldie" of the title, who is lynched along with her husband, Cy Harper, and unborn baby. In this story, Grimké references slavery in the character of Victor's old Aunt Phoebe. Her husband and children sold away during slavery, Phoebe is neither nostalgic about the past nor able to forget its sorrows. She reveals murderous Lafe's whereabouts to Victor. See "Goldie," in Grimké, *Collected Works*, 282–306.
52. Brenda E. Stevenson, *Life in Black and White: Family and Community in the Slave South* (New York: Oxford University Press, 1996), 245.
53. Garner's story inspired Toni Morrison's investigation of the psychology of slavery for her novel *Beloved*. See Mark Reinhardt, *Who Speaks for Margaret Garner?: The True Story that Inspired Toni Morrison's* Beloved (Minneapolis, MN: University of Minnesota Press, 2010); Steven C. Weisenberger, *Modern Medea: A Family Story of Slavery and Child-Murder from the Old South* (New York: Hill and Wang, 1998); and Cynthia Griffin Wolff, "Margaret Garner: A Cincinnati Story," *The Massachusetts Review* 32.3 (Autumn 1991): 417–40.

CHAPTER 4

"A Woman was Lynched the Other Day": Memory, Gender, and the Limits of Traumatic Representation

Jennifer D. Williams

Hollow dresses dangle from makeshift branches
That cast shadows on white walls.
Mirrored reflections multiply these lifeless frocks
and turn the onlooker's gaze upon herself.

I borrow the this essay's title and the following image from Brooklyn-based artist Kim Mayhorn's 1998 multimedia installation memorializing Black women who were victims of lynching and rape in the nineteenth and twentieth centuries (See Figure 4.1). The declaration "A Woman Was Lynched the Other Day" recalls the banner the New York NAACP would unfurl from their Fifth Avenue office when news of another lynching would surface. White letters inscribed on a black background would announce "A MAN WAS LYNCHED YESTERDAY" and ignite a chain of communication that rallied member organizations to don black armbands and march through Times Square chanting "Stop the lynching," former National Council of Negro Women chair Dorothy Height recalls in her memoir (See Figure 4.2).[1]

The gender shift in the title of Mayhorn's exhibit is not inconsequential. Lynching registers in our cultural memory as public acts of racist violence committed against Black men by mobs of white men in purported defense of white womanhood. This familiar narrative eclipses

Figure 4.1 Kim Mayhorn, "A Woman Was Lynched the Other Day," 1998 (Courtesy of Kim Mayhorn)

the lynching and rapes of Black women. Though antilynching literature documented racialized and sexual violence against Black women, it cited such incidents as evidence disproving the myth of the Black male rapist. The lynching of Black women was rarely taken up as a subject on its

Figure 4.2 Flag, announcing lynching, flown from the window of the NAACP headquarters on Fifth Ave., New York City (Library of Congress Print and Photo Collection)

own.[2] To be sure, most racially-motivated lynching claimed the lives of Black men, but between 1880 and 1930, at least 121 Black women were murdered by lynch mobs, according to official documentation by the *Chicago Tribune,* the Tuskegee Institute, and the NAACP. These records only account for reported cases of mob violence resulting in the victims' deaths, and elide other incidents like mob beatings and public rapes perpetrated against hundreds of Black (as well as some white and Mexican) women.[3]

The inattention paid to the lynching of Black women, however, reveals more about the masculinist construction of a history of racial trauma than it does about the infrequency of mob violence that targeted Black women. "[I]f we have 'memory holes' when it comes to the lynching and rape of black women," Jonathan Markovitz maintains in his cultural study of lynching's symbolic meaning, "the explanation for this historical amnesia can be found, at least in part, in the fact that there has been no movement devoted to securing a memory of the suffering of black women that has been comparable in scope to the antilynching movement."[4] Despite recent efforts to restore the lynching of Black women to our cultural memory, such as Mayhorn's installation, The Mary Turner Project, Maria De Longoria's dissertation *"Stranger Fruit": The Lynching of Black Women, the Cases of Rosa Richardson and Marie Scott* (2006), Crystal N. Feimster's *Southern Horrors: Women and the Politics of Rape and Lynching* (2009), and the present volume, the notion of racialized violence as a masculine experience continues to resonate in contemporary culture. "Lynching" has exceeded the physical act itself, to become a gendered sign of racial oppression that enables Black men to claim it as a trope of emasculation over time and in varied contexts.[5]

Lynching has also imprinted Black cultural memory in a way that the more private, and presumably "feminized" trauma of rape has not.[6] Conversely, "Black women have no image, no symbol that they can call up so readily, so graphically in just a word as Black men do with lynching."[7] As Elsa Barkley Brown's reference to the graphic image suggests, much of lynching's cultural power resides in the act's public visibility. Firmly entrenched in modernity's visual regime, lynchings were staged to attract onlookers, at locations like railroad crossings, and were documented in photographs and circulated as postcards until 1908.[8] James Allen and John Littlefield's 2000 exhibition "Witness" (retitled "Without Sanctuary") showcased a number of these postcards and related artifacts to the public for the first time, later publishing 98 of the photographs with essays as *Without Sanctuary: Lynching Photography in America* (2000). As most of the photographs document the torture and mutilation of Black men, Laura Nelson's femininely-attired corpse is a shocking anomaly in the collection (See Figure 4.3).

Laura Nelson was lynched in Okemah, Oklahoma, in 1911. To protect her son, she confessed to shooting a deputy sheriff who was searching her cabin as part of a meat pilfering investigation. Both Laura and her son L.W. were dragged from jail and hung from a bridge. The mob raped Laura before lynching her and her son. In his footnote to Laura Nelson's photo, James Allen calls attention to the photo's ghostly quality: "Grief and haunting unreality permeate this photo. The corpse of Laura Nelson retains an indissoluble femininity despite the horror inflicted upon it. Specterlike, she seems to float—thistledown light and implausibly still."[9]

The empty dress in Mayhorn's installation is an uncanny *evocatéur* of Nelson's photograph, which haunts by virtue of its anti-spectacularity. The disembodied dress materializes the representational void that the silencing of lynched Black women has created. This essay addresses that representational void by turning to literature published during the height of mob violence that depicts the lynching of a pregnant black woman, Mary Turner. Angelina Weld Grimké's "Goldie" (1920), Carrie Williams Clifford's "Little Mother" (1922), and Jean Toomer's "Kabnis" (1923) are narrative acts of witnessing that seek to redress the silencing of Mary

Figure 4.3 Postcard of the lynching of Laura Nelson in Okemah, Oklahoma, May 25, 1911 (Courtesy of Twin Palms Publishers)

Turner as both a victim of mob violence and a woman who spoke out against the lynching of her husband.

Rather than dramatize the spectacular display of Turner's lynching, these works affirm the void that marks the space of loss that language cannot recapture. Further, the engagement with the complexities of language and silence in the aforementioned texts challenges the weight of visual evidence by drawing on an aesthetics of absence.

To achieve an aesthetics of absence, Clifford, Toomer, and Grimké employ narrative strategies of silence and omission that underline the ethics of unrepresentability. Privileging the void offers an approach to the trauma of lynching that does not foreground graphic representations of the tortured Black body. Rather, sound disrupts the silence of the visual and speaks for the dead. These writers' attention to the function of form points toward an alternative ethics of representation based in Black feminist discourse.

Racial Trauma and the Limits of Representation

Trauma generally defines staggering responses to injurious events that are not comprehended the moment they happen, but return belatedly in recurring images, nightmares, and other repeating episodes.[10] The trauma of lynching complicates this definition. The traumatic effects of lynching tend to transpire through acts of secondary witnessing like oral culture, photographs, literature, and journalistic accounts.[11] Repeated acts of witnessing precipitate "a traumatized collective historical memory which is reinvoked at contemporary sites of conflict."[12] African American collective identification with traumatic events that may not have been experienced directly also distinguishes cultural trauma from individualized trauma.[13] However, the quotidian nature of Black suffering has the potential to diminish its "shock value," i.e., its status as trauma. While representations of suffering strive to invoke an audience's empathy on the basis of shared humanity, pornotropic circulations of Black pained and tortured bodies may serve to underline the subhuman status that racist ideology ascribes to Blacks.

Elizabeth Alexander goes on to remind us in her reading of the Rodney King videos that "[b]lack bodies in pain for public consumption have been an American national spectacle for centuries."[14] This pageantry of collective Black suffering moves from auction blocks to public lynchings and rapes, to videotaped beatings by law enforcement officers. Racist spectacles of violence are formative elements in Black collective trauma and are constitutive of Black subjectivity.

What, then, are the aesthetic limitations and possibilities of representing racist violence and how do issues of gender complicate these representations? Historically, African American writers have employed the Black body in pain as a way to "authenticate" racial trauma. Authors of slave narratives recounted scenes of physical and mental violence to arouse the righteous indignation of abolitionists and sympathizers. Frederick Douglass' detailed account of the beating of his Aunt Hester in *Narrative of the Life of Frederick Douglass: An American Slave* is the most remarked upon of these brutal scenes, but as James Olney points out in "'I Was Born': Slave Narratives, Their Status as Autobiography and Literature," the whipping scene is a recurring convention in slave autobiography, and typically the victim is a woman.[15]

It is no wonder, then, that the scenes have genealogical significance. Douglass identifies that "terrible spectacle" of Aunt Hester's vile abuse as the "blood-stained gate" that marked his "entrance to the hell of slavery."[16] That scene of corporeal violence inaugurated Douglass's subjectivity as a slave.

If the brutal flogging of maternal figures instantiates Black men's subjugation in slave narratives, Black men are the archetypal bodies of subjection in literary representations of lynching. Lynching in Black male writers' Post-Reconstruction and Black modern literature represents the denial of freedom and patriarchal citizenship under the threat of death. James Weldon Johnson's ex-colored man abandons the South and the Black race altogether after witnessing a mob lynch and burn a Black man beyond recognition. The mob's methodical lynching and burning of Tom in Jean Toomer's "Blood-Burning Moon" recalls Johnson's vivid portrait. Toomer's story foregrounds the issues of sexuality and economic power that Ida B. Wells exposed in her antilynching campaign. Like Wells, Toomer refutes the myth of the Black rapist and reveals lynching as a tool of economic and social control meant to subordinate Black masculinity.

Though African American male writers tend to take up lynching more than their female counterparts, the antilynching play emerged as a feminist genre of American drama at the turn of the twentieth century.[17] Theatre historian James V. Hatch designates antilynching plays as the second form of protest drama after antislavery plays, and similar in affective appeal. Hence, like antislavery literature, Black women's antilynching dramas tend to emphasize domestic sentimentality and to appeal to white women readers. Angelina Weld Grimké explains her use of maternal empathy in her groundbreaking play *Rachel* (1916) to galvanize white feminists behind the antilynching cause:

> If anything can make all women sisters underneath their skins it is motherhood. If, then, I could make the white women of this country see, feel, understand just what their prejudice and the prejudice of their fathers, brother, husbands, sons were having on the souls of the colored mothers everywhere, and upon the mothers what are to be, a great power to affect public opinion would be set free and the battle would be half won.[18]

Grimké's petition to white women based on the shared value of motherhood follows Harriet Jacobs's entreaty to white women readers to support the abolition of slavery in *Incidents in the Life of a Slave Girl* (1861). By deploying this strategy in a Post-Emancipation context, Grimké suggests that mob violence reinscribes the state of violated maternity that characterized Black women in captivity. The maintenance of Black subjection through extralegal forms of violence, in Grimké's analysis, perpetuates a state of unfreedom comparable to slavery.

Also akin to women's slave narratives, Grimké's play and short fiction touch upon the refusal of maternity as an act of resistance. Whereas Rachel simply foregoes marriage and motherhood, Grimké's protagonist in "The Closing Door" (1919) smothers her baby in lieu of raising a Black boy only to have him killed by a lynch mob. The use of infanticide as a trope found Grimké defending herself against charges of advocating "race suicide."[19] The publication of Grimké's short stories in Margaret Sanger's *Birth Control Review* did not help her defense. Yet Sanger's journal made the story available to Grimké's intended audience: white feminists. The story's publication in a journal committed to women's reproductive rights supports Grimké's suggestion that Black women's maternal rights have been tempered by a history of violation.

By dramatizing the impact of lynching on the mothers, sisters, wives, and grandmothers of male victims, Black women's antilynching plays draw attention to women's grief and loss in the aftermath of lynching. While the lynching victims in these plays are Black men, the dramas unfold in the homes of the victims' families instead of the lynching sites. Georgia Douglass Johnson's *A Sunday Morning in the South* (1925) highlights a grandmother's helplessness in the face of her grandson's arrest and subsequent lynching for the false accusation of raping a white girl. The action of the play takes place in Sue Jones' two-room house. Instead of a maimed body, Johnson's play ends with an aesthetic of visual absence punctuated by sound. Cries of "Lord have mercy" toll from a church in the distance.

The emphasis that Johnson's drama and other women's antilynching literature place on motherhood and domesticity reflects the gender and class conventions of Black women writing in the early decades of the twentieth century. This sense of propriety also made women writers less likely than male writers to represent lynching violence in graphic detail.[20] At the same time, Black women writers' aesthetic detours from the scene of spectacular violence to the space of absence expand the parameters of lynching's injurious effects and the methods of representing them. The focus on those left to mourn the lynching victim establishes lynching as a collective injury rather than a violent affront to Black manhood. The turn to the space of loss also changes the relationship between affect and the aesthetics of representation. Words become inadequate to fill the absence left by the mourned body. A silent pause reaffirms loss and becomes a generative space for a sonic eruption of pain.

The move from scene to sound provides an opportunity to probe Black feminist aesthetic interventions into representations of Black corporeal trauma. The next part of this essay analyzes representations of the Mary Turner lynching, one of the most notorious cases of mob violence which generated activist and aesthetic responses immediately after the crime and continues to haunt Black women's cultural production today.[21] The hesitancy with which the artists in this essay approach Mary Turner's lynching underscores the ethical and aesthetic challenges of representing the unspeakable. Sound intervenes where words fail to articulate embodied pain and to mourn the dead.

"unwise remarks"

The lynching of Mary Turner took place in Georgia in 1918. After a fight between a white plantation owner and one of his Black tenant farmers, Sidney Johnson, resulted in the white man's death, a mob murdered several Black men throughout Brooks and Lowndes counties, including Mary Turner's husband, Hayes. When Mary publicly defended her husband and threatened to press charges against his murderers, the mob set out to silence her. They took her to a stream, tied her ankles together, and hung her from a tree upside down. Then, they doused her clothes with gasoline and set her on fire. One member of the mob took his knife and split open her abdomen, causing her unborn child to fall from her womb to the ground. Another member crushed the child's head with the heel of his shoe. Finally, Mary Turner's body was riddled with bullets. She was in the eighth month of her pregnancy.[22] Following the horrible crime, *The Associated Press* reported that Mary had made "unwise remarks" about her husband's murder, and "the people, in their indignant mood, took exception to her remarks, as well as her attitude."[23]

The "people's" permanent silencing of Mary Turner raised a collective outcry from Black social activists, visual artists, and writers. In *At the Hands of Persons Unknown,* Philip Dray supports, "The horrific details of the mob killing of Mary Turner shocked even hardened antilynching activists," and notes that the attention the case garnered "became an instant rallying point for further agitation."[24] Black news organs, like *The Messenger* and *The Crusader,* cited and recirculated Walter White's detailed exposé in *The Crisis. The New York Times* and the *Atlanta Constitution* also reported the incident and criticized Georgia's state authorities for failing to bring the perpetrators to justice. Organizations such as the National Association of Colored Women, the NAACP, and the Anti-Lynching Crusaders urged Georgia's Governor Dorsey and President Woodrow Wilson to punish the guilty. In spite of public outrage, Dorsey and Wilson's eventual condemnation of the crime of lynching, and Walter White's identification of the persons responsible for the crime, authorities failed to charge or prosecute anyone for Mary Turner's murder.[25]

The creative works that Mary Turner's lynching inspired were a different form of protest that, when taken together, constitute a collective act of mourning and remembrance. Celebrated visual artist Meta Vaux Warrick Fuller was among the first artists to memorialize Turner in 1919 with her sculpture *Mary Turner (A Silent Protest Against Mob Violence).*

The 15-inch high, painted plaster sculpture features a female figure standing atop a base with the inscription, "In Memory of Mary Turner: As a Silent Protest Against Mob Violence" (See Figure 4.4).[26] The figure clutches a small baby at her side and gazes down on a mob surrounded by flames and grasping at her from below. The image detours from conventional lynching representations and recalls the "sorrowful mother" of Christian iconography. Fuller's choice of religious iconography suggests a sense of spiritual transcendence that allows the figure to triumph over her oppressors.[27] The implication of salvation could be perceived as attenuating the violence Mary Turner endured.

At the same time, Fuller's refusal to reproduce Turner's lynching in graphic detail redirects attention from the shock that occurs in the moment of trauma, toward a more empathic and enduring connection

Figure 4.4 Meta Vaux Warrick Fuller "Mary Turner (A Silent Protest Against Mob Violence," 1919 (Courtesy of Museum of African American History, Boston, MA.)

between viewers and subject. Fuller's use of familiar iconography and her citation of "a silent protest" broaden the scope of grievance from Mary Turner's lynching to the crime of lynching more generally. Similar to her mentor Auguste Rodin, Fuller longed to translate affect into physical form. Her skill in doing so gained the attention of the French press, who donned her a "delicate sculptor of horrors."[28]

Yet, the attempt to represent lynching demands a reconceptualization of form. Fuller brought together classical form with modern social commentary to achieve a work of protest that impacts viewers emotionally but does not shock them. What at first glance appears to be a mother cradling her baby becomes more distressing as a viewer's eyes move down toward the sculpture's base and notice the flames that lick the bottom of the figure's dress. The plaque's reference to a silent protest not only merges the mother in distress with the scourge of lynching, but also invokes silence as a way to "voice" resistance. Indeed, a silent protest brings the aural to bear on the visual. The sonic trace of muffled drumbeats sound a requiem for Turner's stolen life.

Fuller's sculpture offers a point of departure for examining the literature of her contemporaries. Like Fuller, Grimké, Clifford, and Toomer come up against the limits of representation in their accounts of Mary Turner's lynching. They mark those limits with narrative omissions, breaks, and gaps. They interrupt the story's telling with hyphens and ellipses. These narrative ruptures call attention to the ineffable. The gaps in narration also beckon readers to fill in the details—to participate in the act of remembering instead of being passive observers of a shocking spectacle. In fact, the writers move away from the scene of violence and appeal to the sound of mourning as an affective transmission of pain.

Sounding the Unspeakable

Angelina Weld Grimké's struggle with representing Mary Turner's lynching seems to have played a part in her writing process. Though most of her poetry centered on themes of love, Grimké explored lynching in almost all her short fiction and drama. She returned to the Mary Turner incident several times, taking it through various incarnations and finally publishing it as "Goldie" in 1920.[29] Her repeated attempts to come to grips with Turner's story can be read as a process of repetition—of working through—that is endemic to mourning.[30]

According to Claudia Tate, Mary Turner's lynching "so severely affected Grimké that not only did she rewrite that story over and over again, but the activity of rewriting it seems to have been more important than her desire to see it in print or performed."[31] Mary Turner's story clearly had an emotional impact on Grimké, yet the letters to the editors of *Atlantic Monthly* and *Birth Control Review* that she included with her stories also affirm her desire to make her artistic protest public.

Grimké's revisions of the Mary Turner story move progressively away from a faithful retelling of the account. "The Waitin" deviates little from the actual event: Mary Greene is lynched for speaking in defense of her husband, her unborn child torn from her womb. In contrast, "Blackness" is a first-person confession of an unnamed northern Black male protagonist who heads south to avenge the lynchings of his former lover and her husband, and then escapes back to the North. The events of the Mary Turner lynching are not introduced until the end of the story, when the narrator tells his friend the scene he witnessed down south:

> "Ripped open—I say—and under her poor little swaying golden feet—her child—unborn—beautiful—tiny hands and feet perfect—one little hand reached up—as though—appealing—the little head—blotted out—crushed—its little brains"—.[32]

The dashes and spacing between the words produce a staccato effect, a textual performance of an impossible confession. This impossibility may explain Grimké's eventual transfer of the scene of violence from the female body to the home.

In "Goldie," Grimké apposes the mob's destruction of the family home to its murder and mutilation of the family itself. Victor Forrest returns south at the request of his sister Goldie Harper, to find the house she shares with her husband Cy Harper abandoned and disheveled: "Chairs, tables, a sofa, a whatnot, all had been smashed, broken, torn apart; the stuffing of the upholstery, completely ripped out."[33] The "ripped out" upholstery supplants Turner's "ripped open" body.

This displacement signifies lynching as a "domestic tragedy."[34] Pertinently, husband and wife are discovered lynched side by side: "Underneath those terribly mutilated swinging bodies, lay a tiny unborn child, its head crushed by a deliberate heel."[35] By representing the Turner lynching as a collective injury and a disruption of Black domesticity, Grimké overthrows the myths of the inviolable Black woman and the rapacious Black man in one fell swoop. But does she also efface Mary Turner as a speaking subject?[36]

Mary Turner was lynched for refusing to be silent. Her insurgency and subsequent punishment by mob law is part of a broader—recorded and unrecorded—history of the use of corporeal violence to discipline unruly Black female bodies.[37] Instead of interpreting Grimké's evasions as silencing Mary Turner, however, it might be more useful to frame her failures of representation through the lens of trauma. Grimké's compulsive returns to Mary Turner's lynching, her determination to remember and bear witness are met by willed and unwilled forgetting, a desire to not tell—to not know. It makes sense then that "Goldie" ends with a sound beyond words. In the woods, a "low keening" can be heard. This moaning, a mourning, anticipates Victor's death "upon another tree," a tree that will join thousands of others to become a "Creaking Forrest."[38]

This creaking ensemble unsilences the dead. Sounds of loss supplant the scene of violence, destabilizing the authority of the visual and the word. It is perhaps fitting that Carolivia Herron's introduction to Grimké's collected works makes reference to the blues "as the African-American epic song" and maintains further that "Grimké sings that song as an artist creating through the triple cultural blows of being black, female, and lesbian."[39] Grimké's "song" is an act of resistance to the mob's silencing of Mary Turner's defiant voice. In the space of absence left by Turner's death, the trees cry out.

Sound displaces the scene of lynching in Carrie Williams Clifford's "Little Mother" as well. Clifford shared Grimké's desire to make art that reflected a commitment to social justice. The poet and activist expresses in her preface to *Race Rhymes* her goal of racial uplift, of calling attention to significant events in the history of the Negro in America (1911).[40] Hence, several of Clifford's poems in *Race Rhymes* and *The Widening Light* (1922) condemn Jim Crow laws and the terror of lynching. *The Widening Light* includes reflections on the East St. Louis riot, the Silent Protest Parade, and the lynching of Mary Turner in its slim 65-page volume.

In *The Widening Light,* "Little Mother" follows a paean to the Silent Protest Parade. Like Meta Vaux Warrick Fuller, Clifford draws together thematically the march against racist violence and the Mary Turner lynching. Clifford writes "Silent Protest Parade" in syncopated rhyming couplets that pick up the beat of the muted drumbeat as the poet describes the marchers:

> Silent, dogged and dusky of hue,
> Keeping step to the sound of the muffled drum,
> With its constantly recurring turn turn, turn
> Turn Turn Turn Turn Turn;[41]

"Little Mother" picks up the aurality of "Silent Protest Parade." A lyrical poem set in rhyming quatrains, "Little Mother" alternates stanzas in a call-and-response pattern. The first, third, fifth, and seventh stanzas warn the Little Mother to "tremble" for her unborn child and his inescapable fate. The second, fourth, and sixth extol the father, Gabriel, and the soon-to-be born baby; describe the sounds hidden beneath the black night and carried by ominous winds; and reveal a captured Gabe being dragged by a sturdy rope. "Hideous sounds and cries" signal the approaching mob and anticipate their revelation of the mother's potential threat: "She is bound to tell!"[42] The threat the Little Mother poses as a speaking subject calls to mind Mary Turner's "unwise remarks," her refusal to remain silent after her husband's brutal murder. Clifford reminds readers that Turner's defiant voice was the impetus for the mob's retaliation. In turn, Clifford makes use of the auditory features of lyric poetry as an alternative means of sonic resistance and mourning.

The varied refrain, "Oh, tremble, Little Mother . . . But tremble, Little Mother . . . Oh, tremble, dark-faced mother" attests to the poem's aural quality. The final stanza also makes a more subtle gesture toward sound. Announcing the Little Mother's death, the concluding lines of the poem shift to italics and address the reader:

> *Oh the human beasts were ruthless,*
> *And there upon the ground,*
> *Two bodies—and an unborn babe—*
> *The ghastly morning found.*[43]

The typeface sets the closing verse off from the rest of the poem, save the last line in the third stanza, "*Why does he stay so late?*" The final stanza is both answer and epitaph. It acts as a marker and speaks for the dead.

Jean Toomer's conceptualization of *Cane* as a "swan song" betrays a concern with the dead as well. *Cane*'s three-part structure blends prose, poetry, folksong, and drama and moves geographically from the rural South to the city streets, and back south again. Set in the Post-Reconstruction era, *Cane*'s southern sections reveal how the economy of slavery continued to shape raced and gendered forms of oppression after emancipation. These structures of oppression meet in the book's lynching narratives. Toomer's attention to lynching is not surprising since he traveled to and worked in Georgia when mob violence was at its peak.[44] More striking is the author's gendered approach to lynching. "Blood-Burning Moon" and "Kabnis," in particular, invert the conventional lynching scenario by engaging Black women as subjects.[45] In light of the dominating female presence throughout *Cane,* scant attention has been paid to what I see as Toomer's politicization of gender and Black collective memory. Yet, as a longtime resident of Washington, D.C., Toomer had ample exposure to the flowering Black feminist discourse around lynching, particularly at Georgia Douglas Johnson's literary salon, a space where the scourge of lynching was discussed and antilynching dramas performed. A year before setting off for Sparta, the trip that inspired *Cane*'s southern set sections, Toomer helped organize a study group with other Washington, D.C. writers, including Carrie Williams Clifford and Angelina Weld Grimké. Among other current topics, the writers studied the history of slavery and the plight of racist violence.[46] It is no wonder, then, Toomer engages Black feminist discourse in his lynching narratives.

The Mary Turner lynching appears as but a subtext in "Kabnis," *Cane*'s closing drama, yet when read in concert with the violated Black women that limn Toomer's entire textual landscape, the Turner lynching becomes an even more potent site of memory. At the end of *Cane*'s opening sketch, "Karintha," for instance, a child falls out of the namesake's womb "onto a bed of pine needles in the forest." Toomer diverts the narrative focus from the fate of the child to a smouldering sawdust pile nearby, implying that the child's remains have joined the "smoke [that] curls up and hangs in odd wraiths about the trees, curls up, and spreads itself out over the valley."[47] That smoke and the image of a falling child resurface throughout "Kabnis," the book's final and longest story. A repeating chorus in "Kabnis", with the alliterative phrase "Burn, bear black children," brings together the death of Karintha's child and the fate of "Mame Lamkin's" and her baby.

A six-part, semi-biographical drama, "Kabnis" centers on a northern Black middle-class man who comes south to teach. After losing his post for drinking liquor on school property, Ralph Kabnis serves as an apprentice to shop owner and wagonmaker Fred Halsey. Under Halsey's tutelage, Kabnis learns how precarious Black life is under Jim Crow and the constant threat of lynching.

The unpredictability of racist terror generates a fear-induced silence throughout "Sempter's" Black community. Professor Layman, a wandering teacher-preacher "who knows more than would be good for anyone other than a silent man," typifies a sense of hopelessness and inaction brought about by southern violence in the Post-Reconstruction era.[48] He functions as the reluctant witness who tells Kabnis about the death of Mame Lamkins:

> White folks know that niggers talk, an they dont mind jes so long as nothing comes of it, so here goes. She was in th family-way, Mame Lamkins

> was. They killed her in th street, an some white man seein th risin in her stomach as she lay there soppy in her blood like any cow, took an ripped her belly open, an th kid fell out. It was living; but a nigger baby aint supposed t live. So he jabbed his knife in it an stuck it t a tree. An then they all went away.[49]

The portrait of Mame Lamkins retains most of the facts of the Mary Turner lynching but none of trauma's affective impact. Yet right after Layman's unaffected telling, shouting from a nearby church amplifies the story and mourns the loss: "A shriek pierces the room. The bronze pieces on the mantel hum. The sister cries frantically: 'Jesus, Jesus, I've found Jesus. O Lord, glory t God, one mo sinner is acomin home."

The text also makes a series of indirect references to Mame Lamkins/Mary Turner's lynching, leading up to Layman's account. Sonic eruptions throughout the drama express, on an affective level, what language cannot convey. Reminiscent of Clifford's "Little Mother," the winds even chant a tainted lullaby for Mame Lamkins's dead child:

> rock a-by baby . . .
> Black mother sways, holding a white child on her bosom.
> when the bough bends . . .
> Her breath hums through pine-cones.
> cradle will fall . . .
> Teat moon-children at your breasts,
> down will come baby . . .
> Black mother.[50]

The image of the Black mother nurturing the white child connects Black women's labor under slavery as nurses for white children to the continued appropriation of Black women's maternal labor in the Post-Reconstruction era. The lines that picture the Black mother swaying, humming to, and nursing the white child contrast with the alternating lines that trail off into ellipses and stress the falling motion of the (Black) baby.

Toomer's acts of indirection and repetition resemble Angelina Weld Grimké's mode of working through the Mary Turner incident as a way of grappling with the aesthetics and ethics of representation. Gaps, elisions, and ellipses create a sense of hesitancy throughout "Kabnis." In the same manner as Mayhorn's empty dress, Grimké's evasions, and Clifford's unarticulated threat, Toomer's textual performances of silence and omission accentuate the unspeakability of the lynching of a mother and her unborn child.

The unspeakable is spoken by the wind's eerie chants and a sister's cries to Jesus. Sounds tell what words conceal. Kabnis's declaration that there is no "mold" to fit the "form" branded into his soul attests to the limits of language to grasp the trauma he has witnessed and wants to capture aesthetically. Identifying the art in his soul with both the lynched mother and her fetus, Kabnis bellows toward the end of the sketch, "I wish t God some lynchin white man ud stick his knife through it an pin it to a tree. An pin it to a tree."[51] Words would have to take on flesh to express the body's pain. Toomer, Grimké, and Clifford's turns to sound—to keening, moans, and screams—are attempts to form words into flesh by conjuring the body's materiality.

The sonic traces of scenes of violence call attention to feelings that endure in the body's absence, when it can neither be looked at nor retrieved through representation. Two years after Mary Turner's lynching, and just a year following the Red Summer of 1919, Mamie Smith's recording of "Crazy Blues" swept the country. Smith's crooned lyrics of lost love and a desire for retribution captured the sentiment of Black communities susceptible to extralegal violence by southern mobs and northern police mobs. If we listen closely, we just might hear Mary Turner's defiant "No!" in the jagged grain of Mamie Smith's voice.[52]

Notes

1. Dorothy Height, *Open Wide the Freedom Gates: A Memoir* (New York: Public Affairs, 2003).
2. Jonathan Markovitz, *Legacies of Lynching: Racial Violence and Memory* (Minneapolis, MN: Minnesota Press, 2004), 22.
3. For a discussion of the "official" compiling of lynching statistics, see Sandra Gunning, *Race, Rape, and Lynching: The Red Record of American Literature 1890–1912* (New York: Oxford UP, 1996) and Crystal Feimster's dissertation *"Ladies and Lynching": The Gendered Discourse of Mob Violence in the New South, 1880–1930* (Princeton, NJ: Princeton University, 2000).
4. Markovitz, *Legacies of Lynching*, 142.
5. Supreme Court Justice Clarence Thomas' description of his sexual harassment investigation as a "high-tech lynching" is the most notorious example of this image's use. Yet, from works of literature like Richard Wright's *Native Son* (1940) to highly publicized incidents of police brutality against Black men, to the hip hop lyrics of Dr. Dre and others, lynching remains an accessible trope for Black men's appropriation and misappropriation.
6. See Hazel V. Carby's *Reconstructing Womanhood: The Emergence of the Afro-American Woman Novelist* (New York: Oxford University Press, 1987) and

Elsa Barkley Brown's "Imaging Lynching: African American Women, Communities of Struggle, and Collective Memory," *African American Women Speak Out on Anita Hill—Clarence Thomas*, ed. Geneva Smitherman (Detroit, MI: Wayne State University, 1995), 100–124.

7. Brown, "Imaging Lynching," 101–102.
8. Jacqueline Goldsby's *A Spectacular Secret: Lynching in American Life and Literature* (Chicago: University of Chicago Press, 2006) places lynching square within the developments of modernity like film and sound recordings.
9. James Allen, *Without Sanctuary: Lynching Photography in America* (Sante Fe, NM: Twin Palms Publishers, 2000), 178n37.
10. Formative criticism in trauma studies includes, but is not limited to Shoshana Felman and Dori Laub's *Testimony: Crises of Witnessing in Literature, Psychoanalysis, and History* (New York: Routledge, 1992); Dominick LaCapra's *Representing the Holocaust: History, Theory, Trauma* (Ithaca, NY: Cornell University Press, 1994); and Cathy Caruth's *Unclaimed Experience: Trauma, Narrative, and History* (Baltimore, MD: Johns Hopkins University, 1996).
11. The term "secondary witnessing" is an extension of Marianne Hirsch's concept of "postmemory," conceptualized in *Family Frames: Photography, Narrative, and Postmemory* (Boston, MA: Harvard University Press, 1997) as a form of traumatic memory that is indirect, secondary, and intergenerational. I borrow the term "secondary witnessing" from Dora Apel's *Memory Effects: The Holocaust and the Art of Secondary Witnessing* (New Brunswick, NJ: Rutgers University Press, 2002).
12. Elizabeth Alexander, " 'Can you be BLACK and Look at This?': Reading the Rodney King Video(s)," *The Black Public Sphere: A Public Culture Book*, ed. Black Public Sphere Collective (Chicago: The University of Chicago Press), 83.
13. See Ron Eyerman's *Cultural Trauma: Slavery and the Formation of African American Identity* (United Kingdom: Cambridge University Press, 2001).
14. Alexander, "Can you be BLACK and Look at This?" 83.
15. See James Olney "'I Was Born': Slave Narratives, Their Status as Autobiography and Literature," *Callaloo* 20 (Winter, 1984): 46–73.

    The recitation of these scenes has sparked a critical dialogue between Saidiya Hartman and Fred Moten that has been useful for my thinking about the gendered implications of representing violence. Hartman's *Scenes of Subjection* questions the desired effect and affect of reciting the beating of Aunt Hester. Moten, on the other hand, interrogates the aesthetic possibilities of this recital and spots, in Douglass' turn from the scene of "objection" to music, an opportunity to engage the originary trauma of Blackness. My intervention in this critical discussion hinges on gendered conventions of spectacular violence in Black literature and culture. I probe this idea further throughout this article.

16. Frederick Douglass, *Narrative of the Life of Frederick Douglass: An American Slave* (New York: Signet Books: 1963), 25.
17. Kathy A. Perkins and Judith L. Stephens have compiled these plays in *Strange Fruit: Plays on Lynching by American Women* (Bloomington, IN: Indiana University Press, 1998).
18. Carolivia Herron, ed., *Selected Works of Angelina Weld Grimké* (New York: Oxford University Press, 1991), 414.
19. Gloria T. Hull, *Color, Sex, and Poetry: Three Women Writers of the Harlem Renaissance* (Bloomington, IN: Indiana University Press, 1987), 121.
20. Trudier Harris, *Exorcising Blackness: Historical and Literary Lynching and Burning Rituals* (Bloomington, IN: Indiana University Press, 1984), xii.
21. A number of contemporary artworks, in addition to Mayhorn's, memorialize the Mary Turner lynching, including Freida High W. Tesfagiorgis' painting *Hidden Memories: Mary Turner* (1985); Marie-Francoise Theodore's award-winning short film *Rebel in the Soul* (2002); and Honoré Fannone Jeffers' poem "dirty south moon" (2005).
22. See Walter White, "The Work of a Mob," *The Crisis* 16 (September 1918): 221.
23. Allen, *Without Sanctuary*, 14.
24. Phillip Dray, *At the Hands of Persons Unknown: The Lynching of Black America* (New York: Modern Library, 2003), 246.
25. For more details about Walter White's investigations, see his book, originally published in 1929, *Rope and Faggot: A Biography of Judge Lynch* (Notre Dame: University of Notre Dame Press, 2001) and Kenneth Robert Janken's *Walter White: Mr. NAACP* (Chapel Hill: UNC Press, 2006).
26. The title of Fuller's 1919 work references the Silent Protest Parade held in New York in 1917. Thousands of African Americans marched in silence down Fifth Avenue after the East St. Louis riots, to protest lynching and Jim Crow racism. They carried banners and signs calling for an end to oppression. The only sound heard during the silent protest down Fifth Avenue was that of muffled drums.
27. Dora Apel, *Imagery of Lynching: Black Men, White Women, and the Mob* (New Brunswick, NJ: Rutgers University Press), 152.
28. Lisa Farrington, *Creating Their Own Image: The History of African-American Women Artists* (New York: Oxford University Press), 67.
29. Grimké reworked the Mary Turner lynching in "The Waitin"' and "Blackness" before "Goldie" (originally titled "The Creaking") was published in *Birth Control Review*.
30. See Sigmund Freud's "Mourning and Melancholia," *General Psychological Theory*, ed. Phillip Rieff (New York: Collier, 1963): 164–179.
31. Claudia Tate, *Domestic Allegories of Political Desire: The Black Heroine's Text at the Turn of the Century* (New York: Oxford University Press, 1992), 217.
32. Grimké, *Selected Works*, 244.

33. Grimké, *Selected Works*, 300.
34. I borrow the term "domestic tragedy" from Claudia Tate's *Domestic Allegories of Political Desire*.
35. Grimké, *Selected Works*, 302.
36. Julie Buckner Armstrong makes a persuasive argument to this effect in " 'The people . . . took exception to her remarks': Meta Warrick Fuller, Angelina Weld Grimké, and the Lynching of Mary Turner," *Mississippi Quarterly* 61. 1–2 (Winter-Spring): 113–141.
37. This history takes various guises: Black women poisoning their captors, the "indecent behavior" of Ma Rainey, and the arrest of Angela Davis, to name a few.
38. Grimké, *Selected Works*, 305.
39. Herron, Introduction to *Selected Works*, 21.
40. See Henry Louis Gates, ed., *Carrie Williams Clifford and Carrie Law Morgan Figgs* (New York: G.K. Hall, 1997).
41. Clifford, *Carrie Williams Clifford*, 56.
42. Clifford, *Carrie Williams Clifford*, 57.
43. Clifford, *Carrie Williams Clifford*, 58.
44. Toomer traveled to Georgia in 1921. The height of lynching was roughly from 1880–1930. Georgia was particularly notorious for mob violence. See William Fitzhugh Brundage, *Lynching in the New South: Georgia and Virginia, 1880–1930* (Chicago: University of Illinois Press, 1993).
45. In "Blood-Burning Moon," a Black man assumes the role of protecting Black womanhood. At the same time, Toomer questions this "protective" impulse. In the story, and throughout *Cane,* male protection of women sometimes serves as an extension of sexual policing, a disciplinary tactic that bolsters male honor while preserving male domination.
46. For more on Toomer's racial and class politics, see Barbara Foley's "Jean Toomer's Washington and the Politics of Class: From 'Blue Veins' to Seventh-Street Rebels," *Modern Fiction Studies* 42.2 (Summer 1996): 289–321.
47. Jean Toomer, *Cane* (New York: Boni and Liveright), 2.
48. Toomer, *Cane*, 86.
49. Toomer, *Cane*, 90.
50. Toomer, *Cane*, 82.
51. Toomer, *Cane*, 110.
52. I borrow this reference to jagged grain from Ralph Ellison's *Shadow and Act* (New York: Quality Paperback Book Club, 1994) and Roland Barthe's *Image, Music, Text* (New York: The Noonday Press, 1977).

Works Cited

Alexander, Elizabeth. 1995. " 'Can you be BLACK and Look at This?': Reading the Rodney King Video(s)." In *The Black Public Sphere: A Public*

Culture Book, edited by the Black Public Sphere Collective. Chicago: The University of Chicago Press.
Allen, James, ed. 2000. *Without Sanctuary: Lynching Photography in America.* Sante Fe, NM: Twin Palms Publishers.
Apel, Dora. 2004. *Imagery of Lynching: Black Men, White Women, and the Mob.* New Brunswick, NJ: Rutgers University Press.
Brown, Elsa Barkley. 1995. "Imaging Lynching: African American Women, Communities of Struggle, and Collective Memory." In *African American Women Speak Out on Anita Hill—Clarence Thomas,* edited by Geneva Smitherman. Detroit, MI: Wayne State University Press.
Clifford, Carrie Williams. 1922. *The Widening Light.* Whitefish, MT: Kessinger Publishing.
Douglass, Frederick. 1968. *Narrative of the Life of Frederick Douglass: An American Slave.* New York: Signet Books.
Dray, Phillip. 2003. *At the Hands of Persons Unknown: The Lynching of Black America.* New York: Modern Library.
Farrington, Lisa. 2004. *Creating Their Own Image: The History of African-American Women Artists.* New York: Oxford University Press.
Hatch, James. 2003. *A History of African American Theatre.* Cambridge, UK: Cambridge University Press.
Herron, Carolivia. 1991. *Selected Works of Angelina Weld Grimké.* New York: Oxford University Press.
Hull, Gloria T. 1987. *Color, Sex, and Poetry: Three Women Writers of the Harlem Renaissance.* Bloomington, IN: Indiana University Press.
Markovitz, Jonathan. 2004. *Legacies of Lynching: Racial Violence and Memory.* Minneapolis, MN: Minnesota Press.
Tate, Claudia. 1992. *Domestic Allegories of Political Desire: The Black Heroine's Text at the Turn of the Century.* New York: Oxford University Press.
Toomer, Jean. 1975. *Cane.* Introduction by Darwin T. Turner. New York: Boni and Liveright.

CHAPTER 5

The Politics of Sexuality in Billie Holiday's "Strange Fruit"

Fumiko Sakashita

> Southern trees bear a strange fruit,
> Blood on the leaves and blood at the root,
> Black body swinging in the Southern breeze,
> Strange Fruit hanging from the poplar trees.
> Pastoral scene of the gallant South,
> The bulging eyes and the twisted mouth,
> Scent of Magnolia sweet and fresh,
> And the sudden smell of burning flesh!
> Here is a fruit for the crows to pluck,
> For the rain to gather, for the wind to suck,
> For the sun to rot, for the tree to drop,
> Here is a strange and bitter crop.[1]

In her final speech before the Passage of Resolution 39, the U.S. Senate's 2005 apology for lynching, Senator Mary Landrieu asserted: "Jazz legend Billie Holiday provided real texture in her story and song 'Strange Fruit.'" In a review of various historical moments of lynching and antilynching efforts on the state and national level, Senator Landrieu introduced the lyrics of the song and further observed that "[s]omething in the way she [Holiday] sang this song . . . must have touched the heart of Americans because they began to mobilize, and men and women, White and Black, people from different backgrounds, came to stand up and begin to speak."[2] Attributing in an anecdotal way the formation of public actions against lynching to the power of Holiday's singing, Landrieu seemed to agree with most former studies of the song that have focused on the racial and gender politics in Holiday's rendition. This essay sheds new light on the politics of sexuality embedded in Holiday's early nightclub performance of "Strange Fruit." By examining her rendition outside of the conventional discussions of the song as a protest narrative, I complement and complicate the existing interpretations of Holiday's "Strange Fruit."

Past studies have explored the politics of race, class, and/or gender of "Strange Fruit." Some scholars, including Michael Denning, David W. Stowe, and David Margolick, have pointed out the song's cultural political power as an antilynching and social protest song, and have linked it to the historical context of antilynching struggles in the cultural activism of the labor movement (Popular Front) in the 1930s, which Denning labeled the "cultural front" where the song was written and performed. "Strange Fruit" was composed by the Jewish-American schoolteacher turned political activist Abel Meeropol (known by the pseudonym Lewis Allan) around 1937. Holiday began to sing the song in 1939 at New York's Café Society Downtown (hereafter Café Society), the first racially-integrated nightclub that opened outside of Harlem, and it quickly came to be known as an establishment that welcomed "labor leaders, intellectuals, writers, jazz lovers, celebrities, students and assorted leftists."[3]

Other scholars like Angela Y. Davis and Dawn-Wisteria Bates have offered an alternative analysis, one that emphasizes, from the racial and gender perspective, the political aspect of Holiday's performance of the song, refuting previous studies by mostly white male critics and biographers alike that downplayed Holiday's political role in her rendition of the song.[4] "Strange Fruit" has been covered by a number of performers, but it is notable that among them are many Black female singers, including Nina Simone, Diana Ross (who played Holiday in *Lady Sings the Blues*), Abby Lincoln, Miki Howard (who played Holiday in Spike Lee's *Malcom X*), Cassandra Wilson, Dee Dee Bridgewater, and India Arie, who either recorded the song or covered it for live performances, suggesting that there has been a Black feminist embrace of the song following Holiday's versions. Crowned as the "Best Song" of the twentieth century in *Time* magazine's last issue before the new millennium, and selected as number one of the "100 Songs of the South" by the *Atlanta Journal-Constitution* in 2005, one can hardly deny that Billie Holiday's "Strange Fruit" maintains lasting impact and influence both in popular culture and in academe.[5]

On the other hand, "something in the way" Holiday sang the song might also have "touched the heart of Americans" in a quite different way. Recall, for example, how the song was used in the 1986 film *Nine and A Half Weeks,* which depicted a short-lived erotic and sado-masochistic relationship between New Yorkers John (played by Mickey Rourke) and Elizabeth (Kim Basinger). In the scene where John invites Elizabeth to his friend's boathouse on their second encounter, he plays Holiday's "Strange Fruit" after making the bed, suggesting the erotic engagement afoot between the two. Why was this particular song—the song about the brutalized Black body in the southern landscape—selected for this scene to portray the white New Yorkers' erotic love affair? The combination of the song and the scene seems incongruous, yet this seemingly inappropriate matching—the way in which Holiday's "Strange Fruit" is eroticized in the recent cultural representation of the urban white couple's sexual relationship—merits further analysis to consider how Holiday's rendition of the song conjures up something sensual in modern-day white imagination. Lynching's erotic nature, however disturbing,—the rape rationale, the nudity, sadistic torture delivered against the victim's stilled body—seemed, for this filmmaker, to mirror the sexual encounter between man and woman, far removed both temporally and geographically from the site of the song's gruesome murder scene.[6]

Indeed, eroticization of the song was often the case in contemporary reception of Holiday's live performance of it. Some audiences imagined race, sex, and violence in the South in quite an erotic way through the lyrics of "Strange Fruit" and within the nightclub space. Historian Jacquelyn Dowd Hall has stated that Holiday "made famous the indelible image of 'strange fruit' of race and sex in the American South," but while she suggests "the imagery of lynching—in literature, poetry, music, in the mind of men—was inescapably erotic," not many studies have closely examined Holiday's "Strange Fruit" from this perspective, thus failing to grasp more comprehensive and complicated politics of race, class, gender, and sexuality in her performance.[7] Although mostly overlooked or only briefly mentioned in past studies, such receptions make sense, I contend, given that by the time of the song's debut by Holiday, American society had become quite familiar with negative sexual stereotypes of Black men and women, and with the spectacle-like characteristics of lynching alleged sexual criminals. These erotic reactions remind us of what cultural critic bell hooks has observed about representation of African Americans. hooks contends that there is a connection between "the maintenance of white supremacist patriarchy" and "the institutionalization via mass media of specific images, representations of race, of blackness that support and maintain the oppression, exploitation, and overall domination of all black people."[8] The eroticization of "Strange Fruit" deserves further scrutiny to elucidate how the consumption of the lynching story helped maintain white supremacist patriarchy. Close attention to the politics of sexuality in Holiday's rendition of the song shows us the nuanced ways in which Holiday meant to resist the commodification of lynching and objectification of the Black body.

This essay reconsiders Holiday's "Strange Fruit" from the perspective of sexuality by thoroughly examining the song's development; its relationship to the historical context of lynching; the lyrics' meanings and symbolism; the public reception of the song in the media and by nightclub audiences; and the way Holiday performed the song—both her bodily presence and the musical interpretation she introduced in the nightclub setting. I explore how Holiday's rendition of "Strange Fruit" reconstructed and reinforced in the public mind a stereotypical image of race, sex, and sexuality in southern lynching. Specifically, I demonstrate how Holiday's performance of a song by a left-wing Jewish composer, carefully directed by the progressive Jewish club owner to draw political attention to the predominantly white audience in the entertainment space, sometimes received a different reception. After discussing the song's historical context—the history of the complex elements that tied racial and sexual politics together through lynching—I argue that "Strange Fruit" was consumed in a manner most similar to the way in which the spectacle of lynching was consumed by white mobs. It is through the vicarious experience of this secondary lynching presented by Holiday's "Strange Fruit" that white supremacist patriarchy was maintained. I further examine how Holiday's rendition of the song, being complicit with the production of such voyeuristic pleasure on the one hand, simultaneously subverted the commodification of lynching and the sexual stereotyping of Black men and women. Here, I draw on the theory of a counterstrategy to contest the racialized representation introduced by hooks, who emphasized the need for the struggle to "critically intervene and transform the world of image making authority," and by cultural critic Stuart Hall, who proposes to contest the stereotype from within. I contend that Holiday's very presence as a Black woman, and her artistry—her politics of sexuality—changed the whole dynamics of white male-controlled representations of lynching, thus challenging the institutionalization of exploited images of African Americans.[9]

Lynching and Rape: Sexual Context of "Strange Fruit"

By the time of Holiday's debut of the song in 1939, the image of the Black rapist had been well entrenched in American society, thanks to denigrating popular depictions in the media. Alleged rape of white women by Black men became one of the strongest racial/sexual images associated with southern lynching. According to historian Sharon Block, as early as the Revolutionary era, rape narratives offered a discursive site to define white manhood and citizenship, and since the Post-Reconstruction period, the Black rapist image dominated this narrative.[10] The more Black men gained political and economic equality with white men, the more they were regarded as a sexual threat against white women.

Thus, whites rationalized lynching in the name of justice against sexual crimes and protecting white womanhood in particular. Lynching worked as a device for whites to preserve their supremacist patriarchy in southern society, especially after Reconstruction. A large number of narratives of the "black beast" or "black rapist" were published at a time when southern whites needed an excuse for lynching African Americans.[11] People had already experienced such an image not only through newspaper accounts of actual lynchings, but also in the representation of lynching in literature and film, most notably D. W. Griffith's *The Birth of a Nation* (1915), Hollywood's first feature-length megahit film based on Thomas F. Dixon, Jr.'s *The Clansman* (1905) and both hyperbolization of the perceived Black male sexual threat against white womanhood.[12] Although antilynching sentiments were widely shared on the national level (the 1937 Gallup Poll showed that 70 percent of Americans supported federal antilynching legislation), a 1939 anthropological study found that nearly 65 percent of southern white respondents believed that lynching for rape was justifiable.[13]

In this way, lynching and rape had become inseparable in the American imagination and public discourse. The rape myth so dominated society that advocates working to end the grisly practice focused their energies on refuting it.[14] It is well known that pioneer antilynching activist Ida B. Wells had challenged the myth of the Black rapist in the early 1890s, but even 40 years later, antilynching activists continued to fight against this pervasive stereotype.[15] In 1935, for instance, the National Association for the Advancement of Colored People (NAACP) sponsored the antilynching art exhibit "An Art Commentary on Lynching," and published an accompanying pamphlet by writer Erskine Caldwell denouncing the familiar reasoning that lynching existed "to protect the honor of Southern womanhood." Such rhetoric, Caldwell concluded, served "merely [as] an excuse designed to cover up the true intent and purpose" of killing African Americans.[16]

The Association of Southern Women for the Prevention of Lynching (ASWPL), founded by southern white woman Jessie Daniel Ames in 1930, criticized the existent image of vulnerable white women who needed white men's protection from Black men's sexual assaults.[17] Whether to reinforce or to refute the rape myth, discourse was created around this image. As Jacquelyn Dowd Hall makes clear, "rape and rumors of rape became a kind of acceptable folk pornography in the Bible Belt," but some reactions to Holiday's "Strange Fruit," as will be shown later, clearly reveal that these pornographic images of savage Black men raping defenseless white women gained widespread acceptance outside the South as well.[18]

The castration of Black men likewise became a well-circulated type of "folk pornography." As seen in the lyrics of "Strange Fruit," hanging and burning were familiar aspects of lynching, but lynching very often included mutilation, particularly of Black men's genitals. Historian W. Fitzhugh Brundage has shown that, across the South, castration occurred in one in every three lynchings.[19] The 1934 lynching of the alleged Black rapist Claude Neal in Greenwood, Florida, for example, haunted the whole nation on account of the detailed description of his castration reported not only in newspapers but also in the NAACP's antilynching pamphlet.[20] As historian Amy Louis Wood observes, castration, as the most powerful symbol of lynching, has "affected the cultural memories of both blacks and whites, more than any other aspect of lynching."[21]

Such a sadistic punishment came out of the white obsession with presumed Black male hypersexuality. The ritual of lynching reflected whites' imaginary fear of and desire for the Black male body.[22] The white imagination turned Black men into sexual objects or, worse, reduced them into merely parts of man—genitalia. As Frantz Fanon has posited pointedly, while projecting their sexual desires onto Black men and acting as if they truly had those desires, white men fixate Black men at the genitals.[23] Similarly, Kobena Mercer has argued that the "essence" of Black male identity is placed in the "domain of sexuality" and adds that "black men are confined and defined in the very being as sexual and nothing but sexual, hence hypersexual."[24] In other words, as Trudier Harris writes, lynching in general, and castration in particular, functioned as nothing more than "communal rape" of Black men—rape in terms of assaulting Black male sexuality.[25]

Fanon's question rightfully articulates this point: "Is lynching of the Negro not a *sexual* revenge?"[26] Rape and alleged rape of white women by Black men had caused lynching that emasculated Black men's bodies in sadistic, sexual ways in the public arena. Although the number of lynchings declined in the 1930s, public obsession with Black male sexuality still continued. It was this social context that impacted the sexual images of "Strange Fruit."

Receptions and the Lyrics: Eroticization of "Strange Fruit"

As many studies have demonstrated, Holiday's early rendition of "Strange Fruit" came out of the peak of a nationwide antilynching campaign, along with the emergence of the Popular Front culture of the 1930s. The lyrics first appeared as a poem entitled "Bitter Fruit" in the *New York Teacher,* a 1937 Union publication.[27] Lyricist/composer Lewis Allan and his wife Anne regularly performed "Strange Fruit" at leftist gatherings a year before Holiday first sang it.[28] Allan later recalled, "I wrote *Strange Fruit* because I hate lynching, and I hate injustice and I hate the people who perpetuate it."[29] Café Society's owner Barney Josephson described the song as "agitprop" and "a piece of propaganda" meant to stir the listeners to action.[30] Affiliates of the antilynching campaign and the labor movement understood correctly the intentions of the composer and the club owner in the song's performance. In 1939, the New Theatre League published the song as sheet music while the leftist magazine *New Masses* called Holiday's rendition "a superb outcry against lynching."[31] That year, the NAACP executive director, Walter White, also praised the song.[32] In February 1940, the Theater Arts Committee (TAC), a Popular Front affiliate, sent a copy of "Strange Fruit" to U.S. senators, urging them to vote for the passage of the Gavagan Anti-Lynching bill, also known as the second NAACP bill.[33] First and foremost, then, the song served as a protest narrative.

Others, while aware of the song's protesting message, belittled Holiday's political awareness as the song's performer. For instance, in *Time*'s April 1939 report on Holiday's first recording of "Strange Fruit," the magazine mocked the songstress and denounced her song as a "Strange Record." The author ridiculed both Holiday's femininity and her artistry, declaring Holiday "a roly-poly young colored woman with a hump in her voice. . . . She does not care enough about her figure to watch her diet, but she loves to sing." Even as *Time* extended a backhanded compliment by acknowledging that Holiday loved to sing, the article minimized "Strange Fruit's" transgressive impact, describing the song as "dirge-like blues melody" (which the NAACP would distort into "a prime piece of musical propaganda"). By dismissing Holiday as someone who "liked its . . . melody" but was "not so much interested in the song's social content," the white-made *Time* author undercut Holiday's political potential as a feminist and civil rights advocate, as well as an artist and singer.[34]

Moreover, *Time* presented Holiday—and her uniquely unsettling rendition of the song for the Vocallion Company—as puppetry for the NAACP and its leftist supporters. Angela Y. Davis criticizes the way in which many white male critics and biographers asserted that Holiday never understood the meaning of the song without white men's tutelage. Club owner Josephson, for instance, claimed to have suggested Holiday perform "Strange Fruit." Biographer John Chilton has described how, although at first Holiday was slow to understand the song's imagery, "her bewilderment decreased as Allen [*sic*] patiently emphasized the cadences, and their significance." Similarly, Donald Clarke labeled Holiday a nonpolitical person who "never read anything but comic books" and "didn't know what to make of" the song when she first looked at "Strange Fruit." Davis writes: "Chilton's, Clarke's, and Josephson's stories capture Holiday in a web of gendered, classed, and raced inferiority, and present her as capable of producing great work only under the tutelage of her racial [and gender] superiors."[35] *Time*'s description clearly exhibited such a view by contrasting Holiday's alleged unawareness of the song's political content with the record company Vocallion's awareness.

This depiction of an ignorant, happy-go-lucky type of heavyset Black woman reminds us of the stereotypical Mammy image widely publicized in popular culture, most notably in the Hollywood film *Gone with the Wind,* released that year (1939). It simultaneously conjures up the seductive Jezebel image, deriving from the fact that the word "hump" connotes a woman as purely a sexual object.[36] Not only the love songs Holiday sang prior to "Strange Fruit," but also her lighter skin might have reinforced such a lascivious image.[37] As Farah Jasmine Griffin rightfully observes, "Billie Holiday emerged at a time when the dominant cultural stereotypes of black women were Mammy and Tragic Mulatto."[38] Record producer Jerry Wexler's comment on the song summarizes the *Time*'s reaction to Holiday's performance: "It's so un-Billie Holiday. It's got too much of an agenda."[39] Similarly, a critic with *DownBeat* magazine reviewed Holiday's recording, writing: "Perhaps I expected too much of *Strange Fruit . . .* which, via gory wordage and hardly any melody, expounds an anti-lynching campaign. At least I'm sure it's not for Billie, as for example, *Fine and Mellow* is."[40] For such critics, political consciousness was not what Holiday represented—nor what they were prepared to see in her.

Able to wrest these stereotypical images from her performance, it should not surprise us that nightclub audiences who gave the song a cursory listening might not have understood its clear protest message. Kenneth Spencer, a notable African American actor of the 1940s-1950s, commented in 1942: "Yes, 'Strange Fruit,' that casually bitter song by Lewis Allan, is a strange song for a night club entertainer to be singing, and stranger still is the fact that the white people at Café Society Uptown call for it every night."[41] The nightclub setting very likely provided room for the audience to receive the song as merely entertaining. One audience member recalled "the contrast between the tragic song of protest sung with the deep feelings by a Negro woman who felt [the] horror of a lynching, and the patrons out for a good time[,] drinking and[,] at times[,] yakking, some of them oblivious to the message of the singer." He "wondered then whether it made sense to sing such a song in such a milieu."[42] The club owner, Josephson, stated that "Strange Fruit" was performed under carefully directed staging ("I insisted she [Holiday] closed every show with it ['Strange Fruit'] every night. Lights out, just one small spinlight, and all service stopped . . . . There were no encores after it. My instruction was walk off, period"), so that "people had to remember 'Strange Fruit,' get their insides burned with it."[43]

Judging by some audience members' descriptions, Josephson's mission—and Holiday's "nightly" mournful crooning—might have fallen on deaf ears. Some in the audience clearly thought that Holiday's performance evoked an erotic image of lynching. In her autobiography, *Lady Sings the Blues* (1956), Holiday recalled how one woman in a Los Angeles audience requested her to sing "Strange Fruit" by asking, "Billie, why don't you sing that sexy song you're so famous for? You know, the one about the naked bodies swinging in the trees."[44] While Bates and Davis have dismissed the woman's reaction as "pathological" and "impervious to her [Holiday's] message," Davis has further made an intriguing observation: "What is interesting about this anecdote . . . is the bizarre and racialized way the woman links the song with the ubiquitous engagement with sexuality in Holiday's work."[45] For that white listener, "Strange Fruit" had become a "sexy song" confined by its reference to naked "black bodies swinging in the trees." Thus, the erotic nature—the folk pornography—trumped the violence described in the song and sanitized its bizarre and pathological landscape.

Even in progressive places like Café Society, Holiday received similar reactions. Songwriter Irene Wilson recalled how a white male southerner had once shown Holiday "some 'strange fruit' " after her performance at Café Society, and described how "he made this very obscene picture on his napkin and the way he had it, honey, it was awful!"[46] One can only speculate what kind of "very obscene picture" he drew, but it was possibly male genitalia, which is later described as "strange fruit."[47] This white man's perception of the song is even more pornographic, suggesting that lynching conjured up a certain erotic image in the presumed progressive and leftist nightclubs.

Focusing on how its lyrics were composed helps us further understand how "Strange Fruit," probably contrary to the composer's intention, was perceived sexually at the time. Composer Allan once mentioned his encounter with an actual lynching photograph that inspired him to write the song, and recalled that, after seeing the lynching image, he "suddenly saw all lynchings—as strange, strange fruit."[48] This powerful, yet somewhat bizarre analogy merits further attention. In Allan's imagination, the particular brutalized Black body in the photograph turned into a mere object (labeled as *strange* fruit) in a very poetic and sexual manner. While "Strange Fruit" describes the literal image of the Black body hanging from the tree, it may conjure up forbidden fruit, a biblical metaphor that represents seduction and the object of desire, yet abstinence.

This notion of taboo is often powerfully melded from Adam and Eve's original sin to narratives of lynching. In the case of the latter, the taboo rests with the sexual relationship between white women and Black men. Indeed, given that southern white women symbolized the South itself in southern legend, the southern landscape filled with the "Scent of Magnolia" possibly connotes southern white womanhood and white female sexuality.[49] Pay particular attention to the contrast between "Scent of Magnolia sweet and fresh" and "the sudden smell of burning flesh," which alludes to forbidden fruit of sweet and seductive white female sexuality for Black men (who were not supposed to have the fruit of the white female body, but could not help wanting it in the white imagination), and describes the hideous outcome of such Black men's sexual desire. The cost of coveting that fragrant fruit is clear: sudden death. Its cause—Black male sexual transgression—and effect—violence and murder brought onto Black men because of their own impetuousness—are compellingly coupled by Allan's use of "and" in his lyrics and Holiday's "then" in her performance.

Another important juxtaposition occurs between "Pastoral scene of the gallant South" and "bulging eyes and twisted mouth," in which the adjective "gallant" possibly signifies white southern manhood and masculinity—the image of the chivalric New South—analogous to how the "Scent of Magnolia" represents southern white womanhood. These four lines, alternating between romanticized and sexualized images of the South (represented by southern white masculinity and white female sexuality), with the sadistic flashback depictions of the images of the brutalized Black body, complete the lyrical description of the prevalent lynching discourse of Black men being persecuted by white men for their alleged crime of raping white women. They stimulate the erotic imagination, as evidenced by how the song describes only a black body, a sexless object, yet some audiences imagined a sexualized Black *male* body. Of course, Allan must have relied on those peaceful scenes of the South for the stark contradiction they made of the gruesome reality of lynching, but the way the lyrics are phrased could imply otherwise.

Equally perplexing, while lynching pictures usually captured the process or immediate aftermath of lynching, as well as the white mobs happily pictured with the hanging bodies, the presence of those spectators is erased or absent from the song. A possible exception is the reference to white manhood in the phrase "gallant South," but it does not fully depict the white mobs' direct and often gruesome role in lynching African Americans. Overall, the lyrics describe the southern landscape of lynching's aftermath, particularly in the first and last parts, while the middle focuses on lynching's eroticism in a series of flashbacks capturing the ongoing event. Due to the absence of mobs and the poetic description of lynching, the lyrics, as a whole, give an impression that it is more a meditation on lynching, particularly its sexual aspects. Clearly, some in Holiday's audience found the song highly sexual despite the fact that the lyrics never illustrated overtly sexual imagery. Envisaged sexuality and lyricism might have embodied somewhat erotic tones. The imaginary lynching in the song reproduced the racial/sexual image of southern lynching that was prevalent enough in contemporary American society.

Bodily Presence and Performance: Holiday in the Contested Space of Spectacle/Witnessing

Just as lynching—the public spectacle of sadistic punishments—became a new space of consumption where Blacks themselves became commodities (the lynching scenes were often pictured with the spectators, and

Figure 5.1 Billie Holiday at Café Society, 1939. Frank Driggs Collection, Institute of Jazz Studies, Rutgers University

the victims' body parts were brought back as "souvenirs"), the image of the South and of southern lynching were commodified and consumed through Holiday's rendition of "Strange Fruit."[50] The performance of the song was essentially a consumer spectacle. For instance, in 1939, the *New Yorker* advertised the song by asking: "HAVE YOU HEARD? 'Strange fruit growing on Southern trees' sung by Billie Holiday at Café Society."[51] The way it was advertised ("HAVE YOU HEARD?") alludes to newspaper accounts that announced scheduled lynchings. The advertisement was intended to attract, and did eventually attract people who had never heard "Strange Fruit" to come listen to Holiday singing, thereby experiencing what a southern lynching was like. Paradoxically, Holiday's rendition of "Strange Fruit" in nightclub settings became a similar lynching spectacle. The public space for enjoyment, where Holiday narrated the story about southern lynching, produced a kind of secondary lynching (See Figure 5.1).

The picture of Holiday's performance at Café Society set the atmosphere for her rendition of "Strange Fruit," and this scene of people surrounding a Black person (Holiday) in the entertainment space evokes for many the actual lynching spectacle evident in many existing lynching photos.[52] In such a space, Holiday was not only the narrator of lynching, but also embodied the Black victim, male and female. Indeed, this nightclub picture shares some similarities with the typical photographs of a lynching spectacle—in terms of their spatial composition—although the photos' different characteristics—as commemorative and documentary—have offered the camera different gazes (lynching pictures and postcards usually captured the spectators looking back at the camera). The audience surrounding Holiday at Café Society unintentionally supplemented the absence of white mobs in the lyrics, turning the club space into the spectacle of secondary lynching, albeit a benign one staged in New York. Nightclubs might not have offered a carnival-like atmosphere, but the song did help the predominantly white audience to participate vicariously in southern lynching, or its rejection as foreign to northern sensibilities.

What makes this situation even more complicated, however, is that it was Holiday, a Black woman, who represented through song this spectacle of southern lynching. A pointed remark by Robert O'Meally, who stated "that song, with its imagery of trees that 'bear' and 'fruit' that is 'plucked' or 'dropped,' also gave expression to her role as a woman who discerned a sexual motive in the act of lynching," suggests Holiday's role as a successor to Black female predecessors who disclosed lynching's true purpose behind the myth of the Black rapist.[53] They challenged white justification of Black men raping white women by focusing on the cases of lynching and rape of Black women. For instance, Ida B. Wells wrote in 1895 that "the same crime [rape] committed by white men against Negro women and girls, [wa]s never punished by mob or the law."[54] The National Association of Colored Women (NACW) passed a resolution protesting the lynching of two Black women in 1914, and campaigned, among other organizations, for further investigation into the lynching of a pregnant Black woman in 1918.[55] The Anti-Lynching Crusaders, an NAACP-affiliated organization formed by Black women in 1922, greatly contributed to fundraising for the passage of the Dyer antilynching bill that year. In all these cases, Black women activists persistently made Black women lynching/rape victims visible.[56]

As some scholars have argued, the dominant discourse of lynching by whites has excluded Black women by focusing only on white male chivalry, white female victims, and Black male rapists.[57] Until recently, the historiography of lynching has overlooked the fact that Black women were also frequent victims of lynching and rape throughout U.S. history.[58] Under slavery, the sexual abuse of Black women never fit into the category of rape, not only because of their status as white slaveholders' property but also due to their dominant image as immoral. This image of sexually-loose Black woman functioned as an excuse for slaveholders to repeatedly impregnate enslaved females for profit.[59] American justice hardly persecuted the perpetrators of the postbellum rape and lynching of Black women, and even lynching of Black men was attributed to Black women's lack of virtue and alleged promiscuous nature.[60]

As Hazel V. Carby rightfully asserts, "rape of black women has never been as powerful a symbol of black oppression as the spectacle of lynching."[61] Indeed, what is striking about the lyrics of "Strange Fruit" is that the gendered-ambiguous "black body" in this fictional southern lynching fails to represent the Black female experience, thus reproducing another lynching narrative similar to the white racist dominant discourse. Under such circumstances, Holiday's bodily presence in this consumer space—the fact that the audience witnessed and listened to a Black woman telling a story of lynching—adds to the interpretation of the song's more complicated dynamics of race, gender, and sexuality. In the consumer space of a nightclub setting that resembled the scene of a lynching spectacle where Holiday was surrounded by the predominantly white audience, not only did she represent Black male victims and/or their mothers, wives, daughters, and sisters, she also possibly embodied Black female victims of lynching *and* rape.

Holiday's presence as a Black woman in the song's performance as well as her bodily politics of sexuality through attire, expressions, gestures, and musical artistry, contributed to recuperating a hidden transcript of the buried history of Black sexual oppression.[62] While nightclubs offered a space where Black female sexuality was objectified and consumed, Holiday subverted the white gaze and challenged the negation of Black female sexuality through her artistic qualities.[63] Evelyn Cunningham, a prominent Black woman reporter for the *Pittsburgh Courier* in the 1940s, recalled that "many times in nightclubs when I heard her sing the song it was not a sadness I sensed as much as there was something else; it's got to do with sexuality."[64]

Although Cunningham mentioned sexuality in a sense that she "never had the feeling that this [rendering of 'Strange Fruit'] was something she [Holiday] was very, very serious about," her comment raises the possibility that Holiday's performance was, as Angela Davis has proposed, deeply rooted in the blues tradition. It was in this tradition that Holiday challenged the negation of Black female sexuality in the dominant discourse of lynching. In her analysis of Holiday's love songs, Davis argues that some of Holiday's renderings represented "a juxtaposition and performance of the conflict between representations of women's sexuality in the dominant popular musical culture and those in the blues tradition—the former denying female agency, the latter affirming the autonomous erotic empowerment and independent subjectivity of female sexuality."[65]

This was clearly the case in Holiday's rendition of "Strange Fruit." Despite the fact that the media and audiences, intentionally or not, downplayed her agency as a Black woman and reproduced the discourse of lynching through consuming her nightly performances, Holiday resisted these limitations by her very presence as an embodiment of Black female sexuality. While Holiday's sexuality was exposed and objectified in nightclubs, it was through this attention to her sexuality—and sexual freedom expressed overtly in her love songs—that Holiday could remind the audience of the sexual exploitation and captivity of Black women so long and so deeply suppressed in the white supremacist discourse of lynching. It is significant that Holiday protested the white supremacist discourse of lynching through the musical affirmation of sexuality rather than the politics of respectability, which was a strategy of collective racial uplift often used by educated Black female reformers to counter the denigrated image of Black women by over-desexualizing Black womanhood.[66] While organizations such as the NACW and the Anti-Lynching Crusaders deployed this strategy, Holiday's politics of sexuality stood out as a strategy to challenge negative stereotypes of Black women in quite a different manner. By affirming the autonomy of Black female sexuality, something Black women had never attained under slavery, Holiday offered her Black foremothers a symbolic liberation from bondage of the long-overlooked history of their sexual exploitation.

Holiday's attire, a vital part of the performance, clearly exemplifies the affirmation of Black female sexuality. Her Grecian-style stage dresses were, most of the time, very fitted to her voluptuous body and showed her curves. The sleeveless long white dress in the picture above, for instance, exposes her arms and accentuates her breasts with its tightened belt. Holiday's hair was usually swept up neatly, showing her full face and neckline. She often wore various kinds of artificial flowers in her hair, most notably gardenias, or magnolias that represented white female sexuality in the lyrics of "Strange Fruit." Holiday was possibly claiming that Black women, too, could be represented by this emblematic southern flower, thus embodying southern womanhood. Also, Holiday's facial expressions and gestures during her performance of the song—her closed eyes, slightly uplifted chin, and half-opened mouth—further played up her sexuality.

It is important to note that Holiday usually performed "Strange Fruit" at the very end of the show, as the club owner Josephson explained, after singing several other songs in her repertoire that were mostly torch songs. Having heard other love songs that openly expressed Black female sexuality, the audience might have received "Strange Fruit" not as a clear protest message but rather something similar to a love song.

What, perhaps, ultimately determined most audience's experiences of "Strange Fruit" is Holiday's musical artistry, i.e, the way she utilized her voice, tone, phrasing, timing, and intonations in the rendition of the song. Through this performative presentation of the song, Holiday refused to simply reproduce the fictional lynching scene based on the dominant discourse of lynching to be consumed. Holiday first recorded "Strange Fruit" on April 20, 1939, soon after she started performing it regularly at Café Society. This particular recording explains the mood around the earlier time the song was performed and received.[67] A cursory listening to this version might give us an impression that Holiday's overall melancholic tone sounds almost like that of the other love ballads in her repertoire, in contrast to the later versions in 1945 and 1956, for example, in which both Holiday's hoarse warbling voice and the dramatic arrangement of an accompanied trumpet and piano demonstrate much more gripping strength.[68] But this very gloomy timbre in her voice, which expressed love, pain, and despair for Black women in her early torch songs, echoes Black women's same feelings about the loss of their loved ones in "Strange Fruit." The way in which the voice of a Black woman (Holiday) describes the landscape of southern lynching in a calm, objective, and meditative manner amplifies her sorrow, and Holiday's musical phrasing and intonation of each word deepens it even more.

In the 1939 recording of "Strange Fruit," Holiday's lyrical performance of the song begins after a minute-long slow introduction of a trumpet solo accompanied by tenor and alto saxophones, followed by a piano solo backed by bass, guitar, and drums. Her simple, descriptive way of singing the first line ("Southern trees bear a strange fruit") that makes the listeners wonder about "a strange fruit," immediately changes by the second verse. Here, Holiday sings most of the words ("Blood" "on" "the"/"blood" "at" "the") with staccato phrasing, conveying musically the scene of blood dripping from the strange fruit. We do not know what this fruit is until the third line: "Black bodi[es] swinging in the Southern breeze." Note that Holiday changes the singular "black body" in the original lyrics into plural "black bodies" in her performance, making clear that this violence is often repeated against many African American men and women's bodies alike.

This slight lyrical alteration successfully inserts in the lyrics a much more horrifying image of lynching, thus reinterpreting lyricist Allan's view.[69]

With Holiday's emphasis on "black bodies" and her stretching out the words "swinging," "Southern," and "breeze," it sounds like the gentle wind is blowing Black bodies, thus perfectly depicting a horrifying picture of hung bodies. It also makes the scale of lynching larger: like the tree's many branches, there swing the many nameless victims across time.

In the song's second section, where the lyrics portray the flashback of lynching paralleled to southern scenery, her rendition makes more palpable, although subtle, the stark contrast between the serene southern landscape and the gruesome lynching scene. Holiday overstretches "pastoral" and emphasizes the peaceful scene in the South while she rises and drops the pitch in the pronunciation of "twisted," thus illustrating the victim's mouth being crooked with pain, as well as the stillness and silence that follow violence and death. In the following line, after stretching "Magnolia," she pauses for a moment before quietly adding "sweet and fresh," as though evoking the sexuality of southern white womanhood.

The last section of the song, portraying the lynched body's predictable fate—"a fruit for the crows to pluck/ for the rain to gather/ for the wind to suck/ for the sun to rot/ for the tree to drop"—is the climax of Holiday's lyrical performance. While stretching each noun and verb, she gradually raises her voice as the song goes, much like the soul leaving the victim's body or the crows taking flight after their grisly gouging on African Americans' remains. In the last two lines, Holiday slows down and makes long pauses between each section. Her phrasing of the words, the way she overstretches "rot," "drop," "bitter," and "crop" even more, dramatically heightens the atrocity of lynching. In particular, Holiday's intonation of "drop"—first rising then falling down slowly in a parabolic way—induces imaginatively the moment the body is being dropped from the tree. Although the lynched body is already dead, it appears to have been killed once again by her powerful performance. It is this musical interpretation of "Strange Fruit" that allowed Holiday to contest the audience's voyeuristic gazing on imaginary lynching and her sexuality.

Indeed, Holiday's musical revisiting of the southern landscape of lynching raises the specter once again for the audience of another imaginative scenario, where a Black woman standing in front of the lynched body hanging from the tree recalls her encounter of the lynching practice and prays for the dead with deep sorrow and anger—did she run into the ongoing incident? Did the mob force her to look? Or did she have to bear witness because the alleged sexual criminal was someone she knew, or her very loved one?

Considering Holiday's performance as well as her bodily presence in the nightclub helps us see more clearly the multilayered dynamics of this contested terrain, where the audience vicariously witnessed the southern lynching while simultaneously seeing Holiday, a Black woman, looking at the lynching. On the one hand, Holiday's rendition of "Strange Fruit" offered a cultural space where audiences imagined and consumed race, gender, and sexuality through southern lynching. Her performance sometimes unwittingly helped reinforce the existing discourse of lynching, whereby Black men were said to threaten white womanhood sexually, and allowed the audience to participate imaginatively in an actual lynching. It reconstructed, reinforced, and commodified the image of southern lynching in the popular mind outside the South. The song first appeared when racially and sexually stereotypical images of lynching and of Black men and women were well propagated in society while antilynching feeling was simultaneously emerging among the public. Holiday's "Strange Fruit" grew out of such a unique historical conjuncture, and her performance itself functioned as a conjunctural space where those contested ideas and perceptions of lynching, race and sex were encountered, contested, and intertwined.

On the other hand, Holiday's performance—her physical and vocal presence in the story of a lynching—revealed further complicating politics of race and sexuality in the actual and imagined lynching. While the media and audience commodified lynching stories that exploited Black male sexuality and negated Black female sexuality in the realm of popular culture, Holiday subverted the institutionalization of racialized and sexualized images of "black body" by her very sexuality, thus challenging white supremacist patriarchy. Furthermore, her bodily presence in the vocalist reproduction of southern lynching made Black women and Black female sexuality visible in the dominant lynching discourse that had long obscured their presence. For Holiday, as a Black woman, to sing "Strange Fruit" was not only to protest against racial violence: it also allowed her to give voice to her silenced sisters who had been continuously denigrated as racialized/sexualized others. In the cultural space of her performance of "Strange Fruit," Holiday's body became the principal site where she contested racialized representation of lynching from within.

Holiday's rendering of "Strange Fruit" likewise offers another interpretation on the politics of sexuality from the perspective of white women.

It created a cultural space where, by listening to Holiday's musical affirmation of women's sexual autonomy, white women could also participate, albeit differently from Black women, in resisting white patriarchy that suppressed female sexual subjectivity. While southern white men had long exploited Black women sexually and excluded them from the category of rape victims in the lynching narrative, they attempted to control white women's sexuality by confining them to the protective rhetoric of innocent rape victims. Hence, on the one hand, Holiday's public avowal of Black women's sexuality resisted the sexual objectification of Black women and the historical silencing of their sexual abuse as examined here. White women's affirmation of sexuality through consuming Holiday's performance, on the other hand, liberated themselves from the imposed notion of rape victimhood. Although the consensual sexual relationship between white women and Black men had often existed in the United States, it became one of the key threats to the weakened white patriarchal positionality, particularly since Post-Reconstruction. According to historian Martha Hodes, ideas about "the agency of white women" in such interracial liaisons had been replaced by new ideas about "the dangers of empowered black men" (the image of the Black rapist) by the 1890s. But the notion and reality of consensual relationships between Black men and white women, by their persistence into the twentieth century, carried within them the germ of another subversive force: the agency of white women.[70] Thus, by consuming "Strange Fruit," white women could subtly validate the proscribed interracial sexual relationship Holiday elegized in the song. In so doing, they undermined the taboo of Black-white consensual liaison, thereby subverting white patriarchal norms.

In this case, the request for the "sexy song" by a white woman in Los Angeles makes more sense; indeed, it would seem that she valued it as the genuinely sexy song that it was. She said "sexy" because of "the naked bodies swinging in the trees," thereby emphasizing not only the brutality inflicted upon these black bodies but rather their nakedness, which conjured up something erotic and seductive in her mind. She actively asked for Holiday's musical rendering of what she considered the sexy, naked bodies of Black men.

It is this very act of this white woman, her affirmative and autonomic desiring for imagined (and possibly actual) Black male sexuality that white men had long tried to suppress through the rape myth. Thus, through the act of musical consumption, Holiday's white female audiences acquired a new vehicle for challenging the dominant social norm of women's sexuality that restricted female agency. And they were able to do so without damaging their respectable womanhood. The picture of Holiday at Café Society included here clearly captures how comfortably well-dressed, decent white female audiences consumed Holiday's overtly sexual performance of both love songs as well as "Strange Fruit" that musically described Black male and white female sexuality, forbidden interracial sex, and sadistic violence as an outcome of such a relationship. From the perspective of the politics of sexuality, the complicit relationship between Holiday and these white women becomes more apparent. Through the performance and consumption of the song about lynching in nightclub spaces, both parties gained access to agency in affirming female sexuality and eventually challenged the white supremacist patriarchy that suppressed, albeit differently, Black and white female sexuality.

In the arena of actual politics, middle-class Black women had tried but largely failed during the 1930s to foster interracial cooperation with southern white women in the antilynching movement. But such an alliance became possible, if not always successful, within the imagined realm through cultural politics.[71] Holiday's "Strange Fruit" contributed to creating an alternative transgressive interracial culture and sisterhood between Black women and white women through the politics of sexuality. Both the song "Strange Fruit"—and Holiday's performativity that suffused the song—thus opened multiple windows of subversive possibilities.

Acknowledgement

Many people offered valuable comments and insights during this essay's production. I acknowledge with gratitude the support I received from Piril Hatice Atabay, Daina Ramey Berry, Gavin James Campbell, Hazel V. Carby, David M. Carletta, Aimé J. Ellis, Darlene Clark Hine, Masahiro Hosoya, Masumi Izumi, Sarah Jane Mathieu, Lloyd P. Pratt, Sayuri Guthrie-Shimizu, David W. Stowe, Yusuke Torii, Alan Trachtenberg, and Jonathan Veitch. I dedicate this essay to my mentor, the late Dr. Aimé J. Ellis, whose academic legacies I will carry forward.

Notes

1. Lewis Allan, *Strange Fruit* (New York: New Theatre League, 1939), Abel Meeropol Collection, Box 14, Folder 14, Howard Gotlieb Archival Research Center, Boston University.

2. *Congressional Record*, 109th Congress, 1st Session (June 13, 2005), S6366. The resolution officially apologized to the victims of lynching and their descendants for the Senate's failure to pass the federal antilynching legislations over a century.
3. David Stowe, "The Politics of Café Society," *Journal of American History* (March 1998): 1391. The latest book on Café Society has corrected the notation of the club name as the original "Cafe Society" while I use the former in this essay. Barney Josephson with Terry Trilling-Josephson, *Cafe Society: The Wrong Place for the Right People* (Urbana, IL: University of Illinois Press, 2009).
4. Michael Denning, *Cultural Front: The Laboring of American Culture in the Twentieth Century* (London: Verso, 1997), 324–361; Stowe, "The Politics of Café Society," 1384–1406; Angela Y. Davis, *Blues Legacies and Black Feminism: Gertrude "Ma" Rainey, Bessie Smith, and Billie Holiday* (New York: Pantheon, 1998), 181–198; David Margolick, *Strange Fruit: Billie Holiday, Café Society, and an Early Cry for Civil Rights* (Philadelphia, PA: Running Press, 2000); David Margolick, *Strange Fruit: The Biography of a Song* (New York: The Ecco Press, 2001); Dawn-Wisteria Bates, "Race Woman: The Political Consciousness of Billie Holiday" (Master Thesis, Sarah Lawrence College, 2001); and Joel Katz, directed, *Strange Fruit* (California Newsreel, 2002). See also Kathy A. Perkins and Judith L. Stephens, eds., *Strange Fruit: Plays on Lynching by American Women* (Bloomington, IN: Indiana University Press, 1998), 15–20; and Darlene Clark Hine and Kathleen Thompson, *A Shining Thread of Hope: The History of Black Women in America* (New York: Broadway, 1998), 259–260.
5. *Time,* December 31, 1999; "100 Songs of the South," *Atlanta Journal-Constitution* (*AJC*), n.d. but in 2005, http://alt.coxnewsweb.com/ajc/swf/songsofthesouth/index.html (last accessed on July 20, 2011). The *AJC* calls "Strange Fruit" an "anti-lynching song," commenting: "When Billie Holiday took it [the song] on, it became one of the most powerful pieces of popular music ever recorded. The chilling images are made even more horrifying by Holiday's reportorial, matter-of-fact delivery." Other songs among the Top Five include Sam Cooke's "A Change Is Gonna Come," Nina Simone's "Mississippi Goddam," and "We Shall Overcome," showing the *AJC*'s inclination to political songs.
6. Adrian Lyne, directed, *9 ½ Weeks* (MGM, 1986). In this scene, when John asks Elizabeth "Do you like music?," the camera briefly captures him smiling at her and zooms into her perplexed look while the song plays "Southern trees bear a strange fruit." John says, "It's Billie Holiday," showing her the record jacket with a seductive look (and the song goes: "blood on the leaves and blood at the root"). Elizabeth tries to change the topic to break the sexual tension by asking him what he does for a living while the song plays: "black body swinging in the Southern breeze/ Strange Fruit hanging from

the popular trees," and the song fades away as their conversation continues. John's blatant seduction scares Elizabeth and she leaves the boathouse, but this critical scene predicts their subsequent sexual relationship.

7. Jacquelyn Dowd Hall, *Revolt against Chivalry: Jessie Daniel Ames and the Women's Campaign against Lynching* (New York: Columbia University Press, 1979, 1993), 150.
8. bell hooks, *Black Looks: Race and Representation* (Boston, MA: South End Press, 1992), 2.
9. hooks, *Black Looks*, 4. Stuart Hall explains of this strategy that it "positively takes the body as the principal site of its representational strategies" and "deliberately contests the dominant gendered and sexual definitions of racial difference by working on black sexuality." Stuart Hall, ed., *Representation: Cultural Representations and Signifying Practices* (London: Sage Publications, 1997), 274.
10. Sharon Block, "Rape without Women: Print Culture and the Politicization of Rape, 1765–1815," *Journal of American History* (December 2002): 849–868. Diane Miller Sommerville emphasizes that the rape myth was constructed after Reconstruction, warning that historians have sometimes confused the postbellum stereotype of Black rapists and the antebellum image of libidinous slave men. Diane Miller Sommerville, "The Rape Myth in the Old South Reconsidered," in Darlene Clark Hine and Earnestine Jenkins, eds., *A Question of Manhood: A Reader in U. S. Black Men's History and Masculinity*, Vol. 1 (Bloomington, IN: Indiana University Press, 1999), 438–472.
11. Hall, *Revolt against Chivalry*, 145–149; Joel Williamson, *The Crucible of Race: Black-White Race Relations in the American South Since Emancipation* (New York: Oxford University Press, 1984), 116–118, 183–185, 306–309; Martha Hodes, *White Women, Black Men: Illicit Sex in the 19th-Century South* (New Haven: Yale University Press, 1997), 198–207; Leon F. Litwack, *Trouble in Mind: Black Southerners in the Age of Jim Crow* (New York: Alfred A. Knopf, 1998), 301–307; Jonathan Markovitz, *Legacies of Lynching: Racial Violence and Memory* (Minneapolis, MN: University of Minnesota Press, 2004), 8–11; and William D. Carrigan, *The Making of a Lynching Culture: Violence and Vigilantism in Central Texas, 1836–1916* (Urbana, IL: University of Illinois Press, 2004), 149–154.
12. The film was repeatedly released in 1924, 1931, and 1938. John Hope Franklin, *Race and History: Selected Essays 1938–1988* (Baton Rouge, LA: Louisiana State University Press, 1989), 14–17, 22. On the Black rapist image in *The Clansman,* see Sandra Gunning, *Race, Rape, and Lynching: The Red Record of American Literature* (New York: Oxford University Press, 1996), 28–43. For the themes of lynching and rape in literature, see Trudier Harris, *Exorcising Blackness: Historical and Literary Lynching and Burning Rituals* (Bloomington, IN: Indiana University Press, 1984); Gunning, *Race,*

Rape, and Lynching; Robyn Wiegman, "The Anatomy of Lynching," *Journal of the History of Sexuality* 3.3 (1993): 445–467; and Crystal N. Feimster, *Southern Horrors: Women and the Politics of Rape and Lynching* (Cambridge, MA: Harvard University Press, 2009).

13. Hortense Powdermaker, *After Freedom: A Cultural Study in the Deep South* (1939, New York: Russel & Russel, 1968), 54–55, 389; George H. Gallup, *The Gallup Poll: Public Opinion, 1935–1971* (New York: Random House, 1972), 48.
14. Jonathan Markovitz argues that while antilynching activists were concerned with racist representations of/racial violence against both Black men and women, they were forced to combat mainly the rape myth (thus less able to confront racist representations of Black women) because the major justification for lynching was Black male sexuality and criminality. Markovitz, *Legacies of Lynching*, 3, 8–18.
15. On Wells' antilynching campaign, see Hazel V. Carby, " 'On the Threshold of Woman's Era': Lynching, Empire, and Sexuality in Black Feminist Theory," *Critical Inquiry* 12 (Autumn 1985): 262–277; Gail Bederman, *Manliness and Civilization: A Cultural History of Gender and Race in the United States, 1880–1917* (Chicago: University of Chicago Press, 1995): 45–76; Patricia A. Schechter, "Unsettled Business: Ida B. Wells against Lynching, or, How Antilynching Got Its Gender," in W. Fitzhugh Brundage, ed., *Under Sentence of Death: Lynching in the New South* (Chapel Hill: University of North Carolina Press, 1997), 292–317; and Jacqueline Goldsby, *Spectacular Secret: Lynching in American Life and Literature* (Chicago: University of Chicago Press, 2006), 43–104.
16. Erskine Caldwell, "A Note," *An Art Commentary on Lynching* (1935), Papers of the NAACP, Group I, Box C-206, Manuscript Division, Library of Congress.
17. Jessie Daniel Ames, "Can Newspapers Harmonize Their Editorial Policy on Lynching and Their News Stories on Lynching?," speech delivered at the Southern Newspaper Publishers' Association Convention, May 18, 1936, reprinted in Ames, *The Changing Character of Lynching: Review of Lynching, 1931–1941* (1942, New York: AMS, 1973), 58; ASWPL, "Southern Women Look at Lynching" (Atlanta, 1937), 4–5; and Jacquelyn Dowd Hall, " 'The Mind That Burns in Each Body': Women, Rape, and Racial Violence," in Ann Snitow, Christine Stansell, and Sharon Thompson, eds., *Powers of Desire: The Politics of Sexuality* (New York: Monthly Review Press, 1983), 338.
18. Hall, *Revolt against Chivalry*, 150.
19. W. Fitzhugh Brundage, *Lynching in the New South: Georgia and Virginia, 1880–1930* (Chicago: University of Illinois Press, 1993), 66.
20. NAACP distributed and sold over 15,000 copies of *Lynching of Claude Neal.* James R. McGovern, *Anatomy of Lynching: The Killing of Claude*

Neal (Chapel Hill: Louisiana State University Press, 1992), 126–131; Grace Elizabeth Hale, *Making Whiteness: The Culture of Segregation in the South, 1890–1940* (New York: Pantheon, 1998), 222–227.

21. Amy Louise Wood, "Lynching Photography and the 'Black Beast Rapist' in the Southern White Masculine Imagination," in Peter Lehman, ed., *Masculinity: Bodies, Movies, Culture* (New York: Routledge, 2001), 204.
22. Hazel V. Carby, *Race Men* (Cambridge, MA: Harvard University Press, 1998), 46–47; Williamson, *Crucible of Race*, 306–310.
23. Frantz Fanon, *Black Skin, White Mask*, translated by Charles Lam Markmann (New York: Grove, 1967), 165.
24. Kobena Mercer, *Welcome to Jungle: New Positions in Black Cultural Studies* (New York: Routledge, 1994), 174.
25. Harris, *Exorcising Blackness*, 23.
26. Fanon, *Black Skin*, 159. Emphasis is added.
27. *New York Teacher*, January 1937, 17, Abel Meeropol Collection, Box 14, Folder 15.
28. Denning, *Cultural Front*, 327.
29. *PM*, September 23, 1945.
30. Josephson quoted in Denning, *Cultural Front*, 327.
31. *New Masses*, June 20, 1939, 55.
32. "Night Club Singer Records Song About Lynchings In South," *New York Age*, June 17, 1939.
33. *TAC*, n.d. but after March 1940, Abel Meeropol Collection, Box 15, Folder 27. For the Gavagan bill, see Robert L. Zangrando, *The NAACP Crusade against Lynching, 1909–1950* (Philadelphia, PA: Temple University Press, 1980), 161–162.
34. *Time*, June 12, 1939, 66.
35. Davis, *Blues Legacies*, 184–187. In her intriguing exploration of the myths that surround Holiday, Farah Jasmine Griffin praises Davis' discussion for its contribution to rescuing Holiday from those white critics and biographers. Farah Jasmine Griffin, *In Search of Billie Holiday: If You Can't Be Free, Be a Mystery* (New York: Ballantine Books, 2001), 130–131.
36. On the images of Mammy and Jezebel, see Deborah Gray White, "Jezebel and Mammy: The Mythology of Female Slavery," in *Ar'n't I a Woman?: Female Slaves in the Plantation South* (New York: W.W. Norton, 1985, 1999), 27–61. In the United States, the usage of "hump" in the sexual sense dates from the 1910s. Jonathon Green, *Cassell's Dictionary of Slang* (London: Cassell, 1998), 624.
37. In her 1937 performance at the Fox Theatre in Detroit, for example, Holiday had to "black up" her face because her skin color was too light. Donald Clarke, *Wishing on the Moon: The Life and Times of Billie Holiday* (New York: Penguin, 1994), 130.

38. Griffin, *In Search of Billie Holiday*, 28. Griffin, too, mentions *Gone With the Wind* as well as *Imitation of Life* (1934), which she points out "reproduced the stereotype of the oversexed, over-ambitious 'tragic mulatto' " (29).
39. Wexler quoted in Margolick, *Strange Fruit: The Biography*, 60.
40. *DownBeat*, July 1939.
41. *New York Post*, February 11, 1942, Abel Meeropol Collection, Box 15, Folder 27. Café Society Uptown opened on 58th street in October 1941.
42. Margolick, *Strange Fruit: The Biography*, 35.
43. Josephson quoted in Denning, *Cultural Front*, 327.
44. Billie Holiday with William Dufty, *Lady Sings the Blues* (1956, New York: Penguin, 1992), 84.
45. Bates, "Race Women," 19; Davis, *Blues Legacies*, 195.
46. Wilson quoted in Margolick, *Strange Fruit: The Biography*, 37.
47. In his analysis of the modern-day representation of Black men, Kobena Mercer describes that "the lynching of black men routinely involved the literal castration of the other's 'strange fruit.' " Mercer, *Welcome to Jungle*, 185.
48. "Of 'Strange Fruit' (the song)," an unidentified article clip, n.d. but after 1944, Abel Meeropol Collection, Box 15, Folder 27. Although journalist David Margolick speculates that Allan was possibly inspired to write the song by a widely-publicized photograph of the 1930 lynching in Marion, Indiana, this photograph of two lynched men is less likely the one Allan referred to, given that Allan described what he came across as "a lynching of *a* human being." Margolick, *Strange Fruit: The Biography*, 21. Emphasis is added. It is possible, however, that Allan saw the same photograph in different framing showing only one lynching victim, just as writer Jacquie Jones did. Jacquie Jones, "How Come Nobody Told Me about the Lynching?" in Deborah Willis, ed., *Picturing Us: African American Identity in Photography* (New York: The New Press, 1994), 153.
49. W. J. Cash, *The Mind of the South* (New York: Alfred A. Knopf, 1941, 1962), 115–116. Mary Jane Brown argues that it was a crucial aspect of southern legend "that the *delicate flower of southern womanhood* needed protection from rapacious black males . . . ." Brown, *Eradicating this Evil: Women in the American Anti-Lynching Movement 1892–1940* (New York: Garland, 2000), 27. Emphasis is added.
50. Hale, *Making Whiteness*, 200–239; Amy Louise Wood, *Lynching and Spectacle: Witnessing Racial Violence in America, 1890–1940* (Chapel Hill: University of North Carolina Press, 2009), 2–15.
51. *New Yorker*, March 18, 1939, 68. It reprinted the lyrics incorrect, combining two lines in the first section into one and using a different verb—"growing." This indicates the advertiser's indifference to the lyrics' detail.

52. On lynching photographs, see Dora Apel, *Imagery of Lynching: Black Men, White Women, and the Mob* (New Brunswick, NJ: Rutgers University Press, 2004), 7–45; Wood, *Lynching and Spectacle*, 103–109; Goldsby, *Spectacular Secret*, 214–281; and Dora Apel and Shawn Michelle Smith, *Lynching Photographs* (Berkeley, CA: University of California Press, 2007). A collection of lynching photos and postcards is available in James Allen et al., eds., *Without Sanctuary: Lynching Photography in America* (Santa Fe, NM: Twin Palm, 2000).

    Although I admit that a contemporary lynching photograph could best underscore the relationship of victim to spectators in comparison with the photo of Holiday at Café Society, it is my decision not to use/abuse any lynching photos in this essay. As a scholar of lynching, I would like to call our attention to the fact that we often include, too easily, images and depictions of lynching into works as historical documents without fully noticing the possibility of running a risk of triggering an exploitative and/or voyeuristic gaze, thus possibly reproducing the white supremacist ideology that was originally inscribed in those representations. For discussions regarding the scholarly use of representations of lynching and other brutalization of the Black body, see Hale, *Making Whiteness*, 306; Saidiya V. Hartman, *Scenes of Subjection: Terror, Slavery, and Self-Making in Nineteenth-Century America* (New York: Oxford University Press, 1997), 3–4; and Wood, "Lynching Photography," 207–208.
53. Robert G. O'Meally, *Lady Day: The Many Faces of Billie Holiday* (New York: Da Capo Press, 1991), 130.
54. Ida B. Wells, *A Red Record* (1895), reprinted in Jacqueline Jones Royster, ed., *Southern Horrors and Other Writings: The Anti-Lynching Campaign of Ida B. Wells, 1892–1900* (Boston, MA: Bedford, 1997), 127.
55. NACW Convention Minutes (1914), 25. Records of the NACW, reel 1; Rosalyn Terborg-Penn, *African American Women in the Struggle for the Vote, 1850–1920* (Bloomington, IN: Indiana University Press, 1998), 96.
56. Rosalyn Terborg-Penn, "African-American Women's Networks in the Anti-Lynching Crusade," in Noralee Frankel and Nancy S. Dye, eds., *Gender, Class, Race and Reform in the Progressive Era* (Lexington, KY: University Press of Kentucky, 1991), 157–158; and Brown, *Eradicating this Evil*, 115, 144–148. For other cases of Black women's role in the antilynching movement, see Markovitz, *Legacies of Lynching*, 18–23.
57. White, *Ar'n't I a Woman?*, 176–177; Nell Irvin Painter, "Who Was Lynched?" *Nation* (November 11, 1991): 577; and Weigman, "The Anatomy of Lynching," 446 n. 1. Rosalyn Terborg-Penn points out that the history of antilynching movements also overshadowed Black women's contributions to them. Terborg-Penn, "African-American Women's Networks," 159.
58. 76 Black women were lynched between 1882 and 1927. Walter White, *Rope and Faggot: A Biography of Judge Lynch* (1929, Notre Dame: University of

Notre Dame Press, 2001), 267. For examples of Black female lynch victims, see Gerda Lerner, *Black Women in White America: A Documentary History* (New York: Vintage, 1972), 161–162; and Terborg-Penn, "African-American Women's Networks," 150–153.

59. For the sexual exploitation of female slaves, see Harriet A. Jacobs, *Incidents in the Life of a Slave Girl* (1861, Cambridge, MA: Harvard University Press, 1987), 27–36, 51–52; Thelma Jennings, " 'Us Colored Women Had To Go through a Plenty': Sexual Exploitation of African-American Slave Women," *Journal of Women's History* (Winter 1990): 45–74; Melton A. McLaurin, *Celia: A Slave* (New York: Avons, 1991), 22–37; Nell Irvin Painter, *Soul Murder and Slavery* (Waco: Markham, 1995), 15–21; and Daina Ramey Berry, *Swing the Sickle for the Harvest Is Ripe: Gender and Slavery in Antebellum Georgia* (Urbana, IL: University of Illinois Press, 2007), 77–88.
60. For rape of Black women after emancipation, see Lerner, *Black Women*, 149–161, 172–190; Susan Brownmiller, *Against Our Will: Men, Women and Rape* (Toronto, ON: Bantam Books, 1976), 133–140; Angela Y. Davis, *Women, Race and Class* (1981, New York: Vintage, 1983), 175–177; Litwack, *Trouble in Mind*, 342–349; and Nell Irvin Painter, *Southern History across the Color Line* (Chapel Hill: University of North Carolina Press, 2002), 121.
61. Hazel V. Carby, *Reconstructing Womanhood: The Emergence of the Afro-American Woman Novelist* (New York: Oxford University Press, 1987), 39.
62. I am referring to anthropologist James C. Scott's concept of "hidden transcript" that represents "a critique of power behind the back of the dominant." James C. Scott, *Domination and the Arts of Resistance: Hidden Transcripts* (New Haven, CT: Yale University, 1990), xii.
63. Farah Jasmine Griffin points out that Holiday is a "salable commodity" just like other American icons. Griffin, *In Search of Billie Holiday*, 32. David Margolick writes that Holiday was often referred to in the press accounts as "the buxom, colored songstress" or "the sepian songstress." Margolick, *Strange Fruit: Billie Holiday*, 62. For example, in its review of the performance by the all-white Artie Shaw Orchestra at the Savoy Ballroom in Chicago on October 22, 1938, *Billboard* magazine described Holiday as "his [Artie Shaw's] sepia songstress Billie Holliday [*sic*]." *Billboard*, October 29, 1938, 11.
64. Cunningham quoted in Margolick, *Strange Fruit: The Biography*, 61.
65. Davis, *Blues Legacies*, 175. Davis argues that the blues departed from other contemporary popular music in terms of its "provocative and pervasive sexual—including homosexual—imagery" (3) and that its distinctiveness came from the unique historical context of African Americans who had been long denied their sexual autonomy. Davis, *Blues Legacies*, 3–24. Michael Denning also examines the relation of Holiday's love songs to the blues, but from the perspective of the Popular Front culture. Denning, *Cultural Front*, 344–347.

66. Evelyn Brooks Higginbotham, *Righteous Discontent: The Women's Movement in the Black Baptist Church, 1880–1920* (Cambridge, MA: Harvard University Press, 1993), 185–299. Another strategy often used to desexualize Black womanhood was the "culture of dissemblance," the attitudes of Black women that created the appearance of public openness but actually, shielded reservedly the truth of their inner lives from their oppressors. Darlene Clark Hine, "Rape and Inner Lives of Black Women in the Middle West: Preliminary Thoughts on the Culture of Dissemblance," in Beverly Guy-Sheftall, ed., *Words of Fire: An Anthology of African American Feminist Thoughts* (New York: New Press, 1995), 380–387.
67. For reviews of Holiday's rendition by music scholars and critics, see Margolick, *Strange Fruit: Billie Holiday*, 65–67.
68. Billie Holiday, "Strange Fruit" (recorded on April 20, 1939), in *Billie Holiday Strange Fruit 1937–1939* (Jazzterdays, 1996); "Strange Fruit" (recorded on February 12, 1945), in *Billie Holiday Verve Story Vol. 1: Jazz at the Philharmonic* (Polygram, 1994); and "Strange Fruit" (recorded on June 7, 1956), in *Lady Sings the Blues* (Polygram, 1995).
69. Indeed, many contemporary media, including the aforementioned *Time* that reviewed the 1939 recording, reprinted this part of the lyrics as "black bodies." Perhaps Holiday regularly sang it as such in nightclubs, judging from the comment by a woman in Los Angeles ("naked bodies"). Today, Holiday's lyrical version seems more popular than the original.
70. Hodes, *White Women, Black Men*, 176–208.
71. ASWPL did challenge the southern patriarchal system by refuting the rape myth, not necessarily because white women affirmed their sexual autonomy but rather because they attempted to emphasize their respectable womanhood. Their antilynching efforts mainly aimed at educating the southern white community about uncivilized and un-Christian acts of lynching because lynching, from their perspective, was a moral-threatening problem for the white community that respectable white women should solve; it was not a problem because of the victimization of African Americans.

    Thus, the ASWPL's strategy of moral uplift did not entail such actions as organizational support for the federal antilynching legislation that would directly challenge state power. Sachiko Hishida, "Jinshu-kan Kyouryoku eno Kitai to Zasetsu: 1930 nendai no Han-rinchi Undou wo Jirei ni [The Hope and Failure in Interracial Cooperation: A Study of the Anti-lynching Movement in the 1930s]," *The Journal of American and Canadian Studies* 23 (2005): 78–92.

CHAPTER 6

Gender, Race, and Public Space: Photography and Memory in the Massacre of East Saint Louis and *The Crisis Magazine*

Anne Rice

> Did any of the early twentieth-century black photographers attempt to record images reflecting the omnipresent and devastating racism of those years? . . . Were any visual challenges inspired by the 1916 lynching of Jesse Washington, who was burned to death in Waco, Texas, before a cheering crowd of 15,000 white people—men, women, and even children? Included in the "Harlem on My Mind" exhibition was a photograph of a march in Harlem protesting the East St. Louis race riots of 1917. How many more images remain to be discovered which evoke the presence of and resistance to the terrible violence of 1917 and the murderous Red Summer of 1919?
>
> Angela Y. Davis, "Underexposed: Photography and Afro-American History."

> Visual records at times display a power too difficult to bear at points within the unfolding of memory.
>
> Barbie Zelizer, "Reading the Past Against the Grain."

Remembering East St. Louis: The Silent Protest Parade

It is an iconic photograph (see Figure 6.1) of the first great American Civil Rights March, the Silent Protest Parade down New York's Fifth Avenue on July 28, 1917.

Behind drummers solemnly summoning the attention of the crowd march some of the country's most prominent African American

Figure 6.1 Silent Protest Parade 1917

men: world-renowned scholar and *Crisis* editor W.E.B DuBois, Rev. Hutchens Chew Bishop, rector of Harlem's St. Philip's Episcopal Church, realtor John Nail and his son-in-law, author and activist James Weldon Johnson. Behind them flow row-upon-row of children carefully shepherded by women, their white costumes contrasting with the men's dark suits. A sign from within their midst reads in large letters: THOU SHALT NOT KILL.

The entire year had been filled with news of terrible lynchings, each surpassing the next in wanton cruelty. The Silent Protest Parade grew out of planning for a public protest after 15,000 white people—including women and children—led by the victim's mother gathered in Memphis that May to watch Ell Persons burn to death for supposedly raping and murdering 16-year-old Antoinette Rappell. By July, as organizers were pondering the form their protest should take, word flooded in from East St. Louis, Illinois, of a horrific massacre: On July 2, hundreds of white men, women, and children had rampaged through East St. Louis, beating, shooting, and drowning African Americans and burning entire neighborhoods to the ground.

Many hundreds more watched and cheered as the rioters pulled Black people off streetcars to hang them from telegraph poles and streetlights.

The mob set Negro homes on fire, and then shot people as they tried to flee. Several witnesses saw the police actively aiding the rioters, and when the Illinois militia arrived, they proceeded to disarm the African American community, jailing those who were victims of the mob and, in some cases, actually pushing Blacks seeking protection back into the crowd at bayonetpoint.[1]

In an era in which white women regularly witnessed and participated in racial violence, their sadistic killing of Black women and children in East St. Louis shocked the nation.[2] In the end, at least 6,000 people fled the city and over $400,000 worth of property lay in ruins. Government hearings gave a low estimate of 39 African American fatalities, but the newspapers put the number closer to 200, and W.E.B. Du Bois would insist on a death figure of 125 for as long as he lived.[3]

The killing a day earlier of police detectives mistaken for joyriders who had shot up a Black neighborhood provided the immediate catalyst, but the larger cause was race hatred, resentment over the loss of "white" jobs to African American strikebreakers, and the growth of Black political power.[4] A wartime demand for industrial labor, intensified by curtailed European immigration and American military recruitment, prompted thousands of African Americans to head northward in search of jobs and relief from southern Jim Crow segregation. When they arrived in East St. Louis, they found themselves caught in the conflict between organized labor hostile to Black efforts to join unions and industrialists determined to break those unions by employing Blacks for lower wages. The eruption of violence in July followed a series of attacks upon the African American community in East St. Louis in which police did little to intervene. Inflammatory newspaper reports of Black "criminality" and union meetings calling for the deportation of southern Blacks simmered the cauldron of white animosity to its boiling point in July. The first of the large wartime "race riots," East St. Louis provided traumatic and inescapable evidence of increased African American vulnerability to white terror across the nation. At the same time that state-sponsored war propaganda celebrated white female purity and motherhood, government at all levels continued a systemic tradition to withhold protection of African American mothers and children from lynch mobs and rioters.[5] African American men were asked to fight for democracy abroad yet denied the most basic citizenship rights, including the right to their own lives.[6]

Of course, African Americans always vigorously and courageously resisted these terrible conditions. This photograph of the Silent Protest

Parade remains alive in collective memory as a powerful symbol of the era. In a recent example, the photograph introduces Julian Bond's foreword to *NAACP: Celebrating a Century, 100 Years in Pictures* (2009). Apart from the founders' portraits next to the Table of Contents, it is the collection's first image. Twenty pages later it appears again as a two-page frontispiece to a section entitled 1909–1919, visually encapsulating the volume's version of NAACP (the National Association for the Advancement of Colored People) history—strong men in the lead, who both protect and are supported by militant women and children, waging a courageous and dignified battle for citizenship rights against overwhelming odds. In other instances, this photograph offers visible affirmation of survival that makes it easier to contemplate atrocity. For example, in Karla Hollaway's *Passed On: African American Mourning Stories,* a volume replete with images of lynching, this is the only photograph illustrating the events of the East St. Louis riot, the unharmed bodies, moving freely in space, placed in dialogue with a coroner's graphic testimony of terrible bodily harm.[7]

Yet with all the compelling reasons to concentrate on this photograph and the story it tells about African American bravery and survival, what gets left out when we do so? The question Angela Davis originally asked in 1983 about African American photographic resistance surfaced with renewed urgency when *Without Sanctuary,* an exhibition of lynching photographs and postcards—primarily featuring the bodies of murdered African American men—began touring the US in the year 2000. The widely-publicized emergence of images of white men, women, and children enthusiastically torturing African Americans to death and willingly posing next to the bodies of the people they killed, prompted a public re-examination of the past that culminated in a 2005 Senate apology for its failure to pass federal antilynching legislation, the first apology it had ever made for its treatment of African Americans.[8] Since *Without Sanctuary,* scholars have meticulously examined the production and consumption of lynching photography, with particular attention recently paid to Black activists' use of white supremacist images in their fight to end lynching.[9]

White photographers, however, were not the only ones to hold Black victims in their gaze. By restoring this iconic image to its original context in the NAACP's September 1917 *Crisis Magazine*, this essay highlights African American photographic practices that forced viewers to look again at what it might mean to be an object of white violence. The issue features a remarkable photo-essay entitled "The Massacre of East St. Louis" by W.E.B. Du Bois and white suffragist Martha Gruening, along with scathing editorials and photographs of the Silent Protest. With a circulation record of nearly 50,000 and a wide distribution to lawmakers, the September 1917 issue represents NAACP antilynching propaganda at its most effective and illuminates the complex intersections of gender and mass racial violence. Often cited by historians, this special issue sought to go beyond factual recording to preserve a record of the thoughts and sense experience of the riot's victims. Through their choice of photographs, layout and accompanying text, both in the photo-essay itself and the larger content of the issue, Du Bois and Gruening make the Black female body the focal point of their coverage, challenging understandings of African American victimization and survival, and providing a fascinating window into the early uses of photography in the struggle for African American Civil Rights.

Investigating the Riot: Negro Women at the Forefront

Stories of white women, often with their children in tow, attacking and murdering Black women and children saturated contemporary coverage of the riot. But African American women were not merely passive victims as some in Denverside defended their neighborhood with guns, and at least one woman escaped rape by pulling a revolver on her attacker.[10] Negro women also formed the first wave of lynching investigators, and much of the testimony they gathered and presented before Congress came from female survivors. When the fearless anti-lynching crusader Ida B. Wells-Barnett arrived from Chicago the day after the riot, conductors warned her that the danger was so great "they had been locking the porters in the coaches as the train ran through East St. Louis."[11] Wells-Barnett got off anyway and walked along the main street to City Hall. Once there, she met a group of Black women, without their hats and wearing two-day old clothes, returning from St. Louis to see what the mob had left behind. A Red Cross official commandeered a truck, placed a soldier at either end with a gun and extra rounds of ammo, and ordered the driver to take them to their destroyed neighborhood, with Wells-Barnett coming along for the ride.

Wells-Barnett's 1917 pamphlet, "The East St. Louis Massacre: The Greatest Outrage of the Century," takes readers on a tour of a dozen ruined homes which the mob had set fire to from the back, forcing occupants into the deadly street. Most of Wells-Barnett's companions were lucky enough to have escaped ahead of the fires. Those who had remained in their homes and somehow survived recounted harrowing tales of watching in horror as mobs that often included their white neighbors murdered people they knew, including children. In this important and heartrending historical document, Wells-Barnett describes the gendered spaces of the ruined homes, measuring the riot's devastation through domestic loss. Respectable and upwardly mobile, her companions include homeowners and renters who took pride in the possessions for which they had worked so hard. The women wander through these spaces gazing in sorrow and anger at new furniture reduced to ashes, good rugs and Sunday clothing trampled underfoot by the mob, and phonograph records smashed to pieces across the floor.

Later that day, when Wells-Barnett crossed the river into St. Louis, she found thousands of similarly traumatized people: "Every which way we turned there were women and children and men, dazed over the thing that had come to them and unable to tell what it was about," she wrote later. "They lined the streets or were standing out on the grassy banks of the lawns that surrounded the city hall or stood in groups discussing their experiences . . . These people who had been robbed of everything except what they stood in."[12] The traumatic distress so evident among the survivors Wells-Barnett encountered in the streets of St. Louis reverberated throughout the entire Black community in America, who experienced this murderous assault in the northern "promised land" as a tremendous psychological blow.

African American women responded with poetry and plays and works of art expressing their anguish and outrage over this betrayal, particularly in terms of the assault against women and children.[13] Their political response was also both immediate and well-orchestrated, channeling grief into grievance as they wrote letters, gathered petitions and testified before Congress. When the US Senate Rules Committee held a special hearing the month after the riot, two African American women appeared to offer testimony at Missouri Senator Leonidas Dyer's request.[14] Nannie Burroughs, founder and head of the National Training School for Girls and Women, appeared in her capacity as superintendent of the National Association of Colored Women's Department for the Suppression of Lynching and Mob Violence to present over 7,000 petitions signed by both Black and white Americans protesting "the outrages perpetrated upon other American citizens in East St. Louis" and urging their support of Dyer's resolution for a congressional investigation. "At least 100,000" more of these petitions from throughout the country, she added, had already been collected to be sent to Congress. In her testimony, Burroughs repeatedly insisted on Negroes' right to "feel perfectly safe to live and labor—and we do not feel that way now—as American citizens."

Howard University professor and Red Cross worker Hallie E. Queen then shared survivor testimony and her own experiences in the immediate aftermath of the violence, noting that "everyone admits that women were far more vile in this riot than were the men and far more inventive of cruelty." As the sole Negro member of the Red Cross Civilian Relief Committee sent to the city, Queen received permission to carry on investigations and to make a report. In her Senate testimony, she produced, as evidence, photographs she had been "allowed to take under military escort as a member of the Red Cross" though civilians and reporters were forbidden to do so.[15] The photographs she held up before the committee included scenes of crowds, mostly women and children, fleeing across the bridge into St. Louis, a burned-out flat once occupied by female schoolteachers, and the charred remains of libraries and schools—visual examples of women and children's spaces destroyed in part by other women who had children and protected spaces of their own.

Her report mailed two weeks later to Illinois Senator L.Y. Sherman, "East St. Louis as I Saw It," presented interviews with survivors and included her appeal for help for Daisy and Cora Mae Westbrook, the schoolteachers who had lived with their mother and adopted child in the burned home in the photograph Queen had introduced in her house testimony.[16] Queen's report can be found in Sherman's papers, which contain extensive firsthand accounts of the riot, including an appeal by Senia W. Madella, a Black woman from Washington, D.C., also on behalf of the Westbrooks and enclosing Daisy Westbrook's letter to Madella's daughter, Louise, describing herself as haunted by the horrors she witnessed and traumatized by the destruction of her hard-earned possessions and probable loss of her job: "Louise it is so hard to think we had just gotten to the place where we could take care of our mother & grandmother well, & to think, all was destroyed in one night."

By 1910, as W.E.B DuBois observed, "over half of the colored female population as against a fifth" of white females left their homes each day to "toil and toil hard."[17] Scholars have long analyzed the riot in terms of industrial labor history, yet Black women's testimony is striking for its representation of women victims as workers, including schoolteachers and domestics as well as factory hands. With their husbands, but often on their own, these women, as Queen put it, had often begun "to acquire better homes, furniture, and clothing than the whites." During the riot, jealous white women looted the homes of their Black neighbors. Wells-Barnett records, for instance, the distress of Mrs. Lulu Thomas, who, having escaped with only the clothes she was wearing, returned to find a white neighbor parading around in Thomas's finest dress.

In *The East St. Louis Massacre,* Wells-Barnett takes pains to foreground female trauma and loss. Unlike Queen, Wells-Barnett did not rely on extensive photographic evidence to document the devastation. In fact, the pamphlet's only illustration is a photographic portrait of Wells-Barnett herself adorning the frontispiece. Wells-Barnett had used her portrait once before in an antilynching pamphlet—on the front cover of *Southern Horrors. Lynch Law in All its Phases* (1892), a pamphlet that claimed authority from its author's own narrow escape from lynching when angry whites destroyed her paper, the Memphis *Free Speech,* and from her continued vulnerability to retaliation. In *The East St. Louis Massacre,* Wells-Barnett similarly establishes her authority as a reporting witness by describing her courage in the aftermath of the violence and including documents of her meetings with governors and generals alongside mainstream newspaper reports of her activities, such as an article from the Chicago *Herald* naming her "one of the foremost colored women in America." The first image her reader sees upon opening her pamphlet is that Wells-Barnett's portrait is a model of Black female respectability. She looks not at the camera, but to the side and slightly upwards at an object in the distance, her hair genteelly swept up, a modest broach fastening the neck of her impeccable shirtwaist. Embodying the respectability her companions worked so hard to attain, only to find themselves brutally under attack, Wells-Barnett thus puts herself forth as a witness—the voice and face of every woman the mob had tried to erase.

A July 10th meeting between a committee of her sponsoring organization, the Negro Fellowship League, which offered aid and protection to migrants in Chicago, and Illinois Governor Lowden was "very satisfactory," Wells-Barnett recalls, until the Governor "took occasion to advise us against incendiary talk."[18] Wells-Barnett fired back that "if he had seen women whose husbands had been beaten to death, whose children had been thrown into the flames and in the river, whose women had been burned to death, he would not say it was incendiary to talk about such outrages."[19] Taking up a challenge from the Governor, she thereupon returned immediately to East St. Louis with committee member Delores Farrow, collecting testimony from 50 survivors to prove the Illinois militia as both negligent and complicit in the riot.[20]

Martha Gruening: Forgotten Antilynching Crusader

On July 8, 1917, NAACP Publicity Director and *Crisis Magazine* editor W.E.B. Du Bois arrived in East St. Louis to begin his own investigation, accompanied by Martha Gruening, secretary to NAACP Public Relations Director Herbert Seligmann.[21] Like Wells-Barnett, Gruening refused to remain silent about government outrages. A key member of the NAACP antilynching team since 1911, and the adoptive mother of an African American son, Martha Gruening, along with her companion, Helen Boardman, devoted her life to the antiracist struggle, making it central to her feminism, pacifism, and labor activism. As a Smith undergraduate, she organized the college league of the National American Women's Suffrage Association (NAWSA), breaking with NAWSA over its refusal to seat an African American delegate at its 1912 convention held in Atlanta to placate increasingly powerful southern members. Gruening's essay "Two Women's Suffrage Movements" in the 1912 *Crisis* "Women's Suffrage Number" reminded readers of the movement's abolitionist roots and denounced its modern turn from racial justice.[22]

Gruening had had a busy month before arriving in East St. Louis. On June 2, 1917, she had been arrested on charges of circulating anticonscription literature.[23] A week before leaving for East St. Louis, she and Boardman, who was also active in the No Conscription League, had testified for the defense in the trial of Emma Goldman and Alexander Berkman for conspiracy to violate the Selective Service Act.[24] For what proved to be the last issue of Goldman's magazine *Mother Earth* (August 1917), Gruening contributed a blistering account of the riots.[25]

Given the considerable dangers posed to African Americans, in the early years of the NAACP, factfinding missions to the sites of lynchings and race riots often fell to white sympathizers, particularly women. The organization had strong connections with the suffrage and peace movements through founding member Mary White Ovington and DuBois, who was a lifelong supporter of women's rights.[26] Like Wells-Barnett, these female lynching investigators had a background in investigative journalism, often writing for mainstream publications, yet their contributions to the NAACP have largely been forgotten. In 1916 and 1917, white pacifist feminist journalists conducted three important NAACP fact-finding missions: Elisabeth Freeman visited Waco to investigate the burning alive of Jesse Washington in May 1916.[27] Wellesley graduate and muckraking journalist Mary Alden Hopkins travelled to Gainesville, Florida, to report in the October 1916 *Crisis* on the murders of five people, including Mary Dennis, pregnant mother of two, and Stella Long, mother of four. Then, in July 1917, Gruening accompanied DuBois to East St. Louis to interview hostile militia and other whites in the aftermath of the riot.[28]

Building a Movement: Antilynching Photography in *The Crisis*

Both the Freeman and the DuBois/Gruening investigations resulted in photo-essays that drove a huge spike in donations to the NAACP while Hopkins' investigation, for which no photographs appear to have been available, ran only two pages and received significantly less publicity. The hanging of five people in Florida, including a pregnant mother, is as shocking and terrible a story as the burning alive of a teenager in Texas but, without visual evidence, the NAACP declined to make the Gainesville lynching central to its publicity campaign.

From the medium's beginning, white supremacists used photography to spread a message of violence and hate. Yet they produced and distributed lynching photographs in ways that withheld them from public view. The police and mayor of East St. Louis certainly understood the power of photography, confiscating the cameras of newspaper reporters and newsreel crews who attempted to record the murder and mayhem.[29] It is little wonder, then, that the Black press actively sought out and published images of violence against African Americans, even when the editors knew that some readers would object.

Throughout the pages of *The Crisis,* DuBois used photography to visualize an ideal middle-class respectability that challenged photographic stereotypes.[30] Yet *The Crisis* also featured gruesome images of African American abjection and death. How did such chilling evidence of white depravity function next to the idealized images of the bourgeois nuclear family, the perfect children and the proud graduates and business owners? Anne Elizabeth Carroll argues that the magazine's impact depends on the "cognitive dissonance created by such juxtapositions," enabling *The Crisis* to "launch a vicious critique of the treatment of African Americans," but also "to assert African Americans' ability to overcome such treatment" and to motivate readers to act.[31] Whereas the spectacle lynching and its reproductions were designed to reinforce notions of white supremacy and cohesiveness, the NAACP provided a counterspectacle of Black achievement and group identity in the pages of *The Crisis* and in public demonstrations such as the Silent Protest Parade of 1917. Crucially, in doing so, *The Crisis* also offered readers a document of their lives as these "disturbing juxtapositions" formally echoed the "discontinuities and shocks" inherent in the experience of living in America as a person of African descent.[32]

Although little documentation remains of the East St. Louis investigation, the extensive file on Waco in the NAACP archive at the Library of Congress illuminates the importance of visual evidence to the antilynching campaign. In a May 16 letter to Freeman, Executive Secretary Roy Nash offers explicit instructions to dig up evidence against the mob, including the photographs he was sure they had taken. He also asked her to find "photos of the places mentioned, the town, the courthouse, the suspension bridge, the scene of the murder, and any of the actors" to "make the thing vivid for news."[33] During her 10 days in Waco, Freeman collected anecdotal accounts, interviews, trial transcripts and 6 photographs by Waco professional photographer Fred Gildersleeve. DuBois compiled these photographs, with selections from Freeman's report and from white newspapers, into a special supplement for the July 1916 *Crisis,* entitled "The Waco Horror."[34]

Like all photo-essays, "The Waco Horror" can be 'read' photographically, with the viewer looking at the photographs in sequence, independently of the accompanying text. Cinematic in its progression and pacing, Dubois's photo text refutes the filmic glorification of lynching popularized by *Birth of a Nation,* which DuBois blamed directly for the increase in the number and ferocity of lynchings.[35] The sequence of images leads from a single photograph of Baylor University to multiple images of the main institutions of the town, and then to a single shot of the city hall behind which Jesse Washington was burned alive. There then follow the six Gildersleeve photographs of the murder in progress: no longer just pieces of the collection being hawked on the Waco streets, here they become part of a new event, with "each image placed so as to resonate with its fellows as the pages are turned, making the collective meaning more important than the images' individual meanings."[36]

Dubois's placement of these images deviates from the actual chronological sequence of the murder. Jacqueline Goldsby explains that lynching photographs "figure the dead as signs of pure abjection, who radiate no thought, no speech, no action, no will; who through their appearance in the picture's field of vision, become invisible." By altering the sequence and scale of the photographs, DuBois instead pulls the viewer inexorably toward the victim, his captioning and surrounding text disrupting the "scopic aggression" that thwarts "sympathetic identification."[37] Arranged for maximum dramatic effect, the photographs begin with long shots of the crowd, but each subsequent photograph moves closer and closer to the lynched body of the boy and the movements of the men and boys who are killing him. The accompanying text focuses on the cowardice and complicity of law enforcement, mob leaders, and the people of the town who stare so frankly at the camera, smiling with glee, one man lifting his hat in mockery. The final page features the largest photograph—a close-up of Washington's body crushed beneath smoking logs, the chain used to lift him in and out of the fire still attached to his neck. Beneath it, for full dramatic effect, Du Bois has written a single word, "Finis."

The September 1917 Issue

The East St. Louis photo-essay is integrated into the September 1917 issue, taking up about one-third of its 62 pages. *The Crisis* issue's front cover (see Figure 6.2), the first of a series of six "studies of Negro life by

Figure 6.2 Cover of September 1917 *Crisis:* Blanch Deas, of the Negro Players. A study from life by Frank Walts

Frank Walts," features a charcoal drawing of an alluring young woman identified in the Table of Contents as Blanch Deas of the Negro Players.

In choosing to integrate the photo-essay into the regular issue—it occupies an entire section reserved for NAACP news—DuBois signals to *Crisis* readers that while the emergency is acute, life can and must go on. The Editorials section immediately preceding contains four outraged and anguished opinion pieces about the riots, lynching, segregation and racial injustice, but there are also four "uplift" pieces as well—urging readers to put their commerce "in the hands of colored people," soliciting photographs of "real, living, moving children" for the next month's Children's Number, and offering suggestions for helping southern migrants. The final snippet, "Prizes," addresses a reader's complaint that first prize for an article on "The Best Summer I Ever Spent" was wrongfully awarded to a submission three times over the stipulated word count.[38]

This last bit of information faces the first page of "The Massacre of East St. Louis," which features a photograph of a solitary figure lying beside streetcar tracks and struggling to get up and flee for his life (see Figure 6.3).

This eruption of terror in the midst of the trivial textually echoes the shock of the riot itself. Leaning on one arm, the man reaches forward with the other, trying to pull himself up. He has lost his hat; his trousers are torn at the knees, his legs positioned strangely beneath him. Behind

Figure 6.3 Cover image of NAACP special report on East St. Louis

him, across the tracks, an ad painted on the side of a building advertises "Detroit Special Overalls", which smaller letters proclaim are "Union Made," an ironic commentary on "the jealousy of white labor unions and prejudice" that DuBois blames for the riot.[39] Adjacent to this wall, a white man stands, hands in his pockets, watching the scene unfold. Except for this lone observer, the image is a reversal of the Waco photos, where white men push their way into the frame, clamoring to have their deeds recorded.

Picturing the Riot

Even though business and political leaders knew well who had started the trouble and people easily recognized neighbors and friends among their number, most of the mob remained officially "unknown." Sympathetic police, moreover, "either failed to record the names of arrestees or later destroyed arrest records" of whites detained in the riot.[40] Mayor Mollman's secretary, Maurice Ahearn, further assured this official "anonymity" by ordering police and guardsmen to arrest anyone with a camera. Still, there were many photographs, and even newsreels taken of the riot and its aftermath.[41] While the newsreels were banned in East St. Louis and nearby Belleville, they were shown elsewhere in the nation and remained in circulation until at least the 1930s, when professors of sociology at Columbia and the University of Michigan conducted a study in which students were shown a film of the riots and given a survey asking them to rate their "sympathetic reaction" to the victims.[42] People throughout the country were therefore able to see images of the mob and of the riot's aftermath on the screen, in newspapers, and in national periodicals.[43]

The ambiguity of photographic evidence makes the context in which it is placed crucial to interpretation. As John Berger explains, "In the relation between a photograph and words, . . . the photograph, irrefutable as evidence but weak in meaning, is given a meaning by the words. And the words, which by themselves remain at the level of generalization, are given specific authenticity by the irrefutability of the photograph. Together the two of them become very powerful; an open question appears to have been answered."[44] *The Independent* of July 14, 1917, for instance, portrayed the riot as a regrettable response to an influx of "several hundred thousand negroes from southern plantations" to the urban north, with East St. Louis receiving "more than its share." In a section entitled "The Story of the Week," readers learned that after "a mob of armed negroes" started the fighting, "in retaliation the white men of the city slums resolved to wipe out the negro quarter." The story is illustrated by a photograph of white men running past a building's smoking remains. Its caption reads: "Twenty-five negroes were killed and a large section of the black quarters wiped out by fire in the three-day massacre. The chief incentive seems to have been labor rivalry rather than race hatred." Readers are therefore instructed not to believe what might seem evident before their eyes; these white men rioting through a devastated Black neighborhood represent a labor disturbance gone wrong rather than a largescale lynching party. The term "black quarters," moreover, recalls the spatial layout of a southern plantation and reinforces the idea of white men's right to take control of this space.

The Crisis coverage of East St. Louis, on the other hand, reframed the news photographs it published to emphasize Black subjectivity in the midst of the horrendous violence. "The Massacre of East St. Louis" devotes 9 of 19 pages to photographs, including 1 composite of 6 images of survivors and the militia. DuBois chose their placement and sequence carefully in relation to the text, which is organized by three consecutive kinds of testimony: white newspaper accounts; testimony gathered by Martha Gruening from white participants and eyewitnesses as well as Black survivors; and, finally, page after page of reproductions of transcripts of survivor testimony taken by an NAACP investigative team consisting of DuBois, Gruening, 5 paid employees and 25 volunteers from African American organizations in St. Louis. In the first section, DuBois weaves together different stories and versions of the riot from white reporters, juxtaposing them with photographs from the St. Louis papers.

A photograph from the *St. Louis Star,* captioned "The Fire" (see Figure 6.4), is taken from a vantage point near a bridge on the Missouri side, showing a distant landscape alight, sky filled with flames and smoke. On the facing page are graphic and disturbing accounts from eyewitnesses caught in the middle of the mayhem on the other side; accounts underscoring that "the violence was not confined only to men. Women were, in many cases, the aggressors and always ready to abet." DuBois cites a *Globe-Democrat* story of a woman who "wanted to 'cut the heart out' of a Negro, a man already paralyzed from a bullet wound, who was being then maltreated at the hands of a mob." Their stockings soaked in blood, young girls were described kicking dead men's faces in. Other reports told of white women attacking African American women with their fists, stones, brooms, and sticks. The *Post-Dispatch* reporter Carlos Hurd told of seeing "one of these furies fling herself at a militiaman who was trying to protect

Figure 6.4 "The Fire" as seen across the river from St. Louis *(St. Louis Star)*

a Negress, and wrestle with him for his bayoneted gun while other women attacked the refugee."[45]

Nationally famous for his scoop interview of *Titanic* survivors on the rescue ship *Carpathia*, Hurd was trapped in the riot for two hours, never getting further than a couple of blocks from where he had initially stepped off a trolley car downtown. Although he had covered "natural disasters, murder, major fires, and bitter labor battles," what Hurd saw in East St. Louis left him deeply traumatized.[46] Most disturbing was the lynching of an African American man whose head had been "laid open by a great stone cut." After dragging him to the end of an alley on Fourth Street, the mob tried to hang him from a cable box on a telephone pole. At this point, the rope broke, causing the man and his would-be lyncher to fall to the pavement. An old white man, wearing what appeared to be a street conductor's cap, rushed out of his home to try to stop them, but was "pushed angrily away." (This was one of the few instances of white people actually trying to intervene in the violence.) What happened next Hurd calls "the most sickening incident" he ever saw as one of the lynchers put his fingers inside the man's skull to lift him from the ground. A central problem when publicizing lynchings and race riots is the danger of reproducing their spectacular thrill. Newspaper accounts in many instances were little better than pornography, titillating readers with shocking details of bloody crimes. DuBois, therefore, repeatedly asserts his editorial authority, justifying the inclusion of sympathetic reports like Hurd's: "These accounts make gruesome reading, but they are all true."[47] Just as in the Waco Horror, the images in this photo-essay move increasingly closer in focus as the story unfolds.

The next set of pages features an image (see Figure 6.5) from the *St. Louis Globe-Democrat* of the gutted remains of the Broadway Opera House juxtaposed with newspaper accounts of white mobs setting fire to buildings and dancing diabolically in the light of the flames as they shoot and torture African Americans trying to escape. We learn that "many Negroes were burned to death in the Broadway Opera House, an abandoned theatre structure. Bystanders claimed to have seen men, women, and children seek refuge in the basement of the buildings."[48] The photograph shows men and women standing along the sidewalk, surveying what is most likely a mass grave. Their presence gives a sense of the human scale of the devastation and reminds us of our own voyeuristic position. The streetcar tracks stretching down the middle of the street and out the edge of the frame, the telegraph poles and streetlights, and the tram wires

Figure 6.5 Broadway Opera House after the fire. $700.000 damage was done in this vicinity *(St. Louis Globe-Democrat)*

stretching high over the heads of the onlookers indicate that this carnage happened in a northern industrial city, with ordinary features of the urban landscape transformed into sites of lynching and terror.

The Landscape of Death

Among the most compelling testimonies Gruening and DuBois heard was that of Mrs. Luella Cox, a white member of the St. Louis Volunteers who had been in East St. Louis on business when the riots broke out. Realizing that something terrible was about to happen, she "tried to persuade some of the colored families living in what afterwards became the burned district to flee." Afraid to go out into the streets, they "remained hidden in their houses with what results one can only shudderingly surmise," report DuBois and Gruening. The terrible sights related by Mrs. Cox include the beheading of an African American with a butcher's knife "by someone in a crowd standing near the Free Bridge." Members of the crowd then "laughingly threw the head over one side of the bridge and the body over the other." Mrs. Cox described a crowd forcing the occupants of a trolley car to put their hands out the window; then, hauling African Americans thus identified "out of the car to be beaten, trampled on, shot. A little 12-year-old colored girl fainted—her mother knelt beside her. The crowd surged in on her. When its ranks opened again, Mrs. Cox saw the mother prostrate with a hole as large as one's fist in her head." When the fires started, Mrs. Cox saw a "baby snatched from its mother's arms and thrown into the flames, to be followed afterwards by the mother."[49]

The veracity of Cox's testimony is corroborated by an African American woman who runs up and exclaims "There's the lady that saved me!" as Cox speaks to DuBois and Gruening. At the time of the riot, Gruening and Helen Boardman were compiling evidence that would be published in the NAACP's *Thirty Years of Lynching in the United States, 1889–1918*. A section titled "The Story of One Hundred Lynchings" included the deaths of eleven women, four of whom were pregnant. While these incidents may have been chosen for their shock value in a publication designed to galvanize support to end these terrible crimes, their inclusion may also reflect Gruening's own anxieties over the safety of her adopted son. What were the thoughts of this Jewish mother of a Black male child as she heard of the atrocities committed against other Black children? Perhaps what she heard in East St. Louis prompted her to open an interracial libertarian school in the upstate home she shared with Boardman, and when that failed in 1923, to move abroad and place

Figure 6.6 Looking for the bodies of victims. Six were found here *(St. Louis Star)*

David in a German boarding school, returning only when he had safely reached adulthood.[50]

Luella Cox's horrible revelations of murder and infanticide appear next to an image from the *St. Louis Star* captioned "Looking for Bodies of Victims. Six Were Found Here" (see Figure 6.6).

The photograph shows a pile of ash and rubble below street-level, in which only a few objects such as iron bed frames and other twisted metal can be distinguished. One of the families too afraid to leave may have hidden in the home that once stood here. A group of men and women that may include survivors and relatives, as well as rescue workers, stands around, looking down at the ground, but not actively digging in the rubble. Up on the street, men seem to be hauling something away on a cart. Other people have turned away and are leaving in the opposite direction, as if all the bodies that are going to be found have been found. As with the onlookers at the Broadway Opera House, there seems little left to do here but stand and ponder the landscape of death.

Visualizing the "Psychology of the Quarry": Stories of Survival

The third section of the photo-essay moves from white eyewitness accounts to the testimony of survivors, which takes up nearly half the printed pages of the text. The authors carefully differentiate this testimony from the catalogue of atrocities in the newspaper reports:

> This recital deals only with facts. But stop and picture for a moment Mrs. Cox's day and the memories which must haunt her and all others who spent those awful hours in St. Louis.
>
> First the mob, always a frightful thing—lowering in dense cowardly ranks through the streets. Then the fleeing Negroes, hunted, despairing. A hoarse, sullen, cry, "Get the nigger!" A shower of bricks and stones. The flash of meat-cleavers and pickaxes. The merciless flames. And everywhere bodies, blood, hate and terrible levity.
>
> All our hunting songs and descriptions deal with the glory of the chase as seen and felt by the hunters. No one has visualized the psychology of the quarry, the driven hunted things. The Negroes of East St. Louis have in their statements supplied the lack.[51]

Reporter Carlos Hurd witnessed events as terrible as Luella Cox did, and his coverage was widely quoted, yet the authors chose a female perspective to elicit their readers' empathy. Having established this identification, the text moves in vivid language from white Luella Cox's traumatized memory to the sense impressions of the riot's terrified victims. This new perspective demands a changed rhetorical strategy, one posttraumatic in form: "The following accounts are published in the somewhat disjointed fashion in which they were necessarily collected by investigators. No interpolation whatever is added to detract from their sympathy." The investigator's notes reproduce the telegraphic urgency of the fleeing, panicking victim's sensations. Consider a few lines from Mary Edwards' account, which goes on like this for almost an entire page:

> East end of Library flats caught and heat was so great that father and daughter tried to escape through alley and up street to Broadway but encountered mob at Broadway. Soldiers were in line-up on north side of street and offered no assistance. Ran across street to Westbrook's home with bullets flying all around them and rioters shouting, "Kill him, kill him." Here daughter lost track of father. She beat on back door of Westbrook's home but no response, ran across alley to Division avenue, ran on white lady's porch, but the lady would not let her in. Men were shooting at her for all they were worth, but she succeeded in dodging bullets. Ran across field and got in house and crawled under bed. Mob following right behind her, but lost sight of which house she went in and set fire to each end of flat. Rather than be burned to death she ran out and the mob began shooting at her again. Just at that time a man ran out of the house, and mob let girl alone and started at him. She fell in weeds and lay very quiet. Could see them beating man.[52]

Figure 6.7 Colored man in front of car, being mobbed. Militia looking on (International Film Service)

Facing this testimony, a photograph shows a streetcar attack (see Figure 6.7), the caption reading: "COLORED MAN, IN FRONT OF CAR, BEING MOBBED, MILITIA LOOKING ON." Members of the militia stand with their guns against their shoulders, some in a very relaxed stance, with one knee bent, weight shifted to the hip, watching the violence unfold as if at a sporting event.

The victim, set upon by the crowd with no one to help him and nowhere to escape, is as isolated a figure as the injured man in the first photograph. Credited to *International Film Service,* which produced animation shorts for newsreels, this may be a still from a film of the riot.[53] It is the only shot of the mob in action, and its placement, roughly in the middle of the photo-essay, visually marks the divide between destruction and survival.

Picturing Survival

Turning the page from this snapshot of a murder in progress, the reader finds a composite image made up of six photographs: two close-ups of injured men in wheelchairs; two of groups of survivors milling around in St. Louis; and two of the militia who have finally restored "order" to the city. The facing page is taken up with survivor testimony, harrowing tales that nevertheless include rescue, escape, and endurance (see Figure 6.8).

Figure 6.8 Composite image featuring six photographs of the riot's aftermath

In the next set of pages, the survivor testimony faces an image (see Figure 6.9) from the *St. Louis Star* captioned "At the Municipal Lodging House, St. Louis, Mo."

The clearly posed image features African American bodies on display as objects of charity. Positioned in a semicircle, one group on benches or on their knees, the others standing behind them, these anonymous men and women are arranged to make a visual statement of Black bodies under discipline and control—and of order restored. Each holds a piece of bread or a cup in their hands. Two men in front of the basket are kneeling with their backs to the camera, taking pieces of food and holding them up to their mouths. Most of their eyes do not meet the camera.

Figure 6.9 At the Municipal Lodging House, St. Louis, MO *(St. Louis Star)*

Taken from its original context in the *St. Louis Star,* the photograph here is placed next to graphic and heartbreaking testimony that reminds us of the chaotic events that drove these people to seek shelter at the Lodging House. Survivors describe hiding in terror from the mob, being refused shelter by white neighbors, frantically trying to rescue their children, and watching family members die. The transcription of the survivors' testimony produces a rupture in DuBois and Gruening's commentary, acknowledging the inability of language to contain atrocity. After telling of a man shot in the back by a white friend with whom he was walking down the street, the text merely notes: "Comments are needless." The addition of photographs of survivors marks this shift from textual to visual commentary. As the bodies of the victims come more closely into view, their words speak for themselves, with only a terse and formulaic introduction: "The testimony of . . . "

"Comments are Needless": Portraits of Survivors

Photographic coverage in "Massacre" culminates in two full-page female portraits—a young amputee named Mineola McGee and an elderly burn victim named Narcis Gurley (see Figures 6.10 and 6.11).[54]

McGee, a chambermaid employed at $3.50 per week, had been in East St. Louis for 5 months when the riot broke out. The day after the riot,

Figure 6.10 Mineola McGee. Shot by soldier and policeman. Her arm had to be amputated

McGee remembered, "between seven and eight o'clock, as I was on my way to work (at Mrs. Gray's) I was shot in the arm, as I was about to enter the door. The only men whom I saw were a soldier and policeman, and I think I was shot by one of the two."

McGee fainted when she was shot, recovering consciousness in the patrol wagon on the way to the hospital, where surgeons amputated the part of her arm that had not been blown away. At the time of her interview, she had no insurance to pay the hospital bill and had not been able to find her aunt and uncle and several cousins.[55] A full-page portrait of McGee faces her testimony. Posed against a white backdrop (possibly the hospital wall), she looks directly into the camera. One hand rests on her nightdress; a bandage can be seen around her neck, stretching to her shoulder, which is heavily wrapped and elevated. Beneath this shoulder

Figure 6.11 Narcis Gurley. 71 next birthday. Lived in her home 30 years. Afraid to come out until the blazing walls fell in

dangles an empty sleeve. The caption reads: "Mineola McGee. Shot by soldier and policeman. Her arm had to be amputated." Her expression is somber; her eyes, piercing. Photographed from below, the portrait emphasizes the girl's quiet dignity and strength.

Directly beneath the McGee testimony appears the story of Narcis Gurley, who "had lived 71 years to come at last to this." A resident of East St. Louis for 30 years, Gurley earned her living by keeping roomers and doing laundry. She told Gruening:

> Between five and six o'clock we noticed a house nearby burning and heard the men outside. We were afraid to come outside and remained in the house, which caught fire from the other house. When the house began falling in, we ran out, terribly burned, and one white man said, "Let those old women alone." We were allowed to escape. Lost everything, clothing, and household goods."[56]

The text directs the reader to see Gurley's portrait on the following page, forcing the reader to turn from one portrait to the other as she reads, thereby reinforcing the connection between these two female survivors. Gurley's three-quarter length portrait, also taken slightly from below, shows her sitting against the same white backdrop, her arms loosely crossed to show the horrible burns covering them from wrist to elbow. She wears a housedress and headscarf; there are earrings in her ears and a ring can be seen on one burned hand. Like McGee, she looks directly into the camera. The portrait emphasizes Narcis Gurley's dignity, but her eyes are full of pain.

There is no known record of who took these portraits which are unique in the photographic record of the East St. Louis massacre. Was there an African American portrait photographer in the group of 30 who assisted DuBois and Gruening? Among all the photographs introduced as evidence before Congress, there are none of survivors, though there are images of the mob in action and dozens (some taken by white studio photographers) documenting the riot's aftermath through block after block of empty, destroyed property. The portraits of McGee and Gurley figure the riot's cost in human rather than monetary terms, their monumental scale in relation to the other images in the essay emphasizing the importance of physical presence, enabling them to stand in for other bodies that have been destroyed or disappeared.

We know from Gruening's article in *Pearson's* that the NAACP had access to images of the riot DuBois chose not to use, including one showing policemen keeping the mob away from a dead body lying on the pavement. In emphasizing the bodies of survivors rather than of the dead, it is, moreover, the female body to which the text directs our gaze. "Massacre" features two other close-up views of injured survivors, again a pairing of young and old. In the composite photograph on page 230 appear two men in wheelchairs with the captions "Frank Smith, burned" and "Amos Davis, 84, shot" (Figure 6.8). The scale of these images (each occupies one-eighth of the page) and their inclusion in a grid with photographs of displaced people in the St. Louis streets, and of militia camping in and standing guard over the deserted riot area, emphasizes their evidentiary over their communicative value. The placement of Frank Smith's testimony on the same page as Mineola McGee's (with four pages and two photos between his image and his words) also indicates its importance, primarily as an illustration of the larger story of the riot.

There is no testimony from Amos Davis, who would die from his wounds a few weeks after the riot.[57] In each of the photographs, which are shot from below, the men are propped up in wheelchairs placed against a brick wall, possibly in the courtyard of the hospital. Twenty-five year resident Frank Smith, who was "frightfully burned" because he "waited until the last possible moment" to flee from his blazing house into a gun-wielding mob, lies back with his eyes closed, his head inclined slightly toward the camera. Bulky bandages swaddle both arms as they rest on the arms of the chair. The cropping of the image just beneath draws maximum attention to his wounded limbs. Similarly positioned in his chair, Amos Davis turns his head to face the camera, as if responding to a photographer's command. Even in an image of reduced size, pain and suffering are etched upon his face.

Why were the portraits of the wounded women rather than of these men chosen to illustrate the riot's human toll? Photography historian Graham Clarke defines the portrait as "a sign whose purpose is both the description of an individual and the inscription of social identity."[58] In the early part of the twentieth century, Black women, in particular, used "self-consciously constructed photographs to promote themselves—in their business and their social and civic activities." The pages of *The Crisis* were filled with portraits of prominent African American women and men, often including women's images in the section praising the "Men of the Month." If such portraits represented "an important political force," with the photographic image "a vehicle" for exhibiting black women's "collective power," what do these portraits of an injured chambermaid and laundress represent? African American leaders called for a collective response to the East St. Louis massacre, one that subjugated differences in class and political beliefs to the claims of race. Yet this collective response maintained a pronounced emphasis on gender difference.

These women workers whose wounds render them unfit to labor are surrounded by none of the traditional props of portraiture, yet the dignified poses construct them as subjects in their own right, possessed by] a painful knowledge that both corroborates and exceeds the testimony surrounding them.[59] What they have seen and endured is written on their bodies, which thus figure as composite texts, fusing determination and pride with searing memories of harm. DuBois asked readers to picture the riot through a witness' eyes and imagine the hunted victim's terror. As Susie Linfield has observed, "the very specificity of the photograph is also one of its great strengths. Photographs—especially portraits, though not only they—demand that we encounter the individual *qua* individual. . . . This encounter is not a form of sentimentality but, on the contrary, a rigorous challenge."[60] The photographer's focus on the steady eyes of the women prompts an identification between viewer and subject, thereby implicating us in the act of witnessing. The moment our eyes encounter theirs, the distance imposed by media representations and stereotypes of race and class collapses.

Why does the sequence of images end with the injured body of Narcis Gurley? In the days before the Civil War, abolitionists circulated copies of a portrait of "Gordon," also known as "The Scourged Back." Taken by the Matthew Brady studio and frequently reproduced by commercial photographers as *cartes des visites*, in the photograph, a man exhibits the scars of a terrible beating on his back, his "partially nude body" making "visible the memory of frequent bloody whippings, which caused the formation of thick-skinned (keloid) scars on his back."[61] Captured by the camera, Gordon's body becomes a text proving white depravity, and circulates to bring political change and end suffering. In this famous photograph, Gordon sits with his back to the camera, his head turned in profile, his hand resting lightly on his hip. This terrible wounding written on his body was used to exhibit the horrors of enslavement. In the same way, the wounds written on Narcis Gurley's body, the pain in her eyes, provide bodily testimony of the workings of mob violence.

In the years immediately before, during, and after the World War I, the African American family found itself under terrible siege, in the North as well as the South, and the East St. Louis riot had particular repercussions for women and children, who were targets on a massive scale. DuBois and Gruening's text reinforces this message as the last two verbal images presented to the reader are of old women left homeless by the violence. A quote from the *St. Louis Star* describes an old Black woman passing the police station, "carrying in her arms all that mob spirit and fire had left of her belongings. They consisted of a worn pair of shoes—she was barefooted—an extra calico dress, an old shawl and two puppies. Tears were streaming down her face and she saw neither soldiers nor her enemies as she passed beneath the lights of the City Hall going she knew not where." The last scene, "saddest of all," is Gruening's account of an old woman she saw "poking about in the desolate ruins of what had once been her home . . . not a fraction of their possessions remained." At 65, the woman cannot begin to fathom how to begin anew. " 'What are we to do?' she asked Miss Gruening. 'We can't live South and they don't want us North. Where are we to go?' "[62]

As for white East St. Louis, Gruening found the city "unrepentant, surly, a little afraid that her shame may hurt her business, but her head is not bowed." The aftermath of East St. Louis, which writer Jessie Fauset compared to the Turkish slaughter of Armenians, Russian pogroms, and Belgian atrocities in the Congo, left American Negroes "fatalists" who could "no longer expect any miraculous intervention from Providence."[63]

Amidst the devastation, African Americans in St. Louis and throughout the nation formed a network to help the survivors face the material and legal challenges before them. Both Gurley and McGee would sue the city for damages under an Illinois law that allowed victims of mob violence to collect from the municipality where they were injured. McGee also received $2,500 damages from the State of Illinois in a 1921 settlement.[64] In the thousands of pages of transcripts from the House Select Committee hearings on the riots, Mineola McGee is the only African American woman to give testimony. In a published report marked by its racism (the opening paragraphs appear to place blame for the riot at least in part on the "swarms" of Negroes entering the city) and filled with lurid accounts of white slavery, gang rape, prostitution and even necrophilia, the committee seems to have been genuinely moved by McGee's presence, calling attention to this unpunished attack by soldiers against a defenseless and innocent girl four times in their lengthy report.[65] Their outrage and sympathy for McGee did not, however, prevent them from rendering her testimony, which appears in standard English in the transcript of the hearing, as an unpronounceable minstrel show dialect.

Silent Protest Parade

On July 28, 1917, 10,000 African American children, women, and men streamed down New York's Fifth Avenue in complete silence, except for the sound of muffled drums. To help spectators make meaning of their presence, they carried signs appealing to President Wilson to address lynching, mob violence, segregation and disenfranchisement. Signs carried by children dressed in white asked "Mother, Do Lynchers Go to Heaven?" Others read "Pray for the Lady Macbeths of East St. Louis" and "Give Us a Chance to Live." Other signs reminded spectators of African American accomplishments, citing the numbers of African American doctors, lawyers, millionaires, and Ph.Ds. Several boasted of the long record of African American military service, including one that read "We have fought for the liberty of white Americans in 6 wars; our reward is East St. Louis."

The Silent Protest Parade was "the march of a whole community in the public space."[66] A flyer dated July 24, 1917, addressed to "The People of African Descent", dictated the Order of the March: "The children will lead the parade, followed by the Women in white, while the Men will bring up the rear." Organizers decreed that "the laborer, the professional man—all classes of the Race . . . the native born, the foreign born, united by ties of blood and color" would all march together on foot. "We march," the flyer proclaimed, "because the growing consciousness and solidarity of race coupled with sorrow and discrimination have made us one."[67]

Spectacles of white supremacy, from race riots to lynchings, to segregation signs, were meant to visually reaffirm white ownership and control over space. The Silent Protest Parade staged a counterspectacle of waves upon waves of African Americans proclaiming, in collective dignity, their right to public space; the power over their own bodies; and the final say in their own representation. As an editorial in the *Washington Bee* declared: "it was not alone on Fifth Avenue that they marched, to be seen by the crowds that happened to be on that thoroughfare," but "thanks to the press and the news service they marched throughout the country in the imaginations of millions of people."[68]

The September 1917 *Crisis* report on "The Silent Protest Parade" reproduced a number of press clippings, a list of every sign carried by the marchers, and a two-page photographic spread of the parade. Although these images are often reproduced, they are almost never considered in the context of the other images commemorating the events in East St. Louis, which appear in the same issue.

By reading them together, however, we restore the context in which these images of affirmation were seen by thousands of people who were so recently traumatized by news of the riots. C.T. Adam's photograph (see Figure 6.12), which appears on page 242 and is captioned "The Negro Silent Parade, at Forty Second Street and Fifth Avenue, New York City," offers an uncanny visual antithesis of the image seen earlier of the "Colored Man, In Front of Car, Being Mobbed, Militia Looking On" (Figure 6.7).

The Adams photograph features rows of women in white, marching in orderly progression, American flags fluttering overhead. A crowd gathers respectfully to view Black women dressed in white, stretched as far as the eye can see, claiming ownership of the most symbolically important street in the country. In the left-hand corner of the photograph, a streetcar has halted in its path on 42nd Street to allow them to pass.

The space on the facing page is divided into two photographs by unknown photographers working for Underwood and Underwood, a pioneering agency in news bureau photography (see Figure 6.13). The top photograph features a close-up of rows and rows of little girls

Figure 6.12 The Negro Silent Parade, at Forty Second Street and Fifth Avenue, New York City (C.T. Adams)

in white, holding hands in perfect formation and watched over by women who call out encouragement alongside. The image beneath is that often-reproduced photograph of African American dignitaries leading the parade, women and children streaming behind. This image offers a powerful visual corrective to the earlier photograph of men standing impotently in the ash and rubble of a ruined African American home: here, the men have been restored to their proper position in the gender hierarchy. The children are safe and nurtured in this northern urban space, their bodies spilling beyond the frame with the promise of the future. Appearing as the final image of the parade, this photograph underlines the men's leadership position in the march.

Yet what is remarkable about *The Crisis* coverage of the parade is these are the only men who appear: all the other photographs feature women and children. There certainly were other photographs of the parade, including the one that caught Angela Davis' attention in the "Harlem on My Mind" exhibition. In that photograph, groups of silent men in dark suits fill Fifth Avenue in orderly horizontal lines, flowing behind men carrying a banner upon which are inscribed the opening words of the Declaration of Independence, proclaiming that all men are created equal (with instructions to "those of African descent" to "tear off" that corner of the document). In front of them, men beat drums to command the

Figure 6.13 The Negro Silent Parade, Fifth Avenue, New York City (Underwood and Underwood)

attention of the crowd, which also seems to be made up mostly of men. In the exhibition and accompanying catalogue, the image is placed in context with photographs of the 369th Infantry Regiment, the "Harlem Hell Fighters," marching first in France and then triumphantly through the streets of New York. Alan Schoener, the white curator of this highly controversial exhibition, identified his task as proving the social and cultural viability of the Black community, with its "continuing leadership tradition." This visual celebration of masculine militancy therefore owes as much to Schoener's understanding of Black nationalism and identity in 1968 as it does to the history of the Civil Rights Movement in the Jazz Age.[69] DuBois' decision to foreground the bodies of women and children, however, reveals the extent to which the riot was perceived in 1917 as an assault against the family that demanded a specifically gendered response. Like the reports of Queen and Wells-Barnett, *The Crisis* coverage foregrounds the bodies of women as victims, survivors, and militants.

Photo-historian Marita Sturken defines memory as "crucial to the understanding of a culture because it indicates collective desires, needs and self-definition." What gets to count as knowledge of the past is always necessarily a political decision based on present needs and desires. Yet as opposed to disavowal or " 'organized forgetting,' . . . cultures can also participate in a 'strategic' forgetting of painful events that may be too dangerous to keep in active memory."[70] What happened in East St. Louis sent a message to African Americans that their lives and their children's lives would not be safe anywhere in the country. Harlem Renaissance aesthetics, particularly in literature and art by women, reverberates with this terrible knowledge.[71] The photographs in "The Massacre of East St. Louis," retaining their power to wound to this day, offered a measure of catharsis while holding dangerous memories for a community struggling to find a way to go on.

It makes sense, therefore, that images of the parade rather than of mutilated female victims survived in the public memory of this event. The reemergence of the corpus of lynching photography, however, demands that we search the archive for images that document white violence from a Black perspective, and ask what they have to tell us. Through their visualization of Black female bodies, as both victims and survivors of violence and as rightful inhabitants of public space, these images help to recover African American women's history that has been obscured and exemplify a history of resistance in Black visual culture that has yet to be fully explored.

Notes

1. Testimony of Hon. William A. Rodenberg, Committee on Rules, House of Representatives, *Riot at East St. Louis, Ill., July 2, 1917,* Washington, D.C., Aug. 3, 1917, 11.

2. See, e.g., Carlos Hurd, "Post-Dispatch Man, An Eye-Witness Describes Massacre of Negroes: Victims Driven from Home by Fire, Stoned, Beaten, and Hanged While Dying, Women Fight Militiamen and Assist in Work," *St. Louis Post-Dispatch,* July 3, 1917, 1; "Man-Hunting Mobs Burn Homes and Slay Fleeing Blacks by Bullet and Rope: Women and Children Join in Blood Orgy as Flames Spread," *St. Louis Globe-Democrat,* July 3, 1917, 1–2, 5; "Mob Burns and Kills; Shoots Negroes as They Flee Homes, Dead in ESL Set at From 15–250, Many Killed and Wounded in All Day Disorders, White Women Help Beat Negresses," *Boston Daily Globe,* July 3, 1917, 1; and "Negro Massacre by Mobs, Rifles and Torch Used in ESL Riots, Dead May Number 75, Women and Girls Aid 'Lynchers,' " *Chicago Daily Tribune,* July 3, 1917, 1.
3. W.E.B. DuBois, *Dusk of Dawn* (Millwood, NY: Kraus-Thomson, 1975), 252.
4. See Martha Gruening, "Democratic Massacres in East St. Louis," *Pearson's Magazine,* 38 (September 1917): 106–108. See also Eliot M. Rudwick, *Race Riot at East St. Louis, July 2, 1917* (Champaign: U. of Illinois P, 1982); Malcolm McLaughlin, *Power, Community, and Racial Killing in East St. Louis* (New York: Palgrave/MacMillan, 2005); and Charles Lumpkins, *American Pogrom: The East St. Louis Riot and Black Politics* (Athens: Ohio UP, 2008).
5. On the wartime celebration of white female purity and motherhood, see Jane Marcus, "Corps/Corpus/Corpse," afterword to *Not So Quite . . .* (New York: Feminist Press, 1989), 241–93; Nancy Huston, "The Matrix of War" in *The Female Body in Western Culture,* ed. Susan Suleiman (Cambridge: Harvard UP, 1986).

   The NAACP's Anti-Lynching Committee's declaration following the riot that "by lynching is understood not only the illegal killing of an accused person but also the killing of unaccused persons by mob violence" signaled a chilling increase in the scope of white terror. Minutes. Anti-Lynching Committee Meeting. Nov. 24, 1917. W.E.B. DuBois Papers. Special Collections and University Archives. University of Massachusetts. 11–10–72.
6. Philip Dray, *At the Hands of Persons Unknown: The Lynching of Black America* (New York: Random House, 2002), 215–252; Herbert Shapiro, *White Violence and Black Response: From Reconstruction to Montgomery* (Amherst: University of Massachusetts Press, 1988), 145–160.
7. Holloway, Karla. *Passed On: African American Mourning Stories: A Memorial* (Durham: Duke UP, 2003).

   Also see my use of this image to illustrate a discussion of Lola Ridge's poem "Lullaby," describing white women throwing infants into the flames. Rice, Anne, ed. *Witnessing Lynching: American Writers Respond* (New Brunswick: Rutgers UP, 2003).
8. Avis Thomas-Lester, "A Senate Apology for History on Lynching: Vote Condemns Past Failure to Act," *Washington Post,* June 14, 2005: A12.

Four years later, the Senate apologized for slavery. Krissah Thompson. "Senate Backs Apology for Slavery: Resolution Specifies That it Cannot Be Used in Reparation Cases," *Washington Post,* June 19, 2009.

9. See, e.g., Amy Louise Wood, *Lynching and Spectacle: Witnessing Racial Violence in America, 1890–1940* (Chapel Hill: UP of North Carolina P, 2009); Dora Apel and Shawn Michelle Smith, *Lynching Photographs* (Berkeley, CA: U of California P, 2008); Jacqueline Goldsby, *A Spectacular Secret: Lynching in American Life and Literature* (Chicago: U of Chicago P: 2006); Shawn Michelle Smith, *Photography on the Color Line: WEB DuBois, Race, and Visual Culture* (Durham: Duke UP, 2004); and Dora Apel, *Imagery of Lynching: Black Men, White Women and the Mob* (New Brunswick, NJ: Rutgers UP, 2004).
10. Testimony of Thomas J. Canavan, *Select Committee to Investigate Conditions in Illinois and Missouri Interfering with Interstate between these States.* Transcripts in Microfilm Collection, *The East St. Louis Race Riot of 1917* (Frederick, MD: U Publications of America, 1985), 1424–48; Ida B. Wells-Barnett, *The East St. Louis Massacre: The Greatest Outrage of the Century* (Chicago: The Negro Fellowship Herald Press, 1917), 7. See also Malcolm McLaughlin, "Women in the Crowd: Gender and the East St. Louis Race Riot of 1917," *Studies in the Literary Imagination,* 40.2 (Fall 2007): 49–73.
11. Alfreda M. Duster, ed., *Crusade for Justice: The Autobiography of Ida B. Wells* (Chicago: U of Chicago P, 1970), 384.
12. Harper Barnes, *Never Been a Time: The 1917 Race Riot that Sparked the Civil Rights Movement* (New York: Walker and Co., 2008), 177.
13. See, e.g., Jessie Fauset, "A Negro on East St. Louis," *The Survey* (August 18, 1917), 448; Carrie Williams Clifford, "Race Hate" and "The Silent Protest Parade" in *The Widening Light* (Boston, MA: Walter Reid, 1922), 15–16; and Alice Dunbar Nelson's "Mine Eyes Have Seen," *Crisis* 15 (1918): 271–275 (Ostensibly a recruitment drama, Dunbar Nelson's one-act play reverberates with traumatic echoes of East St. Louis in its nearly obsessive focus on atrocities against women and children). Meta Vaux Warrick Fuller's choice to title her 1919 statue of a woman clutching her stomach protectively as figures swirl around her lower limbs, "Mary Turner: A Silent Protest Against an Angry Mob," connects the 1918 Georgia lynching of a pregnant woman and her child with the memory of the earlier assault against women and children. The lynching dramas and short stories of Angelina Weld Grimke portray characters living a nightmare of worsening race relations in the North that specifically target defenseless women and children. *Selected Works of Angelina Weld Grimke*, Ed. Carolivia Herron (New York: Oxford UP, 2006).
14. Dyer was so upset by the riot, he would go on to sponsor an anti-lynching measure, first introduced in 1918 and known as the Dyer Bill. Although the Dyer Bill passed the House of Representatives in January, 1922, a filibuster

later that year, organized by white Southern Democrats, killed its passage in the Senate.

15. Testimony of Nannie Burroughs, "Riot at East St. Louis, Ill, July 2, 1917." Head of the National Training School for Girls and Women (and often referred to as the female Booker T. Washington), Burroughs had helped found the National Association of Colored Women, which now boasted a membership of approximately 100,000 women, 6; *Committee on Rules,* House of Representatives, Washington, D.C. August 3, 1917, 18. See also Testimony of Hallie E. Queen, 21.
16. The Westbrook sisters would themselves return to East St. Louis to testify on behalf of Dr. Leroy Bundy, who was accused of masterminding the plot to kill the white detectives. Testimony in re: People vs. Leroy Bundy. Cora May Westbrook, Reel 8: 0374, 0391; Daisy Westbrook, Reel 8: 0381, 0391. Microfilm collection of *Select Committee to Investigate Conditions in Illinois and Missouri Interfering with Commerce between These States* (Frederick, MD: University Publications of America, 1985). Hallie E. Queen, "East St. Louis as I Saw It," Special Report to Laurence Y. Sherman, "East St. Louis Riot" file, Box 205, Lawrence Y. Sherman Papers, Illinois State Historical Society, Springfield.
17. African American women, declared DuBois, "are a group of workers, fighting for their daily bread like men; independent and approaching economic freedom! They furnished a million farm laborers, 80,000 farmers, 22,000 teachers, 600,000 servants and washerwomen, and 50,000 in trades and merchandizing." W.E.B. DuBois, "The Damnation of Women," *Darkwater: Voices Within the Veil* (Mineola, New York: Dover Publications, 1999), 104.
18. Lowden's warning came at a time when African Americans were under increasing scrutiny. Wells-Barnett's militant antiracism earned the suspicion of the Military Information Bureau, which compiled a thick file of her "incendiary" activities, including the entire East St. Louis pamphlet along with a note that said the pamphlet was being used to "stir up a great deal of interracial antagonism." Nannie Burroughs came under government scrutiny after "alarmed whites, in the days following the East St. Louis riot," construed early morning prayer meetings led by the deeply-religious Burroughs as "protest gatherings that might undermine the war effort." See Theodore Kornweibel, Jr., *Investigate Everything: Federal Efforts to Compel Black Loyalty During World War I* (Bloomington, IN: Indiana UP, 2002), 241.

    In her report, Hallie Queen reassures Sherman that "German agents had no more to do with the riot than American agents had to do with the German atrocities in Belgium or the Belgian atrocities in the African Congo." Queen correctly debunks the rumor of German propaganda as a cause for Negro unrest in East St. Louis, a rumor that had been circulating since Wilson's 1916 reelection campaign. But by August of 1917, the U.S. Army Military Intelligence Division (MID) had enlisted Queen to spy on the African

American community in Washington. While Queen did not report on either Wells-Barnett or Burroughs, she did so on numerous others. A'lelia Bundles speculates that Queen's presence at Madam C.J. Walker's Irvington, NY, Christmas party later in 1917 might have been for purposes of espionage. Having lived in St. Louis for 16 years when she was young, Walker was so moved by the stories of close friends there who had aided the riot victims that she began to work tirelessly for passage of antilynching legislation and likely viewed Queen's work in East St. Louis very favorably. Hallie Queen File on microfilm in RG 165, Records of the War Department and Special Staffs; Name Index to Correspondence of the Military Intelligence Division of the War Department Staff, 1917–1941, MII94. Barnes, *Never Been a Time*, 189; A'lelia Bundles, *On Her Own Ground: The Life and Times of Madam C.J. Walker* (New York: Scribners, 2001), 255.

19. Wells-Barnett, "The East St. Louis Massacre," 14.
20. Wife of the artist William McKnight Farrow and a nurse at Provident Hospital, Farrow accompanied Wells because she was eager to help and the Red Cross had told her they were not accepting Black nurses to aid riot victims. Mrs. Delores Johnson Farrow, "Side Lights or Shadows on the Recent Riots at East St. Louis, Illinois," *The Broad Ax*, July 28, 1917. Papers of Ida B. Wells Barnett. Series VIII, Box 8, Folder 10.
21. Although the files relating to the investigation have been lost, a memorandum from DuBois informs the AntiLynching Committee that he left New York on Sunday, July 8, and returned Wed., July 18th, having spent "seven actual working days in East St. Louis." Establishing an office at 2336 Market Street and in the Pythian Hall, Gruening and DuBois hired 5 workers and established a voluntary committee of 25. The team was thus able to collect "personal stories of one hundred fifty of the victims and date showing the circumstances of 1,500 other victims." NAACP Papers. Anti-Lynching File.
22. Martha Gruening, "Two Suffrage Movements," *Crisis* (September 1912), 245–247.
23. "Anarchists Plot Against U.S Army; Arrests for Treason Reach Thirteen," *The Washington Post,* June 3, 1917.
24. See Miriam Brody, "Introduction" in Emma Goldman, *Living My Life* (New York: Penguin, 2006), xxxv.
25. Emma Goldman and Alexander Berkman were tried in New York between June 27 and July 9, 1917, for conspiracy to violate the Selective Service Act. Found guilty, each was sentenced to 2 years in prison and fined $10,000, with their deportation recommended at the end of their term. Gruening's article, "Speaking of Democracy," deplored the "supreme and deadly cruelty of the white race asserting its superiority," which she linked to economic gain. "East St. Louis," Gruening charged, "is an example of that democracy we are to spread over the world.... That is why I want the world made

unsafe for it." Martha Gruening, "Speaking of Democracy," *Mother Earth,* 12.6 (August 1917). Reprinted in *Anarchy! An Anthology of Emma Goldman's* Mother Earth, Ed. Peter Glassgold, 400–404. The August 1917 issue was deemed unmailable by the U.S. Post Office and confiscated.

26. Investigators Mary Alden Hopkins and Martha Gruening belonged, with Ovington, to the New York City branch of the Women's Peace Party (NYC-WPP), the first feminist peace organization in U.S. history. The NYC-WPP, composed of young, educated, and radical women reformers, broke with the national organization over U.S. entry into the war. In the August 1917 issue of the branch's magazine, *Four Lights,* Ovington attacked President Wilson for his indifference to the atrocities in East St. Louis and denounced the participation of U.S. military troops in the riot. The NYC-WPP was "the only peace organization to make such charges." Kaleen L. Endres and Therese L. Lueck, *Women's Periodicals in the United States* (Santa Barbara: Greenwood P, 1995), 110–111.

    While generally praising DuBois as a pioneer in his support for women's rights, Black feminist scholars point out a discrepancy between his philosophy and his practice, particularly in his treatment of his own wife and daughter and in his failure to acknowledge Black women as influences on his intellectual thought and his activism. See Nellie McKay, "The Souls of Black Women Folk in the Writings of WEB DuBois" (1990); Beverley Guy-Sheftall, *Daughters of Sorrow: Attitudes Toward Black Women, 1880–1920* (New York: Carlson, 1990), 13, 161; Joy James, *Transcending the Talented Tenth: Black Leaders and American Intellectuals* (New York: Routledge), 1997; and Farrah Jasmine Griffin, "Black Feminists and DuBois: Respectability, Protection, and Beyond," *Annals of the American Academy of Political and Social Science,* Vol. 568. *The Study of African American Problems: W.E.B. DuBois's Agenda, Then and Now,* ed. Elijah Anderson and Tukufu Zuberi (Mar. 2000), 28–40. See also Garth E. Pauley, "W.E.B. DuBois on Women Suffrage: A Critical Analysis of his Crisis Writings," *Journal of Black Studies,* 30.3 (Jan. 2000), 383–410.

27. British-born Freeman had gone on hunger strike with Sylvia Pankhurst in England, and had been arrested with Upton Sinclair, protesting for miners' rights in front of the Rockefeller mansion. At the time of the lynching, the spirited feminist was on a speaking tour as a paid organizer for the Texas women's suffragist association. See Patricia Bernstein, *The First Waco Horror: The Lynching of Jesse Washington and the Rise of the NAACP* (College Station: Texas A & M U P, 2006).

28. Within a month of her investigation in East St. Louis, Gruening would travel to Houston, Texas, to report on a race riot there involving the all-Black Twenty-Fourth Infantry. Martha Gruening, "Houston: An NAACP Investigation," *Crisis* (November 1919), 14–19. Wells-Barnett would also report on the riot and its aftermath in the *Chicago Defender* (26 January 1918).

29. "Photographers Threatened," *St. Louis Globe-Democrat*, July 3, 1917 (in Tuskegee Institute Clippings File 6:1029). The Grand Jury indicted East St. Louis mayoral secretary Maurice Ahearn for conspiracy, "the specific charge against him being that the mayor used him to muzzle the cameras, and to order destroyed all photographs relative to the riots. The assistance he rendered the mob was valuable, and his only aim was to cripple the grand jury in its search for evidence." "Grand Jury Holds Him Responsible for the Riot," *Chicago Defender* (Sept. 15, 1917).
30. Recent scholarship has begun to refocus our understanding of DuBois as an activist with a highly sophisticated understanding of visual rhetoric. Deborah Willis, *A Small Nation of People: W.E.B. DuBois and African American Portraits of Progress* (Library of Congress, 2003), 51–52; Shawn Michele Smith, *Photography on the Color Line: W.E.B. DuBois, Race, and Visual Culture* (Durham, NC: Duke University Press, 2004).
31. Anne Elizabeth Carroll, *Word, Image and the New Negro: Representation and Identity in the Harlem Renaissance* (Bloomington, IN: Indiana University Press, 2007), 15.
32. Carroll, *Word, Image, and the New Negro*, 28.
33. "Such a spectacle in the public square of a town of over 35,000 inhabitants, a young boy condemned to death and then taken from the court room, affords one of the most spectacular grounds of attack on the whole institution ever presented," wrote Nash. He implored Freeman to get all the facts: "the crime in detail, who the boy was, and who his victim, the Judge and jury that tried the case, the court record, and the ghastly story of the burning." Bernstein, *The First Waco Horror*, 138.
34. The July issue, dedicated to education, provides an important example of a *Crisis* composite text, featuring on its front cover a photograph entitled "Up From Georgia," of six college graduates, thereby emphasizing that progress and uplift continued despite the violent onslaught against the race.
35. W.E.B. DuBois, *Dusk of Dawn* (Edison, NJ: Transaction Publishers, 230).
36. Martin Parr and Gerry Badger, *The Photo-Book: A History, Vol.* 1 (London: Phaidon, 2004), 7.
37. Jacqueline Goldsby, *A Spectacular Secret: Lynching in American Life and Literature* (Chicago: U of Chicago P, 2006), 231.
38. "Prizes," *Crisis* (September 1917), 215–216.
39. DuBois and Gruening, "Massacre," 220.
40. Lumpkins, *American Pogrom*, 115.
41. "Photographers Threatened," *St. Louis Globe and Dispatch*, July 3, 1917; Congressional Report: "When the newspapers were taking pictures of the mob, policemen charged them with their billies, broke their machines, destroyed the negatives and threatened them with arrest if any further attempt was made to photograph the rioters who were making the streets run red with blood." *East St. Louis Riots:*

Report of the Special Committee Authorized to Investigate the East St. Louis Riot. 65th Congress, 2nd Session. Doc. No. 1231 (July 15, 1918).

42. "Belleville Bars Riot Pictures," *East St. Louis Daily Journal,* July 10, 1917, 3; "Moving Pictures of Race Riot," *St. Louis Argus,* July 27, 1917, 1. Gardner Murphy and Rensis Likert, *Public Opinion and the Individual* (New York: Harper & Bros., 1938), 115. Students were shown a film of the aftermath of the riot (which the authors mistakenly identified as taking place in 1925), showing "the burning homes of Negroes, the trucks carrying them in large numbers away from the conflagration, and the Red Cross administering relief. The misery and terror of the Negroes were apparent, and the opportunity for sympathy was directly offered." A second film showed a lynch mob being repulsed by National Guardsmen at a Lexington, Kentucky, courthouse, with "the issue here being primarily the question whether the accused Negro in custody awaiting trial was to be the object of sympathy, or the members of the crowd." The third film in the survey showed fleet maneuvers meant to arouse "loyalty to the flag."
43. Photographs (possibly stills from a newsreel) credited to the International Film Service appeared in a section entitled "The Story of the Week" in the *Independent* (July 14, 1917, 52) and in the "Current Events" photographic section in the *Outlook* (vol. 116, 1917: 438).
44. John Berger, *Another Way of Telling* (New York: Vintage, 1995), 92.
45. DuBois and Gruening, "Massacre," 222.
46. Barnes, *Never Been a Time,* 140–41.
47. DuBois and Gruening, "Massacre," 222.
48. DuBois and Gruening, "Massacre," 224.
49. DuBois and Gruening, "Massacre," 226–227.
50. In his memoirs, the lawyer Charles Recht recalled that Gruening "devoted herself to the unique task of being a white mother to a very dark little boy in a city where prejudice was strong. After the war, to get him properly educated, she emigrated to France, and until her untimely death continued to be a steadfast advocate of Negro rights," quoted in Frances H. Early, *A World Without War: How U.S. Feminists and Pacifists Resisted World War I* (Syracuse: Syracuse University Press, 1997), 28.

    Gruening and David Butt lived abroad from 1923 to 1931, during which time David attended the Odenwald Schule in Germany while she worked as a freelance journalist. Upon their return to the U.S., David enrolled in City College. He died after a long illness in 1936. Gruening appears to have cooled her ties with the NAACP around the time of DuBois's departure. Gruening died from an aneurysm in 1937. Martha Gruening file, Smith College Alumnae Archives, Northampton, MA.

    Boardman undertook several lynching investigations for the NAACP in the 1920s and 1930s. In 1932, the NAACP sent Helen Boardman to investigate charges of peonage and abuse of Negro laborers in the construction of federal flood control along the Mississippi River. The NAACP sent her detailed report to the president, who turned it over to the Secretary of War. She also worked for the Federal Writers Project researching African American history, becoming embroiled with Claude McKay over her attempt to join the Negro Writers' Guild. Langston Hughes, *Collected Works,* Ed. Arnold Rampersad (Columbia: University of Missouri Press, 2001), 90; Helen Boardman, "The Rise of the Negro Historian," *The Negro History Bulletin,* No. 7 (April 1945), 152–153; and Tyrone Tillery, *Claude McKay: A Black Poet's Struggle for Identity* (Amherst: University of Massachusetts Press), 1992, 149.

51. DuBois and Gruening, "Massacre," 228.
52. DuBois and Gruening, "Massacre," 228.
53. A photograph in the "The Story of the Week" in the *Independent,* July 14, 1917, 52, showing men running through a burned-out landscape, seems also to be a frame taken from a film.
54. Gruening repeated these women's stories in other articles she wrote about the riot. Martha Gruening, "Speaking of Democracy," *Mother Earth,* 12.6 (August 1917). Reprinted in *Anarchy! An Anthology of Emma Goldman's* Mother Earth, Ed. Peter Glassgold, 400–404; Martha Gruening, "Democratic Massacres in East St. Louis," *Pearson's Magazine* 38 (Sept. 1917): 106–108.
55. McGee's congressional testimony indicates that she was subsequently reunited with her aunt and cousins.
56. DuBois and Gruening, "Massacre," 235.
57. "East St. Louis Victim Dies," *The Chicago Defender,* January 19, 1918, 2.
58. Graham Clarke, *The Photograph* (New York: Oxford UP, 1997), 112.
59. Photographic portraits in the nineteenth and twentieth century, as Deborah Willis points out, used "props such as drapery, classical columns, and parlor furniture" to offer "a class-based and gendered reading of an individual subject" and to signify "achievement." *Let Your Motto Be Resistance: African American Portraits* (Washington, D.C.: Smithsonian Institute P, 1997), 17. Symbols of social status, wealth and empowerment included such props as lecterns, books, pillars, and framed photographs of ancestors.
60. "To look at a photograph is to begin to engage this individual, concrete experience of suffering, of pain, of defeat." Susie Linfield, "A Witness to Murder," *Boston Review* (Sept./Oct. 2005). Available April 12, 2010 at http://bostonreview.net/BR30.5/linfield.php.
61. Willis, *Let Your Motto Be Resistance,* 16.
62. DuBois and Gruening, "Massacre," 238.
63. Fauset explicitly links this despair to the assault upon mothers and children: "A people whose members would snatch a baby because it was black from its mother's arms, as was done in East St. Louis, and fling it into a blazing

house while white furies held the mother until the men shot her to death—such a people is definitely approaching moral disintegration," *The Survey,* 38 (August 18, 1917), 448.

64. An existing Illinois statute gave mob victims a cause of action against the State for their injuries, with families of the dead as well as living victims given the right to sue. "Negro Girl Shot by Soldier Asks $10,000 from State, Claim of Girl Who Lost Arm During East St. Louis Race Riot Filed in Court of Claims," *Belleville News –Democrat,* 4–26–1920; "Negress Shot in Arm During Riot to Receive $2,500," *Belleville News-Democrat* 1–23–1921.
65. See the testimony of Mineola Magee (no occupation given), October 27, 1917: *Select Committee,* 1346–1373 of transcripts of hearings (reel 2, frames 458–464 of microfilm collection).
66. Allesandra Lorini, *Rituals of Race: American Public Culture and the Search for Racial Democracy* (Charlottesville: University of Virginia Press, 1999), 243–248.
67. NAACP Papers, I: C334.
68. *Washington Bee,* August 11, 1917.
69. Herbert Shapiro's choice of this photograph 20 years later for the cover of his seminal *White Violence and Black Response: From Reconstruction to Montgomery* signaled that the Black response he would analyze therein would largely exclude women's history.
70. Marita Sturken, *Tangled Memories: The Vietnam War, the AIDS Epidemic, and the Politics of Remembering* (Berkeley, CA: U of California P, 1997), 2.
71. See Anne P. Rice, "White Islands of Safety and Engulfing Blackness: Remapping Segregation in Angelina Weld Grimke's 'Blackness' and 'Goldie,'" *Representing Segregation: The Aesthetics of Living Jim Crow, and Other Racial Divisions,* Ed. Brian Norman and Piper Kendrix Williams (Albany, NY: SUNY P, 2010), 93–112. See also Maureen Honey and Venetria K. Patton, *Double-Take: A Revisionist Harlem Renaissance Anthology* (New Brunswick, NJ: Rutgers UP, 2001); and Judith L. Stephens and Kathy Perkins, eds., *Strange Fruit: Plays on Lynching by American Women* (Bloomington, IN: Indiana UP, 1998).

Notes on Contributors

Julie Buckner Armstrong is an associate professor of English at the University of South Florida, St. Petersburg. She is author of Mary Turner and the Memory of Lynching (The University of Georgia Press, 2011), editor of *The Civil Rights Reader: American Literature from Jim Crow to Reconciliation* (University of Georgia Press, 2009), and co-editor of *Teaching the American Civil Rights Movement*: *Freedom's Bittersweet Song* (Routledge, 2002).

Barbara McCaskill is an associate professor of English at the University of Georgia, where she has taught for 19 years. She co-directs the Civil Rights Digital Library and is a recipient of the 2010 Helen and Martin Schwartz Prize for outstanding work in the public humanities. Her research publications focus on African American literary and cultural figures, including William and Ellen Craft, former slaves and abolitionists from Georgia, and the Atlanta-based reporter and activist Joseph Richardson Jones.

Koritha Mitchell earned her Ph.D. from the University of Maryland, College Park, and is currently an associate professor of English at Ohio State University in Columbus. Her primary interests are African American literature of the late nineteenth and early twentieth centuries; racial violence throughout American literature and culture; and Black drama and performance. Her first book analyzes Black-authored lynching drama and is titled, *Living With Lynching: African American Lynching Plays, Performance, and Citizenship, 1890–1930.*

Mitchell is also interested in examining the impact that racial violence has had on artists who work in forms other than drama. For example, see her article "Mamie Bradley's Unbearable Burden: Sexual and Aesthetic Politics in Bebe Moore Campbell's *Your Blues Ain't Like Mine*" in *Callaloo.*

In examining a novel prompted by Emmett Till's murder, this essay builds on the traditions of Black feminist criticism to begin explicating what Mitchell calls "homebuilding anxiety," a concept that will animate some of her future work.

Fumiko Sakashita is an assistant professor of American Studies at Kansai Gaidai University, Japan. Her latest article, "Lynching across the Pacific: Japanese Views and African American Responses in the Wartime Anti-lynching Campaign," appears in the forthcoming *Lynching in Global Perspective: New Approaches and Directions in the Historical Study of Global Violence* (eds. William D. Carrigan and Christopher Waldrep, University of Virginia Press). She has also translated works of David W. Stowe, Hazel V. Carby, Bertram D. Ashe, and Nelson George into Japanese; and co-translated Eric E. Williams' *Capitalism and Slavery*.

Anne Rice is Assistant Professor of African and African American Studies at Lehman College, CUNY (the City University of New York). Rice edited *Witnessing Lynching: American Writers Respond* (2003), the first anthology of literature and journalism about lynching. She has also published essays dealing with lynching and visual culture; most recently, "White Islands of Safety and Engulfing Blackness," an *African American Review* essay (2008) exploring embodied and gendered memory of racial violence in the works of Angelina Weld Grimke.

Jennifer D. Williams is an assistant professor/faculty fellow at New York University's Department of English. Her research interests include trauma and memory studies, feminism, gender and sexuality studies, and travel and migration. Her most recent article, "Jean Toomer's Cane and the Erotics of Mourning," is published in The *Southern Literary Journal* (Spring 2008). Her other published reviews and essays can be found in *Modern Fiction Studies, American Literature, and Africanizing Knowledge* (eds. Toyin Falola and Christian Jennings, 2002). Williams is currently at work on her book manuscript, which examines how post-civil rights writers and artists approach Black cultural memory.

Index

Note: Page numbers in *italics* refer to illustrations.

CPSIA information can be obtained
at www.ICGtesting.com
Printed in the USA
LVOW04s0339080916
503717LV00037B/452/P

9 781349 294633